ON THE COUCH

TALES OF COUCHSURFING A CONTINENT

FLEUR BRITTEN

Collins

Collins
An imprint of
HarperCollins Publishers
77-85 Fulham Palace Road
London
W6 8JB

www.harpercollins.co.uk

First published in 2009 by Collins

10 9 8 7 6 5 4 3 2 1

A catalogue record for this book is available from the British Library

Isbn: 9780007310999

Designed and typeset by seagulls.net
Printed and bound in Great Britain by Clays Ltd, St Ives plc

Mixed Sources
Product group from well-managed
forests and other controlled sources
www.fsc.org Cert no. SW-COC-1806
© 1996 Forest Stewardship Council
FSC

FSC is a non-profit international organisation established to promote the
responsible management of the world's forests. Products carrying the FSC
label are independently certified to assure consumers that they come
from forests that are managed to meet the social, economic and
ecological needs of present and future generations.

Find out more about HarperCollins and the environment at
www.harpercollins.co.uk/green

Fleur Britten is a journalist, and since 2004 has worked for the *Sunday Times* where she is currently senior commissioning editor of *Style* magazine. She is also the author of *Debrett's Etiquette for Girls*, *A Hedonist's Guide to London*, *A Hedonist's Guide to Milan* and *A Hedonist's Guide to Life*. She lives unhedonistically in London

ACKNOWLEDGEMENTS

Couchsurfing debt? Who don't I owe? First thanks must go to Ollie for being my stabilising wheels at the trip's outset, and for then graciously assuming the grim role of remote trip adviser and blog updater (talk about salt in the wound). Then of course there's the 'without whoms': like my agent Cathryn Summerhayes. That she managed to secure a book deal in these times says a lot (except for how kind and compassionate she is too). Like my gifted and lovely editors at Collins, Claire Kingston and Lucie Jordan, who steered this solo sailor away from the doldrums of dross and towards something hopefully readable and not seventeen million words long. There was my Sunday Times editor, Tiffanie Darke, who sanctioned my sabbatical and so kindly supported me. There was Ruby Quince who was there with brilliant, bookish advice at the proposal stage of things. There was Miko's most generous Photoshop rescue service, now that I had to blag it without Ollie's photography. There was *cara* Cara, who reminded me to explore those couches in the first place. And for those couches I thank my hosts … what admirable fellows, to open up their houses, to share with the world their private lives, their emotional space, their hearts. I do – really do – admire them all. As for the founders of couchsurfing, those heroic hawkers of optimism, trust and community (all the things society so badly needs and yet so readily dismisses), I salute you. And thank you.

To Miroslav the Impaler

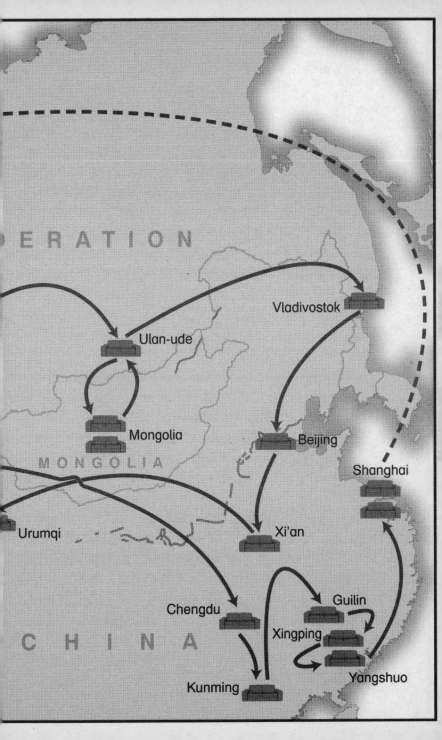

CONTENTS

CHAPTER 1
LONDON: A REVOLUTION TO RIDE

'I have an idea.' I was on the phone to my great friend, Ollie. 'It's a little extreme, but I think you'll like it.'

Ollie and I had been friends for so long that neither of us could quite remember when or where we met. Suffice to say it would have been drunken, at university, about fifteen years ago. We had a shared appreciation of the night, of the world and of the new; especially new chocolate products. Well, today, I had something new for us to try and it wasn't edible.

'Let's go couchsurfing.'

Couchsurfing was not, as might reasonably be assumed, synonymous with bed-hopping, or being a couch potato, but was the name for a one-million-member strong, international 'hospitality exchange' website, connecting people who wanted to stay in other people's homes around the world with people happy to host them; it was like one big notice board. When I'd been abroad before, I had always longed to have tea with a local, or be invited to a party. I'd done some home stays and had once gatecrashed a house party in Berlin after seeing it spilling out of a high window, but when it came to talking to the natives I suddenly felt stuck. Couchsurfing seemed like the ideal mediator.

If Ollie agreed, couchsurfing would become the theme of a ten-week trip to Russia, China, Mongolia and Kazakhstan (Kazakhstan alone boasted an impressive 124 couches). We were both drawn by an irresistible call to the East, intrigued by societies in varying degrees of 'post-communism', and for two years had been discussing planting our flags on what was over one-fifth of the globe's landmass. We wanted to unpick the world's largest country (Russia) and most populated nation (China) from the media myths they'd been reduced to – couchsurfing promised the inside track.

No more homogenous hotels for us, no more formulaic checklists and guidebook dependence deadening the whole experience. Couchsurfing presented a timely switch from passive observation to participation – we'd be hearing the truth, whether settled around the kitchen table, lounging naked in the Russian banya, or relaxed and disarmed on the sofa. And what an apt metaphor the couch was for a warm welcome. Wasn't couchsurfing what holidays were waiting for?

Couchsurfing was founded in 2004 when an American, Casey Fenton, spammed about 1,500 Icelandic students asking them to let him stay. He was inundated with replies, and the idea became a phenomenon. There were devotees who'd sold up everything they owned to couchsurf the world, and couchsurfers offering 'couches' in virtually every country across all continents, from Antarctica to Zimbabwe, where a 'couch' could be a bedroom, a garden, a corner of the floor, or even just a couch. And *all* for free: how timely during these locust years.

With the average age of a couchsurfer standing at twenty-seven, couchsurfing was something of a Generation Y game, but it was by no means exclusively so. There were over two hundred surfers between the ages of eighty and eighty-nine – free spirits didn't become less free with age, if they could help it.

✪

'Sleeping in strangers' houses? Couldn't think of anything worse.' That was the general reaction to my plan, but Ollie was up for it.

'Cooool!' he said boyishly. 'It'll be like *The Hitchhiker's Guide to the Galaxy*. Arthur travelled through time and space on his irrational sofa.'

But Ollie was no Arthur, no stranger to exploration: worldly, courageous and blessed with a preternaturally sunny spirit, there wasn't a better travelling companion to be had.

Ollie had established himself an enviable *modus vivendi*. A freelance ad exec, he earned a handsome wedge for six to nine months of the year, and then travelled on a shoestring for the remainder, photographing his experiences. What he really wanted to do was find more, bigger, better Kodak moments and snap them all – couchsurfing was surely going to throw up some intriguing material for him. I, meanwhile, was a wage slave, a features writer for the *Sunday Times*, and in return for three years' 'good service' I'd been granted a career break. I was desperate to escape the feeling that Planet London – and the *Daily Planet* – was closing in around me. For too long stifled by institution and constantly stressed by killer deadlines, I yearned to recover a sense of self. For a bit.

Ollie and I had had a few adventures together before: regular alpine appointments for pleasure-seeking skiing; Goan New

Year raves with the heroin-addled old-timers; and the cosy thrill of living together (though not like that – 'that' had fortunately never been relevant to us). Ollie – something of a kamikaze skier – had skied off a mountain early in the year, shattering his tibia and fibula so badly he'd had a Terminator-style titanium plate and six screws fitted. By September, he still needed a crutch, walked with a grievous limp, and was more familiar with the physio than with his own mother.

'Are you really sure your leg isn't going to drop off in Outer Mongolia or something?' I asked.

Despite his protestations to the contrary, I was sure I saw flashes of electric white pain behind the brave face. But Ollie got himself thoroughly vetted, and his consultant *promised* he'd be fine.

'Perhaps we could have a sub-theme of communist swimming pools,' Ollie suggested – it was critical that he kept up his physio.

I, too, was damaged – in the cardiac department. One day, eighteen months ago, I met The Emperor. Right then and there he impaled my heart and the rest of the world fell away. We were so high on each other, we'd stay up all night like one long waking dream, reluctant to miss a single second. But then a terrible and destructive war of the wills broke out. The Emperor was Serb – that came with insuperable Slavic pride; he had an artistic temperament – that came with extreme emotions.

Of course, I also had my complications. I was neurotic, sensitive, highly-strung and, like so many girls, prone to overthinking. Plus, I was possessed of a will that wouldn't be broken. So, instead, it was us that broke up. Then, after not very long, we involuntarily gravitated back to each other; he still had my heart, while part of his soul, he said, had been left with me. And so began one very bipolar relationship, as we lurched across the emotionally exhausting canvas of love. He moved in, he moved out, he moved in …

'Cut your losses,' friends advised. 'It's too dramatic.'

At thirty-four I was getting to an age where I couldn't afford to be trapped in this cycle. Ten weeks' absence, I reflected, would have to decide it one way or the other.

✪

So Ollie and I had a revolution to ride. 'Participate in Creating a Better World, One Couch At A Time' was couchsurfing's endearingly cheesy motto. Couchsurfing wasn't only about free accommodation; it had A Philosophy. Through conversation and understanding, it wanted to bridge cultures. What's more, it was an invitation to step out of the monetary economy and into the gift economy, where things were just given, with no expectation of quid pro quo: what timing. Couchsurfing's founding principle was Pay it Forward, a virtuous cycle of 'give and ye might eventually receive'. But reciprocal altruism wouldn't work without a community, and couchsurfing was *all* about enabling one big, happy community. The ultimate antidote to the West's atomised society, its founders even called it a 'love-ocracy'. This was globalisation at its most benevolent.

Hold it! We were about to stay with weirdos that lurked online in a time when 'trusting' was a byword for stupid. How could we be sure it would be safe? Well, plenty of safety measures had been implemented, such as an eBay-style, meritocratic reference system where guests and hosts would write reports on their experiences, marking them positive, negative or neutral. Requesting a couch with lots of negative references would be very 'trusting' indeed …

✪

But most of all there was faith. 'Trust your instincts' was the website's advice. This was especially useful in the absence of choice: in Micronesia, with its one registered couch, there wasn't much else to rely on. And yes, apparently there were those hosts who'd upgrade their guests from the couch to the bed. That couchsurfing was full of young, free travellers, and that the reproof 'Couchsurfing is *not* a dating site' was stamped all over its pages, made it obvious that plenty were at it. It sounded like one big party.

So who was waiting for us out there? Were couchsurfers enlightened new-age ideologues, Freecycling, foraging and living in perfect political correctness? Were they party hardies, hoping to corral all strays on their radar? Or were they, like Ollie and me, keen to reach into new frontiers? What would 'make yourself at home' really mean? Was this really pure altruism, or did they expect something – like sex, for example, in return? The lack of personal space concerned me. How did marathon couchsurfers nourish the complex requirements of the soul?

In addition, we'd be going cold turkey on choice, a luxury we had grown so used to in the Western world. How would we tolerate having to eat that Kazakh camel-cheek stew? What about varying attitudes to hygiene, to punctuality, to alcohol (Russian and Kazakh hospitality were notoriously spirited). And *surely* it was only a matter of time before we'd be embroiled in an excruciating domestic, faced with a malfunctioning toilet, or with intimate body bits we shouldn't see.

And what about our Britishness? Hopeless at instant familiarity, we were the islanders who shook hands at arm's length to avoid the Continent's kiss. And now we thought it would be a good idea to sleep in strangers' homes? What's more, I had an overactive sense of British social protocol – I was *obsessed* with doing the right thing. We'd be constantly on the spot, always having to guess at other cultures' codes of conduct. There was also a moral niggle – as wealthy Brits, we'd be freeloading off our less affluent hosts.

I felt an epiphany coming on – being so out of our comfort zones was going to be an adventure in self-development. We were all going to be on the metaphorical couch.

SEPTEMBER 2008

And so began that cringeworthy business of compiling our profile. As a travel networking site, couchsurfing worked along the same lines as Facebook or Myspace, requiring droll personal declarations, illusory photography and pretentious lists of recherché books, films and musical preferences. It asked for a personal description, a personal philosophy and our 'mission'. I had a self-conscious bash:

Fleur and Ollie

Mission:
12,000 overland miles from Moscow to Mongolia to China to Kazakhstan to China again and then back to London in time for Christmas.

Personal Description:
Open-minded, easy-going and always up for new experiences, we'd like to think that we're the kind of people you can take anywhere. Never say never is our mantra. Except

> to nuclear bombs, maybe. Left to our own devices, you
> might find us watching films, reading, gazing at art, walk-
> ing in the wilderness, debating the issues of the world (in
> a polite British way, of course), and dancing and singing
> wildly to comedy pop (very Brits abroad). OH! And we are
> not boyfriend and girlfriend, but just great, old friends
> (much better that way, non?).

I uploaded a couple of 'sweet' photos of us and sent it into the
ether. At least we didn't have an empty profile any more – the
mark of the much-loathed amateur.

1ST OCTOBER

Now we were ready for a little Russian roulette: Ollie and I must
set up a series of these random acts of kindness across our Trans-
Siberian route. We would meet during our lunch breaks and
look at couches together – but Moscow's 1,890 listed couchsurfers mysteriously scuttled into the darkness in the glare of our
searchlight. Were they dormant? Dead? Or were we asking for
too much?

We had some exacting parameters: they had to be native, we
wanted full security verification, our own room, no language
barrier (we didn't speak Russian) and *no* children of early-morn-
ing screaming age. The Russians had their own conditions: one
redoubtable Muscovite had written a full constitution on her
profile: 'In Russia water is cheap (sorry dear environmentalists)
and I do expect you to look clean and smell nice when you come
out of my flat. Please try to be invisible in all ways. In Russia we
do not call it sexual harassment when a guy opens a door, helps

a girl to put on a coat, helps a girl to carry a shopping bag. This is called GOOD MANNERS. Don't be afraid to show how polite you are.'

She wasn't alone: another supplied a terrifying list of dos and don'ts: 'DON'T bother applying if you're one of those free accommodation hunters who just read about CS in a newspaper. DON'T feel obliged to bring a present. A bottle of crappy wine from a store around the corner is only a waste of money. DO have your own agenda. We are not gonna sit down and smile at you for the spirit of couchsurfing ...'

A culture of kindness? Not necessarily. But then we found the thirty-year-old musician, Olga, who lived in a spacious and central flat, and who 'LOVED' showing people around. And, she'd written, 'every night you can hear horses walking across the yard, so if you are a sound-of-hooves fan, this is definitely the place.'

A match! Well, at least, she matched our requirements, but, with no references and no 'friends', did we match hers? We were ashamed of our virgin profile; but shame, we concluded, didn't seem like a useful emotion – so we overstated the case.

Dear Olga,

I hope this finds you well. We are Fleur and Ollie from London and you are the very first door that we have knocked upon in our first foray into couchsurfing.

So why you?! Well, wouldn't we be mad to overlook someone described as 'the nicest/kindest person I have ever met'?! We are also fully charmed by the idea of horse hooves. You seem fully conversant in the couchsurfing spirit – that it's more than free beds and instant company, but a will to bridge cultures and dispel stereotypes.

Why us? Well, we may be absolute beginners, but we come fully house-trained and domestically skilled and would be thrilled to regale you with tales from London and life.

Well, do let us know if we might have made it through the first round!

Fleur and Ollie

Factually slippery ('domestically skilled'?) and shamelessly jolly, it reminded me of my first job application. But we'd been warned – even by Olga on her profile: 'Unfortunately I still receive many "hi there"-style requests from people with empty profiles saying that they are "cool, open-minded and easy-going ..."'

We'd already fallen into couchsurfing cliché; and I wasn't even easy-going. I quickly deleted the offending article from our profile. Just as with an overly ambitious job-hunt, it all went quiet. We spread our bets.

Hello Maxim!

I hope this finds you well. We are Fleur and Ollie from London and you are the very first door that we have knocked upon in our first foray into couchsurfing ..."

Precisely 23 hours, 13 minutes after Overture Number One, our Inbox had a visitor. I experienced a momentary episode of abnormal heart activity – it felt a little like receiving love-mail.

Hi Fleur and Ollie,

thank you for your very kind request. i will be very happy to host you at my place, and show you a bit around the city. you will find my phone number, address and a link to a google map at the bottom of this message. could you just confirm that you're coming, 2-3 days before. since you're coming on Saturday, I can pick you up outside the metro station. also, if you need some tips or some information about moscow don't hesitate to ask.

see you soon,

Olga

Meanwhile Maxim also wrote back.

Welcome to Moscow!

I like your letter very much!!!! Usually it's OK to be hosted in my flat, in case I'm not hosting or travelling at this moment.

So you can count on me!

Regards. Max

P.S. We have CS meetings on Tuesdays & Thursdays.

Well, we weren't expecting a double-hit, but maybe coming from London boosted our appeal. We decided to stay three days with Olga, two with Max. From reading others' profiles, it appeared that much more at any one place was too much.

We wrote back with more blandishments, and both hosts and guests were suspended in a happy communion of sweet, innocent friend-making. Perhaps they would like something from London, I offered – I didn't believe that they could possibly be happy to just give, give, give and wait for the universe to give back. Paying it back instantly was surely obligado.

Just time to complete one prior experiment before departure: The Emperor and I had agreed to spend three days together –

yes, just three small days – and if we got on, we were go, if not, that would be it – the end of us. War descended within hours. We made up, pretended it hadn't happened and continued, only to fall out again. It was no use. By the end, we had to agree that we had failed.

CHAPTER 2

MOSCOW: UNDER OBSERVATION

11TH OCTOBER

1900 hours, Pushkin Square, Moscow. Night had fallen. In front of us was a confusion of old Soviet apparatus competing with new capitalist trappings: shadowy communist towers illuminated by the neon glow of monuments to money-making; a Vegas-style casino; an American coffee house; fast-food joints. Around the square, glossy European 4x4s beeped at dirty little Ladas. Ollie and I fell silent. Excited yet anxious, it felt like first date territory.

'I'll be waiting for you by the benches near the Pushkin statue.'

The romantic poet would surely have approved of Olga's instructions. And indeed, this was to be a blind-date of sorts, for Olga's profile picture was, enigmatically, of dense foliage.

We scanned the horizon and shrugged. A crowd of disconnected individuals lurked around the benches in dark, heavy clothing. We had no idea what we were looking for – we were the conspicuous ones, be-rucksacked and bewildered. Like exposed rabbits on an empty hill, we could only wait and be hunted.

Suddenly our view was filled with Olga. A slim girl wrapped in a fitted, navy, three-quarter-length corduroy coat, her pale, colourless face luminesced in the darkness, and was framed by a sandy coloured Jim Davidson hairdo, token blond highlights and all.

'Olga! Hello!'

Olga's smile was shy and short-lived. The Slavic hug I'd rehearsed hid behind British prudishness – instead, my left arm shot out to touch hers in odd, lumbering affection. Ollie held out his hand like a man. She took it, and then came to my hand, but it was full of rucksack. The critical moment, fudged. She pointed to the far corner of the square: 'Let's go this way.'

We probably talked about the journey or something, but the sensory overload made me forget everything. Now she was visible in three dimensions, I stared unblinkingly at Olga. Couchsurfing's internet profiles had not prepared me for the storm force of human life: suddenly, couchsurfing seemed to be about choosing a house on the merits of its front door.

Sensitive and birdlike, Olga's chin trembled and her head bobbed when she spoke. She seemed surprisingly nervous; yet, with twenty previous guests, wasn't she the experienced one? When it was my turn to speak, a voice usually reserved for other people's parents came out – I was being so 'good', answering pleasantly about our Russian visas and asking about her work. Was I about to be 'good' for ten weeks?

We turned into a dark cohort of daunting Soviet blocks, whose seemingly lowly status was belied by an assortment of prestigious cars; already I felt the thrill of access. Hotels weren't built in Soviet blocks, after all. We entered a simply tiled, beige stairwell, went into the functional, matchbox lift and out towards a dusty, pleather-padded door, which Olga unlocked before neatly removing her shoes in the hall. We neatly copied her. She handed Ollie a pair of brown leather, open-toed sandals of dubious sexuality, and me some pink towelling slippers. Hit by the smell of a second-hand bookshop, we looked up from our feet. Bearing down on us was an object lesson in cold Soviet life: peeling ochre wallpaper covered with old theatre posters, dusty cabinets and shelves piled with books, old photos and dead flowers. We were in a 1950s time warp.

'Wowwww,' Ollie and I emitted in unison.

'Well,' explained Olga, without uttering the vowel. 'It was my grandparents' place. My mother was born here, my parents used to live here – it hasn't really changed since then.' Her eyes darted around. An only child, she now lived alone. I wondered, was couchsurfing supposed to bring the company she craved?

It was hard to ignore the blood-boiling heat.

'Russia has a centralised heating system,' Olga said, fidgeting with her hands like they didn't belong to her. 'The heating is turned on at the same time every year by the government. Residents have no control. If we go on holiday for two weeks, it is still on.'

Her windows were wide open.

'What about the environment?' I spluttered.

'Mother Russia doesn't worry about natural resources,' she said, her eyes scouring the floor.

I'd read that Russia had the world's largest natural gas reserves and second-largest coal reserves, and was the world's third-largest energy consumer. I opened my mouth, then let it go – best not to insult the host country.

A sinewy silence slipped out. My arms were crossed and clinging on to each other tight, while Ollie was pretend-laughing at thin air. Olga was biting her cheeks tensely. Frozen in this psychological drama, we were all hyperaware of ourselves. I, for one, couldn't quite get those bossy Muscovites' constitutions that I'd read in London out of my head. What would *real* couch-surfers be doing now, I wondered?

'Shall we make our beds?' I offered helpfully. Knowing where I'd be sleeping would be one comfort. Olga directed us straight ahead with an outstretched arm: 'I have bedding if you need.' Ollie and I entered the living room (though any evidence of life here had long since departed) and Olga discreetly left us to it. Yet we continued to behave as if she were still in the room; no conspiratorial whispering – we were still being 'good'.

There, in the darkest corner of a long, low-lit room (most bulbs had blown) was my couch – an actual couch. Apparently from the 1980s (though it looked 1970s – maybe that was the Russian delay), it was a coffin-sized rectangle of foam uphol-stered in a brown and beige, zigzag-patterned, coach-seat fabric. Ollie said he'd prefer the retro, canvas camp bed, which didn't look comfortable but, he insisted gallantly, its wonky elevation would be good for his leg. The fact that Ollie and I would be sharing a room – a first in our long history – was vaguely unset-tling, but it was the least of our new experiences. What was more overwhelming was suddenly finding myself in the slipstream of someone else's life. I was wearing Olga's slippers, breathing her air and shadowing her life. It all felt extraordinarily random.

We regrouped with Olga in the hallway, and handed over our gift. In response to our invitation, she'd politely suggested a book of our choice, and we'd picked a photographic compilation, *London Through a Lens*. She unwrapped it, peered at it, flicked through it, but it was impossible to decipher her half-nod, half-smile and restless hands. Maybe we'd embarrassed her.

'Would you like a drink?' Olga offered.

We repaired to her modest kitchen, which looked unchanged since the 1950s – rose-print kitchen units, an electric oven and a quaint, rounded, ceramic sink – and sat at a humble breakfast table.

'I'd love a drink of water,' I supplicated.

'Oh. That could be a bit difficult.' She looked mildly ashamed. 'You can't drink the tap water here.'

She poured the tepid remains of water from the kettle into a teacup for me. Ollie and I were starving.

'Do you do much cooking?' Ollie asked.

'I don't cook for couchsurfers,' she said with surprising frankness. 'I just cook for myself. It's not so tasty; it's very basic things. But you can help yourself.'

She opened a monastic-looking fridge to reveal eggs, bread and cheese. A sticker on the door read WHERE ON EARTH IS PERTH?

'From a couchsurfer,' she said.

Now that our first living-and-breathing couchsurfer was firmly in our clutches, we cross-examined her with our entry-level questions. Forget Putin and polonium – what we really wanted to know was: how was it with other couchsurfers? Was it strange the first time she hosted?

'It was something unusual,' she said, smiling quietly, 'so I didn't know what to do.'

That was at least reassuring. Telling us how she'd hosted a male English teacher for six days, I wondered how this shy sparrow had coped, and then I thought, maybe it was *our* gaucheness polluting the atmosphere. I was looking forward to when this all felt more normal.

'Did you ever give any bad references?' I asked, trying to feel for the edges of this experiment.

'Most people don't leave negative references unless it's *really* bad,' Olga replied. 'I had a couple of fairly bad guests, though they never broke or stole anything. 'I did hear that one host found their guest shooting up.'

Olga's 'worst ever guest' treated her like his servant, asking her for tea, coffee, to buy his train ticket, 'Can I have my breakfast now?'

'He asked for many, many things like this, and he didn't bring anything,' she said, softly indignant.

Our problem was the opposite: British reserve and a keen concern for etiquette. Perhaps ten weeks of couchsurfing would knock it out of us. Still, at least first-time guests were still grateful. There was obviously some delicate balance to strike, somewhere in between excessive courtesy and taking liberties.

As for sexual harassment, she'd received messages, from mostly Turkish and northern African men, saying, 'You look nice – let's be friends.' Impossible, given that Olga's profile picture was of foliage. I'd noticed girls who seemed naked in their profiles, I said.

'Yes, probably,' she laughed timidly. 'And they never look as good as their picture.'

The 1950s standard wasn't so welcome in the bathroom: there was no lock (the door didn't even shut), the single-ply toilet paper was the colour of Jiffy bag stuffing, and above the sink was an old-fashioned shaving brush, some wooden combs and antique mildew.

Back in the kitchen, the wine came out. 'It's only cheap and sweet,' Olga apologised, adding, 'It's how I like it. Would you like some?'

'Oh – only if you're having some.'

'No, no, please have if you like.' She poured from an open bottle labelled 'La Jeunesse'. Nibbling on past-it black and white grapes, Ollie and I smiled away our hunger. There was a couch-surfing house party that night, Olga said, the leaving party of an Irish couchsurfer called Donna. Result. We'd just inherited her social life – it felt liberating to have to go with it.

En route to the party, Olga pointed out one of the Kremlin's potent red stars atop its spiky towers. A volt of joy fizzed through my body: we had a house party, a hand-holder and a local guide through Europe's largest city. We passed a street kiosk and refu-elled on public-transport-grade potato-filled *pirojki* pies, too flabby and tepid to be savoured.

Inside another anonymous Soviet apartment block, past a four-foot-high mound of coats, twenty-five-odd twenty-somethings were mingling amongst the scatter cushions and up-lighters. The first four guests we encountered had been made redundant.

'Actually, it freed me,' said a Russian in a blazer. 'There's no point for career now. So I just go travelling.'

Donna turned out to be Donagh, a young male architect with warm freckles and black, curly hair, and also an open future – like us, he was heading east on the Trans-Siberian. We rico-cheted around the party as the only itinerants; everyone else lived in Moscow. Wasn't that strange?

'We are networking,' admitted a Siberian lawyer.

Tom, a British accountant, said it was an ex-pat thing.

'Yes,' added the Siberian, crisply, 'Russian girls go to couch-surfing parties to meet foreign men.'

I nudged Ollie.

'Let me tell you about Moscow women,' said Tom. Ollie and I leant in. 'There are more women than men, so while they're better-looking than the men, they have to work a lot harder. It's why you see feisty, dressy Russian women alone in bars – they're competing for limited resources.' But there wasn't a novi Russki in sight: the demographic here was one of middle-class, bright young things, computer literate and emancipated. And English-speaking. Finding a Cossack while couchsurfing was going to be unlikely.

'Oh, you're in really capable hands with Olga,' said Sarah, a bubbly Irish girl with bubbly, coiled hair. 'She's probably the most professional host here. She knows exactly how to be, without being obvious about it. If she doesn't like you, she'll diplomatically let you do your thing.'

With impeccable timing, Olga announced she was going home, adding, 'Who is the most responsible person here?'

She elected Tom to get us home, drew us a map and gave us some keys. Tom took us to a snug indie club where we learned about the Russian mafia non-scene.

'Oh, there is no more Mafia – they just became corrupt businessmen or politicians where there's more power.'

And about the 'blacks': labour migrants from the 'Stans – Tajikistan, Dagestan, Uzbekistan.

'The Russians treat them worse than animals.'

But eventually the public displays of Russian passion around us became insufferable, so he sorted us a 'gypsy cab', a Tajik worker with his own Lada, and we returned to Pushkin Square to make an ill-advised friendship with a burger shack – toxic coiled *sausageskis* in white sliced bread that could have been moulded from foam. Still, slathered in mustard, ketchup and mayo, it became a meal. We'd be back.

12TH OCTOBER

8am. Ollie's alarm was screaming – he'd forgotten to turn it off from the day before. He slept on, but after just four hours' sleep, I couldn't. Grey daylight seeped in and the rain bore down. I peered out of the window. Amongst all the cloned, beige-brick residential blocks, I saw in one corner '1956' picked out in red bricks. In the apartment's oppressive silence, I didn't know what else to do but return to my couch. Only now, sober, did I realise it smelt faintly of unwashed bodies and that under the thin foam was a rigid wooden board – it was like sleeping on a door. In the heat I was too uncomfortable to sleep. I thought about tea and food, and sent texts to The Emperor. We'd become so twinned I was finding it hard to cut off.

Some hours later I finally tiptoed out and stop-started my way towards the kitchen, hesitating outside Olga's bedroom for an argument with myself: say good morning; no, don't bother her. Well, you can't just march into her kitchen. I'm hungover, I'm not in the mood. Well, that's not good manners …

In London, I either lived alone or with The Emperor – I wasn't used to dealing with people not on my terms.

Knock, knock.

'Good morning,' I croaked.

Olga was communing with her laptop at a wooden desk, in a study half the size of our room with a sofa like mine and no other sleeping apparatus – the sofa was her bed.

'Hello,' she replied.

She got up and formally introduced me to the kitchen. A waft of cooked eggs lingered.

We chatted briefly, then she returned to her room. Too

inhibited to whip up a full breakfast, I poured myself a water from the kettle. This, I realised, was the point of Pay it Forward. If I'd hosted first, I'd feel more right to hospitality.

After a time, she returned.

'Have you had breakfast?' she asked.

'Actually, I'd love a cup of tea.' What I *really* wanted was a cappuccino.

'Bfff, of course!' From a tiny pot crammed with loose black tea, she poured a strong, cold shot into a mug and topped it up with boiling water – *chai*, Russian style, no milk. 'Try some kefir as well – it's good for hangovers.'

'Sure!' I pursed my lips to test the buttermilk. It was sour and unfriendly. 'Maybe it needs sugar,' I said, trying to sound optimistic.

The digital age might have brought instant connections, but that didn't mean instant friendship. A force-field of unfamiliarity separated us. Olga hung around, so I had to sing for my breakfast. I didn't feel like small talk, but I was couchsurfing: I had no choice. Eventually, Olga left to see her parents, and in her place, Ollie arose, boldly putting his foot up on the sideboard in the kitchen. He pulled up his trouser-leg to reveal a swelling the size of a computer mouse.

'It's not as bad as it looks,' he said.

It looked hot and angry. I wasn't convinced.

'Chai?' I offered. 'Black, one sugar, coming up.' I ferreted through her cupboards, looking for sugar. It felt strange to sense some kind of ownership over someone else's apartment.

'Arghhhh!' Ollie had found a problem with the tea.

'Did you burn yourself?'

'No – you put salt in my tea. If Olga had made it, I probably

would have politely drank it: 'Hmm, this curious Russian speciality!'"

We made it into Moscow as the sun was setting. We ran dull
errands, refuelled, and then met Olga at the beautiful 1930s
Komsomolskaya metro station under the mosaics honouring its
workforce, the Komsomol (or Communist Youth League). Olga
was going to help us buy our Trans-Siberian rail tickets. 'Always
remember that the host is doing the surfer a favour,' the website
had chided. I couldn't forget. She assumed the mothering role
and we became the children: we'd left our passports and cash
behind, turning a fifteen-minute task into one and a half hours.

'I must have taken seven or eight of my guests to get their
train tickets,' Olga said.

I was confused: I felt guilty, and yet, it seemed, this was standard. The kindness of strangers – it really existed.

We felt an urge to take Olga to dinner. She chose an art-café-
cum-bookshop, Bilingua, and, as we chatted, she told us how she
had a 'very special criterion' when couchsearching. She'd search
for 'Godard' or 'Truffaut' to locate fellow French cinema fans.
She told us about Russia's Country Ambassador, something of a
celebrity in Moscow: a Philippino diplomat who often had four
or five surfers staying at one time; he'd had over a hundred
guests this year.

'I don't like it when homes are like hostels,' Olga frowned.

There was even a couchsurfing monastery, she said, just
outside Moscow: one shared room for couchsurfers, a curfew,
and a task, such as painting the walls. Like opening a *matrioshka*,
those sets of Russian nesting dolls, Olga's twitchy, nervous shell
had fallen away, and she seemed at last relaxed. Finally, the act of
welcoming us into her home didn't appear so masochistic.

We headed back and, unbidden, Olga looked up our train times and wrote out a role-playing station script for next time. And as we ate into her bedtime, my couchsurfing guilt reappeared. Christ, was this going to be like catholic guilt? I went to the kitchen to make tea, and found myself washing up, thinking about the selfish rewards of altruism: had Olga, too, gone to bed feeling good? Outside I heard the ghostly clatter of horses' hooves – Olga had told us earlier that they belonged to gypsy girls who used them to beg. It was my reward.

13TH OCTOBER

Moscow Sights Seen So Far:

- The metro system;
- The railway station;
- A Russki hair salon (I had amused myself with a Moscow makeover, hairspray finish and everything).

Not exactly Top Ten. Couchsurfing, with all its social and organisational demands, was eating into our tourists' needs, but then,we'd seen a very different kind of tourism – intimate tourism.

But we were just getting to know our host and our little party was over: we had to leave Olga's at 7am the next day to meet Max, our second Moscow host ('Please arrive at 8am – I have a very hard day.'). Couchsurfing Rule Numero Uno: guests defer to hosts. Olga assured us she'd get up early to say goodbye. She really was the sweetest thing, I said to myself, mentally composing my very first positive reference.

14TH OCTOBER

'When you come out of the metro, you'll see a supermarket, then we are house 36.' A riddle wrapped in a Soviet apartment block.

Metro – check. Supermarket – check. Time check: 8.10 – a little late. But house 36? House even? Encircled by row upon row of dirty white, high-rise blocks, we were stumped. We sent out a Mayday to Max, but by 8.50 (a lot late), there was still no word. We called him (wasn't that the sound of a man freshly woken?), and received our instructions for the final stage.

The smell came first – the fetid smell of fermenting men. At the foot of the twenty-storey Block 36, four red-faced, leering drunks swayed in the wind; a fifth was retching over clutched knees. We picked our way past the broken bottles, suspect puddles and a dark-skinned, obese woman slumped in the janitor's cabin, and into a lift. One hour late, we got our hands on the prize.

Max, rangy in jeans and a Cambodia T-shirt and with the flat, fringed haircut of a young geography teacher going on fifty, bounced out to greet us with a laughing, long-armed hug. Sleep creases marked his smooth Pinocchio cheekbones. 'Lock the door behind you!' he said merrily, as we followed him through two solid steel doors and straight into a glittering coral-pink hall resembling a camp Santa's grotto. We were equipped with slippers (leather for the boys, flowery pink towelling for the girls), and led off the hall into a small room containing a brown velour 'super deluxe' sofa.

'Yesterday,' clucked Max in a singsong voice, 've vent to ze couchsurfing film night, on ze Irish independence!'

'Oh yes?'

'Ve vatched ze *Bloody Sunday*, khuh khuh!'

We courtiously laughed back, and Max took to his computer. I slumped dysfunctionally on my new bed; I'd had on average four hours' sleep a night at Olga's.

'Zere's anozzer couchsurfer vere you sleep. Yvonne from London!'

I was confused, but too strung-out to pursue. Max fiddled with his computer, putting disks in, taking disks out, taking work calls (aged thirty-five, he worked in logistics, he told us), then, with a grin the size of his face, he presented us with a commemorative Moscow photo disk.

'So, Max, have your other couchsurfers struggled to find your place?' I bleated. 'All the blocks look the same!'

'Khuh khuh! Ve khave a film zat is set around New Year's Ev, ze main kholiday in Russia. So, it's usual to go to ze banya to clean your body and mind at zis time. When you go to ze banya, you take wodka. So, in zis film, four men khad drunk so much …'

To shear back a long and tangled shaggy-dog story, Max was recounting a much-loved Russian film by the director Eldar Ryazanov, which was shown on Russian TV every New Year.

'It's called *The Joke of Your Life*,' he explained.

The plot followed a drunk Muscovite who mistook a Soviet apartment in St Petersburg for his own, as the addresses coincided, the appearances coincided, the interiors coincided; even the key worked.

'It's based on Soviet style of life,' explained Max. 'For foreign person, it's difficult to understand.'

We understood.

Yvonne, a wan, thin girl with straggly, long hair, emerged from the kitchen. So that's where we'd be sleeping; I hadn't done that since drunken student days.

Max hooted, 'Breakfast Included!'

The opposite of Olga, extroverted, jokey and unselfconscious, he made me feel instantly cosy. In the kitchen, against a pumpkin-coloured backdrop, rested a pumpkin-coloured sofa bed. Claustrophobically small, it was in fact rather like being inside an actual pumpkin. What space remained was serried with panpipes, fridge magnets and ethnic masks – Max's apartment was a shrine to travel. If travel was Max's religion, couchsurfers were its disciples – for Russians, visas were difficult to obtain, Max told us, and air travel was expensive: in times of need, couchsurfers brought the world to him.

Max's phone rang again, so we acquainted ourselves with our compatriot. Couchsurfing was an obvious starting point (and current obsession).

'It would be quite lonely without couchsurfin',' Yvonne explained in her London accent. 'I'm twenny-one, I've got £1,000 to travel indefinitely. I'm going to Mongolia, China, India, Tibet, Nepal, Thailand, Laos, Cambodia, Vietnam ... I can teach but I'd rarver not.'

Yvonne's conversational coffers seemed infinite – and so she went on. She'd been staying at Max's for a week, but she'd evidently earned her moral right because she'd hosted a lot in London. She recounted how two guests had paid for her National Express ticket so she could show them Stonehenge, and how one girl had asked for the vacuum cleaner ('My house isn't completely spotless, right') and left after an hour.

Max returned and busied himself with breakfast: tea in glasses and a large bowl of chocolates and wafers.

'Zere's not so much sugar so I khave some khow-do-you-say ... blackberry.'

I gamely put some jam in my tea and took a chocolate for breakfast, but the wrapper wouldn't budge so I aborted. Max spooned soupy chocolate spread straight from a bowl into his mouth. I went to refill the kettle from the tap, but Max leapt up, saying 'No, no!' and ladled a cup of water from a large pan. The point of couchsurfing was being played out – we were experiencing a new 'normality'. A random bloke sloped in, helped himself to tea, offered legal-minimum pleasantries, and sloped out.

'Khe's out-of-verk computer programme,' explained Max. 'Khe's my permanent couchsurfer. Khuh khuh.'

Max's was evidently a hospitality that didn't say no.

With a stomach-turning collection of corpse-long and broken fingernails, Yvonne clawed a number into her mobile.

'So can I crash your language class today?' she drawled into the mouthpiece. 'Cuz you said the ovva day I could sit in on your Russian class?' Yvonne was looking for a pen.

'*Ruchka*!' enthused Max. 'Tsat's 'pen' in Russian. 'Arm' in Russian is *ruka*, so pen is little arm!'

Yvonne scratched down the new word in her exercise book. It seemed they had a good tutor-student relationship going on.

Max had to drive out of Moscow, so we gathered ourselves to leave with him; there were no spare keys and we'd have to stay out all day.

'Zere's a couchsurfing party tonight. Someone is presentation khis trip to China.'

He furnished us with the address, and the three Londoners disentangled themselves from this force of positive energy and returned to the real world.

Passing thunder-faced, potato-bodied babushkas selling kittens in cardboard boxes, we advanced in the drizzle to Red

Square. In my sleep-deficient state, Yvonne's motormouth was bringing out my misanthropy. Gone was my rictus smile – compulsory companionship had gone unquestioned when there was a motive but now I dropped back while Ollie and Yvonne swapped India stories. Yvonne expressed an interest in going to the State History Museum so I expressed an interest in the Kremlin. Bye-bye Yvonne: she'd be moving to a different host later.

✪

Rocking up at a Russian house party felt a little peculiar without Max, and with no introduction other than the fact that We Too Were Couchsurfers. But, we reminded ourselves, couchsurfing was an open community, plus we'd come well stocked with ingratiating party provisions. Inside, we couldn't get past the human log-jam in the hall; the bilingual slideshow on China was taking place in an impenetrable bedroom. Conversation was unavoidable. Finding myself in front of two Californian sisters tucking into bowls of borscht, we got talking. They didn't know anyone either, and were staying at a hostel. Not wanting to be with all the tourists, they had checked out Moscow's couchsurfing group, and this party was posted on it.

A Kazakh girl invited me into a 'secret'; she'd met her boyfriend when couchsurfing with him in Paris.

'We were reading my English-Russian manual together,' she whispered. 'I was very tired so I leant my head on his shoulder ...'

Why the whispering?

'To stop others thinking that they'll find love on the couchsurfing site and messaging random girls.'

I told her we were on our way to Kazakhstan.

'I sympathise,' she quipped. 'In Moscow, nobody ever looks at you in the street. In Kazakhstan, they do. They're checking your nose hasn't turned white with frostbite – it can be -40°C in the winter.'

Beyond the capacity of my imagination, it just sounded exciting. Naivety was remarkably motivating.

'Everyone leave now!' shouted the flushed Russian host. 'We're all going to a café down the road!'

Nobody budged. Nobody could.

Eventually, the host got his way, so we returned to Max's and convened in the kitchen. As we snacked on bread and bananas from our own supplies, Max quizzed us on all matters travel.

'Show me rucksack! Vot about sleeping bag? Khow much you pay?'

We presented him with our gift, a Lonely Planet guide on Thailand (he'd dropped a hint in an email while we were in London) and he yelped with joy.

'Natalie!'

His tiny, mouse-like girlfriend scurried in wearing mint-green loungewear with SWEET GLAMOUR twinkling in green crystals.

'Try ze rucksack!' said Max, excitedly.

My rucksack practically toppled her, but she beamed. Their delight infected us all. Natalie didn't speak English so Max seamlessly ran two conversations without ever revealing the strain.

By 1am, we could delay the inevitability of kitchen camping no more. We pushed the kitchen table right to the wall and unfolded the sofa-bed – the kitchen disappeared. I filled my empty water bottle from the just-boiled kettle – the only drinking water I could find – and the plastic warped. I wasn't used to having to think about where I'd get my water. I sandwiched myself between Ollie and the wall and we killed the lights, but the glow from the appliances' LEDs held their steely gaze on us. I couldn't sleep: the fridge was whirring, I was boiling, I had a dead arm from the wooden 'mattress', and there was a foreign body in my bed snoring. Meanwhile, my mind was imploding from the day's events. Was it really only this morning that we were lost in transit? It felt like we'd lived a week in one day.

15TH OCTOBER

'I vont to khave breakfast!' Max, in football shorts and his Cambodia T-shirt, entered the kitchen – it was rather like joining us in bed. All evidence of the night was efficiently tidied away, and Max set about producing a Heidi-style brunch: watery cabbage soup in need of salt, with trace elements of onion and carrots; smetana; chewy, sour black bread; and spineless 'Russian standard' cheese. Random Bloke joined in, and he and Max chatted in Russian. I was grateful not to have to join in, since I couldn't think of anything to say. I just wanted coffee. Which wasn't included.

Mystified by the ease with which Max played host, I asked, was the concept of couchsurfing intrinsic to the Russian psyche?

'Yes!' he said, practically bursting. 'I met man in Kiev at ze station and khe invited me to stay khis khouse. Russians are wery khospy-table.'

I, too, could accommodate people on my kitchen floor, but it would take a Blitz for that to happen.

'Okay, you do the voshing-up!' Max left the kitchen and it struck me that the couchsurfing dynamic was all about sub/dom. Max was instinctively dominant and we happily submitted.

Maybe it could also work as a dom/dom dynamic, and even dom/sub, with a guest dominating a submissive host. But when both were submissive, as it had been with Olga, it left the relationship needing a kick.

'Perhaps that's what I should do,' Ollie piped up. 'I'll get couchsurfers into my house, and say to them, 'You can stay in my house, but you do the washing-up.'

Max returned with his Moscow guide book: 'You could go here, you could go here …'

Actually, we said, we were interested in the All-Russia Exhibition Centre (a Monaco-sized tribute to Soviet glory). Max seemed unconvinced, but went to print out notes. Now a troika, Max, Ollie and I left the apartment. Feeling shattered, I wished we were *a deux*. We passed the obese woman in the janitor's cabin and Max explained that yes, she did live in that one tiny room.

'Rent is wery expensive in Russia. She's probably from Uzbekistan. Zey take zose jobs.'

Ollie couldn't have told me that, I thought to myself.

Outside, Max hucked and spat on the roadside. I sneezed. Ollie blessed me. 'Yes,' said Max, 'Cheers!'

First we visited Moscow's space park, where a one-hundred metre tall, titanium totem to The Conquerors of Space pointed vertiginously skywards. As we walked down the Avenue of Cosmonauts, Ollie struggled to keep up with Max's long strides; despite our polite requests, the pace never slowed. Ollie wisely sat out the Monaco-sized glory park. Max guided me indefatigably round the eighty-two Stalinist pavilions, Gagarin's *Vostok* rocket and an *Aeroflot Yak-42* (smirking not permitted). Without Ollie to share in deciphering Max's accent, I struggled to understand him, and when I could, I felt too socially retarded to converse, relying simply on a repertoire of, 'Oh yes, wow, how interesting, I see, umm, gosh'. It became increasingly apparent that Max had taken the day off to hang out with us, despite not really rating our choice. The consummate host never let on.

Max peered into a souvenir stand with hungry eyes: 'Now I know vare to send my couchsurfers,' he clucked.

'Do couchsurfers usually bring presents for you?' I asked.

'Sometimes zey offer to buy food, but mostly I say no, pliz. Many zink of it as a place for staying so zere is no obligation to leave presents. But it is a custom of Russia to bring a gift because you don't pay the bill.'

I resolved to keep on giving.

We scooped up a smiley Ollie, and took the scenic monorail (which Max had researched for us earlier) to Moo-Moo, a chain restaurant decked out like a Friesian cow, serving up Russian classics: borscht, cabbage-stuffed bread, kvas (fermented rye bread water), and, of course, vodka. Two men on the neighbouring table asked to join us. 'Sure!' said Max. For the rest of our meal, Max tirelessly translated the glassy-eyed Igor and Sergey's rants on the war in Georgia (and the Western media's blindness to Saakashvili's evil), eulogies to Bulgakov's *The Master and Margarita* ('most important Russian book!') and pushy vodka toasts to 'united nations'. But Max remained the jolly messenger, never getting political. I'd tried to discuss politics with him earlier, but he'd laughed it off; it didn't seem relevant to him. Natalie appeared halfway through, to nibble on an eggcup-sized portion of vegetarian gratin and saucer of salad, after which our hosts skipped off to their Latino dance class.

Couchsurfing was a hungry beast, so Ollie and I busied ourselves in an internet café. There was a constant need to plan ahead, arrange back-up and confirm arrivals. Each acceptance felt like a minor victory. Perversely, however, we found ourselves, like naive kittens, seeking just a little more danger. Our next stop was Yekaterinburg (some 1,814 kilometres east of Moscow), where our host, a journalism student called Polly, would be on holiday in a 'rather fashionable' hotel in Turkey when we arrived, leaving us in the curious company of her pet rat. Danger indeed.

16TH OCTOBER

Max was expecting a Spanish couple – our replacements – to arrive at 8am from St Petersburg. Ollie had suggested we wake at 7am to prepare for them, but given our own delayed arrival, I overruled it. At 8.30, the doorbell rang.

'*Hola! Buenos dias!*' they trilled.

Max, the expert logistician, deftly organised us like human elements in a sliding-tile game, and then began the breakfast ritual. The girl immediately offered to do the washing-up. I was so slow on this sharing and helping thing.

'Do you always like to have surfers, Max?' I asked, when the *amantes* weren't listening. I was shocked by his turnover.

'I need a rest,' he replied. 'Sometimes Natalie don't like zem.'

'Are there ever surfers that you don't like?'

'No, no!' he heehawed like a donkey, before adding, 'Zere vos a Sviss couple cycling viz all zare kit.'

That was as rude as he could bring himself to be about them.

It was checkout time for us – we had a train to catch aboard the world's longest railway. While packing up, it occurred to me that Max must now have something of a collection of *objets oubliés*.

'Ah yes!' he said, convulsing with laughter. 'It's like a muzeum khere. I khave towels, I khave trousers, I khave tooz-brushes ....'

'Actually,' I added, 'I can't find my top.'

'Too late! It's in the muzeum, khuh khuh khuh!'

CHAPTER 3

YEKATERINBURG: THERE'S A RAT IN THE KITCHEN

'Well, *that* was odd.'

Ollie and I were rumbling towards Asia on board the Trans-Siberian Express, and I was grappling with why Max could possibly choose to live in that chaos. We had thirty hours to work it out before it all began again in Yekaterinburg.

'Max is having the time of his life,' Ollie mused, as he stretched out on his sailor-sized bunk. 'He's meeting experienced travellers from all over the world, showing them his city, dodging his shitty job and working from his phone. He's got it all worked out.'

Still, he must have possessed a spare brain lobe to accommodate the madness. Perhaps it was a reaction against Russia's isolationist stance. Whatever, it would be hard to look at a Soviet block and still think 'prison with windows' – we knew now that within their walls could be warm and colourful homes.

Ollie, meanwhile, was getting familiar with my dinner of Russian biscuits.

'I couldn't be my normal cheeky self,' he said, his mouth full.

We were both caught up in manners: this was a shame – cheekiness had its role in social lubrication.

'And you can't be selfish as a couchsurfer,' he added. 'I was really having to push my leg because I felt rude telling Max to keep slowing down.'

He inspected the growth on his knee. It was bulging hard and taut. Ollie strapped a chilled bottle of water to the lump (he'd left his gel pack at Max's) and added, 'It would be really churlish to call a host boring – but Olga wasn't so exciting.'

He was right. That was blasphemy.

As we pulled away from the relatively westernised Moscow, we pressed our noses against the window. Nothing to see but nothing: the Siberian birch, it seemed, had a monopoly over Russia's hinterland. Staring out of the window began to feel like sticking one's head into grey cloud: ready-made emptiness, waiting for our minds' overspill.

But at least, I realised, one part of my mind was filled with peace: The Emperor Department. Usually so fraught with the minutiae of our last five arguments, now it was quiet. There was surely something out there for both of us that was more stable, that was better for us. We should be using this time to heal. I'd been sending trip updates to The Emperor, but now I sent this emotional update, and I felt it strongly. Maybe thousands of miles and all these weeks was the only way to save ourselves from ourselves.

17TH OCTOBER

Our need to get our heads around couchsurfing had left us without much grasp of Moscow: we'd spent much of it in a Petri dish of domesticity. Couchsurfing was meant to be the vehicle, but in Moscow, it had done the driving. I was looking forward to being in Polly's apartment without Polly for a day. She'd despatched her friend Sasha to meet us off the train. All we knew was that her English wasn't very good, and she wasn't a couchsurfer.

As the train slowed down into Yekaterinburg – founded in 1721 by Catherine the Great and where, in 1918, the last Tsar and his family were murdered by the Bolsheviks – my heart sped up. Like looking at a jack-in-the-box, I was expecting the shock, but I knew I'd still jump.

Scanning the busy Friday evening platform for a young Russian woman was like watching an identity parade without witnessing the crime. But this was a redundant task – immediately outside our carriage were three coloured balloons attached to the hands of a smiling sylph with long ballerina hair and a peaches-and-cream, babydoll face.

Sasha's uncontainable excitement proved a handy tool for cutting through any social tensions. We fell into a spontaneous group hug, giggling in idiotic communion, holding our respective balloons. After a physical tussle between us over her insistence on helping with our bags, we headed to the tram stop, engaging in much sign language, and confused yet eager communication: 'I very dream talk of London!'

We managed to gather that she was twenty and, like Polly, halfway through a six-year journalism course. Plus, she explained, by putting an imaginary microphone up to her mouth and adding a few key words, she presented for a local news channel – we were in the company of young ambition. She had a brother and a sister, which was a lot of siblings by Russian standards: 'My father is hero!' she joked. She loved British and American music, but not Russian – hip-hop, lounge, Alicia Keys, Bon Jovi.

'Cool,' we smiled.

We feigned cheery obliviousness to the freezing, thirty-minute wait at the tram stop. Yekaterinburg had a Siberian sense of space. Large, low-rise Soviet blocks inhabited the wide, quiet streets, which were veiled in an icy, dusty mist that whispered hostility. Its cars were thick with the spit of slushy streets. But Yekaterinburg seemed less desperate than Moscow. There were fewer drunks and street folk scratching around for bread money, and a little more laughter and conversation. A small child overheard us talking, and said to us, 'How are you? How are you?' We were more of a novelty here, not least to Sasha.

As night drew its inky curtain across the overcast day, Sasha gave up on the tram, and held out an elegant gloved hand to hail a taxi. Three private cars pulled up in quick succession, and then drove off.

'This is how is be Russian woman,' she sighed. 'They say, 'Oh, you beautiful woman and then ...'' She finished her sentence by motioning a brush-off.

Eventually, we were delivered, via a muddy, rutted track, to an uninvitingly dark and vast residential estate in Central Yekaterinburg, filled with sad, skeletal trees – the perfect horror-movie set.

That is, until we passed through the grim, dingy stairwell. Inside, it was as if we'd booked into a boutique hotel: all dark-wood, floor-to-ceiling wardrobes, blonde-wood floorboards and plum organza curtains. It exuded the distinctive smell of newness.

'It's all Ikea,' Sasha said, proudly.

The bed was pleasingly huge, a king-size surrounded by a dinky white wooden fence and cornflower-blue flocked wallpaper, straight out of Elle Deco. Or Ikea.

Returning my stare, and motionless on its hind legs was a rat, dull brown and threadbare, right in the middle of the floor. Behind bars, thankfully. We approached with caution, eyeing it suspiciously. Sasha, meanwhile, skipped into the kitchen and grabbed a thick red dictionary (or 'diary', as she called it). 'Please make what home!' she grinned, reading from its pages. Then she skipped to the cage and fished out the rat. 'Hello DouDou!' She thrust it towards me. 'Hello Fleur!' I reluctantly fingered its coarse, matt coat, but soon stopped. Then she walked over to the bed, and lowered DouDou on to it. It scampered to the edge. I traced its path without blinking, yet it disappeared. I stared hard at the bedcovers. Eventually, they rippled: it had burrowed underneath.

Pinned to the fridge on squared paper was a note from Polly:

Hi guys! You are Welcome! Well, now you've reached the destination and I hope you'll feel yourself like home.

I don't know in what my flat is because I'm still in Turkey. I hope Sasha keeped it well. There are two most things you need now!

the bed I hope you see it :-)

and the supermarket (about 3 minutes by on foot ...)

[she'd drawn a map.]

So, I will arrive in the morning of 19th and I won't explain you anything else because I hope to see you soon.

Enjoy your first night in Yekaterinburg.

Polly

Sasha hopped into hostess action. Taking leaves from a chic, artisan-looking brown paper bag, she brewed a fragrant floral tea, then interleaved some slices of tomato and bland Russian cheese on top of slices of black rye bread. She neatly sliced an orange, an apple, a pear and a banana and fanned them out on a white Ikea plate (our first taste of fruit this trip).

'Heat, heat!' she urged, adding, 'I can't heat'

'Why not?'

'I used to be model but too fat,' she cried.

I checked her out there and then. Her skinny-cut Hilfiger jeans – no more than a size ten – were cutely crammed, but fat? No. Who had she been modelling for? Amongst others, the *Yekaterinburg Journal*. She could afford an apple slice.

Sasha certainly had a lot of energy stored somewhere. She broke into song (it sounded neither British nor American) and danced as if stirring a giant saucepan with both hands. Ollie and I were rather more sedate (or shy), watching the show. We needed a Wi-Fi zone, so she suggested we went to Rosy Jane, an 'English' pub where she used to work on 'Face Kontrol'. Face Kontrol was Russia's 'survival of the fittest' entry-selection process in its clubs and bars, where 'fit' could be measured in cosmetics consumption. Sasha rose to the occasion with a thick mask of make-up over her perfect complexion and pulled on Polly's black patent-leather knee-high boots. From what we'd seen in Moscow, you weren't a real Russian girl without them.

The door-bitch deemed Ollie and me too *sportif* but Sasha managed to sway her.

Inside the wood-panelled, pub-themed bar, she lit up a Parliament Light.

'Polly no drink no drugs. I am smoking and drinking,' she said gleefully.

She told us about a local music festival: 'Three boys very ill,' she said, pointing skywards. 'Cocaine. Girls eat drugs but they control situation.'

We ordered drinks, chatted for a polite length of time, and then tried to log on, but our own private cabaret refused to stop performing.

'Are your friends coming down?' I asked, thinking that perhaps they could entertain her.

'Russians work, work, work maximum – they don't control time,' she frowned, adding, 'Is a Russian tradition to work when drinking.'

Or drink when working. Behind us, two office girls were dancing shamelessly on an empty dance floor.

Our Wi-Fi needs were eventually abandoned, while Sasha bounded on: 'I will shocked that Polly hosting. Russian tradition to have Russians, but tourist never. We think you're going to steal it.'

Ollie and I laughed in shock. But it was certainly either very amazing or very naive of Polly to agree to us being there without her when we had no references (not that she did, either).

'My parents were worried too,' Ollie said, understandingly, and told us how he'd had to show them our hosts' profiles.

'My mother looked at my father with eyes on stalks,' he explained, 'But my dad said, 'These look like nice people, Jeni. Remember when we were eighteen. Hitchhiking is the same.''

Except that couchsurfing, with its reference system and verification, was way safer.

The English pub succeeded in recreating the essence of an English Friday Night, complete with binge-drinking, elbows at the bar and insufferable disco beats, so we retreated homeward. Sasha threatened to stay the night – not, I think, to check up on us, but because she just wanted more. To my relief, she ordered a taxi and went home.

Now unobserved, Ollie and I made ourselves at home, making tea, casing the fridge (empty but for Clipper organic ground coffee) and cold-reading her white, fitted bookshelves: five Lomo cameras protectively stored in their boxes, a Super 8 and a few books (Kafka, *1984* and some Russian chick-lit). Being able to adjust to an alien environment without the added pressure of having to get along famously with our host, was a welcome reprieve. Ollie and I were now having *fun*.

Ollie swore that he really would rather sleep on the floor to elevate his alarmingly large leg. Meanwhile, the rat seemed to sense the presence of danger, gnawing away at the bars of his cage.

'It's a controversial pet,' Ollie pointed out, 'considering all the rat infestations in the Gulags.'

Controversial – there was a clue about our host.

Spread like a starfish across Polly's bed and now finally alone, I read again the response from The Emperor. 'We both know,' he'd written. 'I've been thinking the same. It makes me so sad … My soul is aching.'

This was supposedly the right response, yet it broke my heart. I indulged in that silent land of tears. By day, as couchsurfers, we were forced to live publicly and so I was forced into coping. That was actually quite useful.

18TH OCTOBER

During a spot of couchsurfing in an internet café, the person sitting next to us happened to be a fellow couchsurfer. A middle-aged Australian kidult who talked too much, he was off to

Krakow for a big party. He was 'surfing' with his Russian girl-friend after a messy divorce. It suddenly felt like we'd joined a secret society. But we had work to do, leaving gushing references for Olga and Max. Displaying true amateurishness, we closed with a kiss.

Sasha had asked us to be part of Polly's surprise welcome home committee for six o'clock. Except that we lost half an hour to trying to locate Polly's block from the scores of other identical beige-brick blocks, all unmarked save for their information boards by the door – all carrying identical flyers. A Ryazanov moment (as we'd had trying to locate Max's apartment) was only spared by comparing an earlier photograph to all the doors until, finally, we had a match.

At Polly's, Sasha and her friend Albina were creating a Post-It collage on the breakfast table in the shape of a giant, umm …

'Da!' shrieked Sasha, holding my hand in kittenish enthusiasm. My hand went Britishly limp. 'It's a 'pennis'!'

'Err, why?'

'It's our fantasy!' she giggled.

I saw right through Ollie's smile into his fear.

Around the apartment were orange balloons and oranges sliced into quarters (orange was Polly's favourite colour). Who got such a homecoming after just a two-week holiday, I wondered. Was this normal in Russia, or was Polly abnormally lovely?

Eventually, out of the kitchen window, I noticed a glossy black Range Rover with blacked-out windows. It seemed to match this luxurious, modern apartment. My eyes locked on to it. Sure enough, out popped an impish, tanned girl with a confident crop and over-sized, tomato red spectacles. She looked up to her apartment and saw me. I waved at her. She waved back.

'She's here!' I hissed.

The girls collapsed into a hysterical fit, started up *Voyage* by Milky Lasers on the laptop, and assumed the 'surprise!' position.

And so two hysterical girls became three, screaming, jumping, hugging. Ollie and I hesitantly joined in. Tomboyish in twisted jeans and a white T-shirt, the 20-year-old Polly burnt bright, flashing her strong, milky teeth and warm, nutty eyes. She babbled spiritedly and quickly launched into a gift ceremony. For Albina: 'The best coffee in Turkey!' For Sasha: Turkish Delight. She turned to us: 'Guys, you both eat meat?' Oh *yes*, we said, as if being offered the keys to paradise. Wow – a Turkish spice gift set. We in turn gave her a bottle of Agent Provocateur perfume, the last of our gift stash from London.

The rat was duly positioned on Polly's shoulder. DouDou, Polly told us, was named after Madame DouDou from the cartoon *Max & Co*.

'You haven't seen *Max & Co*? *Really*?' she said, haughtily.

She fed the rat some Turkish Delight direct from her own mouth, and the Polly Show began. Like small children introduced to TV for the very first time, Ollie and I were mesmerised. Polly was like a Studio Ghibli character – a super-cute, quirky heroine and an army of one.

'I'm not a racist, but Turkey is such a stupid country,' she said, unpacking her suitcase. 'Turkish people are so lazy and stubborn. You only get progress in cold countries, where you have to work and think. They don't have to think because food grows all around them.'

'What about the Greek and Roman philosophers?' I gently challenged her.'

'They were the last ones to do anything intelligent,' she sniffed.

Couchsurfing warfare was surely internecine so we laughed it off, but it soon became obvious that it didn't matter what we said, it was still going to come. English was clearly the lingua franca here, so eventually Albina and Sasha drifted off, leaving Polly to continue uninterrupted.

Eclipsed by her energy, Ollie and I grew increasingly passive, sitting at her new dark-wood breakfast table while she danced around us, regaling us with her riotous political incorrectness. She was outrageous and opinionated; this was entertainment. We were her first couchsurfers, she explained, and she was 'crazy' about speaking English.

Had she received any other couchsurfing requests?

'One Turkish guy, but I didn't respond because Turkish men think Russian girls are prostitutes. Saying yes would be saying yes to sex.'

We howled with laughter.

'I hate Italian men because they stare at Russian women like we're prostitutes. And they are so impulsive; their feelings are too much.' She pulled a comedy face. 'I think I'm talking too much.'

But it didn't stop – the dynamic had been set. After jumping from topic to topic, Polly sat us down in front of her laptop for a comprehensive presentation on her Lomo photography, and then suggested sushi: 'I'm crazy about sushi.' Sure, we said, by now adjusted to going with the flow – it was 10pm. We grabbed a taxi into town.

'If you had a car,' I asked, 'would you give strangers a ride?'

'Only foreigners,' she said briskly. 'It's dangerous to pick up locals, even when it's a couple – there could be sex violence.'

Declaring herself fat-, junk-, alcohol- and meat-averse (although she really missed cow's tongue, she said), Polly liked sushi because it was about the only fun thing left. As we took our seats at Wasabi, Ollie pointed out that this would be only our third meal of the trip. Industrial foodstuffs, sweets and sufferance had been our staples. 'It's very bad for your bodies to live like this,' Polly lectured crossly. She made some bossy suggestions, but quickly returned to her favourite subject: herself. It was such a problem, she told us, because *so* many guys wanted to be with her and she didn't want to be with them. Admiration for our host soon distorted into a sense of asphyxiation. I sank into my wine – at least just listening, and not having to talk, offered some kind of respite.

Wakey, wakey: party time. We were off to Apartment, a nightclub at the top of a cinema complex, which Polly's older-man lover owned. Arriving at Face Kontrol, she dialled her lover's number and pushed her phone at the door police. They spoke to the phone and waved us through. To the tune of European hip-hop and old-skool funk, Ollie and I threw back vodka shots with her art student friends in amongst the garcon-chic guys and vintage-clad ladies. Polly threw some expert shapes for a while and then became entwined in a lover's knot. Ollie and I made do with her friends – we had an instant gang.

'I am an architecture,' said a blonde, goateed Russian with yellow-lensed spectacles. 'But the Russians who have money have no taste, so we are not being asked to build nice buildings.'

Crutches made good dance floor props – Ollie danced unrestrainedly for what looked like way too long. Should I have said something? Nothing he didn't already know.

At 4am, we walked home to a soliloquy on how Polly had spent two years playing the Long Game to win over her lover. Unfortunately, she had to put up with me as a bedfellow that night for some top-to-tail action. My breather from Polly was sleeping with Polly.

19TH OCTOBER

'So guys, how do you feel after all that alcohol?'

'Fine!' we replied, in grinning defiance.

I bounded out of bed to put the kettle on.

'Actually, we don't drink from the tap.'

'But it's okay boiled, no?'

'The government says yes but I say no.'

Faced with this planet-sized ego, my British diplomacy could hold its banks no more. I started experiencing inappropriate compulsions to take her on; the self-doubt that had bothered me in Moscow had summarily been pushed aside.

Breakfast was porridge and politics. What did Polly think of Medvedev? Did Russia regard him as Putin's puppet?

'I met a DJ from Munich who said the same thing, but the election was shown as democratic – maybe it was the truth that lots of people voted for him.'

'Yes', we said, 'but there are ways of pushing the electorate.'

'My generation is tired of politics,' she said with a brush of the hand. 'We don't have a newspaper culture here. The most common news in Russia is rumour. It goes back to Soviet times when the only information was rumour. People would meet in the kitchen, where you'd be sure that no one would go to the government. It still exists now: people don't want their brain to be – what's the word – pressed?'

Did she feel Asian? Apparently not, despite Yekaterinburg sitting within Russia's Asian border. It seemed all Russians wanted to be seen as European. She explained that in Yekaterinburg there were many Tajiks, Dagestanis and Chechens, selling vegetables in the market.

'I'm not a racist,' she said, arching an eyebrow, 'but I don't like them. They're Muslims – they have absolutely different minds. They are used to war so they can't think any other way. They don't trust people. And I don't like the way they treat Russian women. We are nothing to them. They make a lot of sex violence in the night.'

She flicked on the TV to check the outside temperature: 8°C. Polly was going to take us on a guided tour. She'd done a couple of days' training as a guide – that definitely boosted her couchsurfing worth.

'Polly, do you mind if we take a taxi to wherever you're taking us?' asked Ollie. 'It's hard to walk any distance.'

'But it won't work with taxis – we're going to lots of places and they're all close.'

It was even harder for Ollie to put his foot down.

So, in perfect, crisp sunshine, we were escorted to Yekaterinburg's finest by our own private guide. We passed the Black Rose monument to soldiers lost in Russia's Afghanistan War in the 1980s; a traditional, wooden Russian house, home to a fringe theatre; the early 19th-century Ascension Church that survived the communists; a lemon-yellow stucco merchant's mansion handed over to the Young Pioneers; and across to the Church of the Blood. Built in 2003, on the site where the last Tsar and his family were murdered, there were plenty of hip young Russians inside, praying solemnly in rather unhip headscarves and skirts. Religion was very fashionable here, Polly explained.

'I think it's stupid so much money was put into this building. This is a place that makes you look to God, not talk to him.'

At the Metenkov Photography Museum we found an exhibition from a recent local competition.

'Did you enter?' I asked, one eye on a photo of an overweight, topless construction worker.

'Yes, but I didn't like the judges – they were so conservative. They didn't even say anything about my entry.'

I rolled my eyes rebelliously. We took a tram to Lenin Prospekt, location of the City Hall where her mother worked. Just outside, a beat-up old car drove into the back of another. Both drivers laughed and sped off. Polly pointed out her mother's office – as the city's culture minister, she had her own driver, she told us, and a new black Volga.

'The beautiful thing about couchsurfing,' I said, 'is that you form emotional attachments with cities.'

'But you didn't hear about the secret Russian soul?' she said, as if I hadn't heard of Russia. 'You really didn't hear that we have so great literature, that we are so open-hearted?'

'*No*,' I retaliated – that wasn't the point. My point was that our memories wouldn't be of architecture and facts, but of personalities and homes. Couchsurfing gave a place the human touch – that could happen anywhere, and it certainly didn't take a legacy of literature to enable it. Polly's phone rang.

'Christ,' I muttered darkly to Ollie, 'I can't handle any more arrogance, nationalism or bigotry. Oh the irony of the Russians thinking they're the best.'

My British pride was boiling. Ollie defused me with the appropriate pacifiers, while I consoled myself with the fact that at least when hosts could be tolerated no more, it would soon enough be time to leave.

I determined to behave and suspend my ego for our last

supper – Polly took us to a traditional Urals canteen to carb-load before our 25-hour train journey that night to Novosibirsk. She explained all the strange, muddy offerings, helping us to choose rich, oily Uzbek *plov* (lamb pilau with carrots, cumin and paprika), *pelmeni* (meat dumplings), shredded pork in aspic, and sweet pancake filled with horridly sour, granulated milk. Good behaviour was productive – I was sweet to her, she was sweet back; it gained its own momentum. I nearly lost the *plov* when she asked, 'So Fleur, what do you do for a living?' After all this time.

One classic Polly one-liner came as an unexpected after-dinner treat when we popped into the supermarket: to my offer to carry her five-litre vat of water, she replied, 'I'm not a feminist – men should carry heavy things for women. It's not good for women before they are pregnant.'

Priceless. Polly was a raging feminist.

CHAPTER 4

NOVOSIBIRSK: LOSING A LIMB

'Hello Ravil! Just to say that we're on board our train to Novosibirsk and are looking forward to meeting you tomorrow at midnight … could you just confirm that you've received this?'

This was the third unanswered text message that we'd sent our prospective couch. We were hoping Ravil would be our fourth host, but we'd had precisely no replies. The probability of something going wrong – given that the premise of couchsurfing was suspended on the very delicate bridge of altruism between strangers; and that Ravil was holding a Kalashnikov in his profile picture – was soaring. As novices, this seemed like an impending catastrophe. But first we had to exorcise the electrifying effects of Polly. Now at a safe distance, she amused me – surely better provocative and caffeinated than thumb-twiddlingly bland. The problem was that couchsurfing's doses were either overdoses or none at all. Besides, she'd put us up, and in luxury – as our host, she was the sacred cow.

Ollie elevated his leg in a tea-towel sling – the compulsory walking tour hadn't helped; it was obvious that he was hiding the pain.

'You should seriously get your leg checked out, Ollie,' I said. 'You might be doing it permanent damage. Maybe we can ask Ravil to help.' After all, Ravil was a 23-year-old medical student who worked nights at an 'emergency station' in a town renowned for science. *Akademgorodok*, meaning 'academy town', was Novosibirsk's 'utopian science city', purpose-built in 1957 and considered to be Siberia's educational and scientific centre. Ravil lived, sometimes with his mother, in a one-room apartment. It was staggering that people were happy to share such a small space. It was also an indication of Novosibirsk's limited couch-surfing choices.

20TH OCTOBER

We awoke in Siberia. Were the rest of Russia to disappear, it would still be, at thirteen-million kilometres squared, the largest country on earth. There was a text from Ravil: 'ok'. Just okay? It was both a relief and a jolt – no catastrophe, but not exactly much love. All his communication had sounded alluringly bastard-like: our gun man was handsome, intelligent and danger-ous. The tension mounted.

We hurtled over Stalin's mass graves, the iron ore and the permafrost, and spent the day staring out at the monotony of miles and miles of nothing: barren, prehistoric steppe and great tracts of spruce and birch taiga, occasionally interrupted by hope-less, broken railside settlements and the odd, sky-choking indus-trial plant. I zoned out into the waiting abyss in preparation for the next onslaught. Because we'd be arriving at midnight, Ravil had promised (or threatened) 'a bit sleepless night'.

'Fleur! Ollie!'

Standing statuesquely outside our carriage on the stroke of midnight was Ravil, tall and lean in jeans and a beige puffa jacket. Black flashing eyes looked out from beneath a moose-grey beanie. He smiled briefly. I inexplicably squeezed his arm, while the boys shook hands. Ravil led us through Novosibirsk's imposing Stalinist station and out into an empty car park encrusted with a sparkling frost. Russia's answer to the Fiat Panda – an ocean-blue and very muddy Oka – awaited.

'It's the last Soviet car,' explained Ravil in a soft, Americanised accent. 'I bought it for $1,250 – hardly any works and there's probably twenty kilograms of dirt on it.'

'Fuck.' Ravil's engine stalled in front of a police patrol car, right in the middle of a monster junction resembling the confluence of four motorways. After a brief Kubrick moment (specifically, Wendy trying to flee Overlook Hotel in *The Shining*), the car started … and stalled … and started, as it did for the rest of the journey. Similarly, with much prompting, Ravil gave us his potted history. I focused on him furtively in the rear-view mirror while he told us he was a Tatar, a Turkic people originally from the Gobi Desert. It sounded awfully romantic. He was born and raised in south Kazakhstan, and came to Novosibirsk, Russia's third largest city, to study, ignoring his family's wish for him to study in Kazakhstan. It was a child's right to ignore his parents, he said powerfully. Besides, he was 'very clever' and won prizes for biology. His father had passed away a few years ago, and after his death, Ravil's mother, a seamstress, joined him in Novosibirsk.

So could he explain the Kalashnikov?

'It's a filter,' he said brusquely.

Against what?

'There are two types of couchsurfers. Those who judge on first impressions, and those who think about things. There are too many couchsurfers who say how crazy they are. Psychologists will tell you that they're compensating for being pale.'

Right-o, we said, with pointed blandness. And, err, where was the gun now?

'It's from a little training I did in Russian army. I only had to do it for three weeks because I'm doctor. I don't know how to use it – I'm pacifist.'

Somehow though, the presence of the gun never quite left him.

We arrived at his 'open-air garage' at the hospital where he worked. 'I parked so right by the wall,' he chuckled, 'because my fuel lid is broke.' Three belligerent guard dogs ran for us but Ravil said something to them and they loped off. Ollie asked if we could take a taxi to his, but Ravil said no, firmly: 'By the time we find the taxi, we'll be at home.' He set off into the darkness, walking fast and with purpose, like a lone knight. Ollie was instantly left behind, but it was in my interests to make Ravil wait for Ollie – it was much easier to chat with back-up.

Walking down a dark, potholed dirt track, we passed rows of battered tin-can garages.

'Any Homer Simpson activity down here?' I asked.

'Yes,' Ravil replied airily, like I shouldn't need to ask. 'It's well-known fact that Russians drink in their garages to escape their wives.'

He then told us about his $500-a-month job (the best paid at his level, apparently) screening A&E patients: 'I must decide what do the people need – maybe they're too drunk, too drugged, maybe they just need go home.'

Novosibirsk's health sounded pretty wretched, but, he re-assured us, 'because we have such large country, disease doesn't spread like it does in Britain.'

Perhaps that went for social dis-ease too.

I swooned when he told us he was building a house in a village seventy kilometres away. Was that usual? To build your own house in Siberia?

'My father was engineer,' Ravil said, proudly. 'I built one house with my father in Kazakhstan. I don't see any difference between making a computer, a car or a house.'

Ravil had borrowed his friend's couchsurfers to dig there at the weekend: 'There will always be space for surfers there.' Factoring couchsurfing into his house's blueprint – was it naivety or vision? Ravil was nothing if not resourceful.

'Is that a door you're sleeping on?' I asked, when we arrived at his bedsit in an unloved Soviet tenement building on a seem-ingly infinite estate.

'Two half-doors,' he said, with relish. 'It's hard – I like it.'

The doors rested on two mismatched chairs at each end of his 'bed'. In fact, all the furniture was similar to what you might find in a skip. Either Ollie or I would be sleeping on the floor, though these kinds of facts were made explicit on the couchsurfing site. I stuck my head round the oversized wardrobe in the middle of the room to find, hidden in the darkness, an old red sofa.

'It's Mama's bunker,' he smiled.

Even his mother slept on a sofa. Ravil's entire apartment seemed to be a bunker.

Having totally overlooked buying anything in Yekaterinburg, Ollie and I had privately agreed to re-gift Polly's spices – after all, we couldn't travel round Asia with a spice set.

'Thank you,' Ravil said, scrutinising them before adding imperiously, 'We have all these spices here.'

The spices languished by the front door for the duration of our stay.

'You want Russian soup? It's Mama's gift.'

Ravil led us into his phonebox-sized kitchen, lined with smetana and yoghurt pots hatching herbs, lettuces and other edibles. With only room for two, Ollie wedged an armchair into the doorway. Ravil passed him a plank to use as a tray, and we broke plump, disc-shaped Uzbek bread together, dunking it in his mother's wholesome chicken soup. I forgot to concentrate on taste, however, as my senses were distracted by the view: strong, hero's cheekbones, fine olive skin, kitten-tail eyebrows. His hairline was maturely undulated for a 23-year-old, but it added extra gravitas to an already serious soul. The grey patches under his eyes reminded me of that sleepless night that might be waiting for us. I offered to make tea – this ritual at least was a small claiming of kitchen territory – and Ollie went for a smoke on the balcony.

'Don't hurt my bike!' Ravil yelled, jokingly, but not.

I was caught up in my own jarring, one-way sexual tension. This one-room imprisonment, every nuance under scrutiny, didn't help. But it was the diktat on Ravil's profile that wouldn't leave me: he only wanted travellers – not tourists ('even hardcore ones'). Could we stretch to being travellers? We'd needed a couch, so of course we'd say what he wanted to hear. But if comparing stories with travellers was Ravil's motive for couch-surfing, we were going to disappoint. Couchsurfing was a host's market – they could afford to stipulate conditions. Us guests had to be much more accepting.

It was time for the slideshow. Ravil opened up a photo on his computer of himself lying in the middle of an empty road – the classic hitchhiker pose – and began to conduct a sermon on Russian hitchhiking.

'When you hitchhike, everyone is happy to see you,' he said wistfully. 'You don't need money, you don't need a bag. If you think you need something, it's your problem.'

He took his Axe deodorant and sprayed a squirt on to a lit match, creating a jet of fire close to our ears. It would have been laughable were it not for Ravil's silent command over us.

Russia had a hitchhiking guru, Ravil told us, Anton Krotov – a 32-year-old modern-day Kerouac (who looked like the last person you would give a ride to, owing to his abundant Jesus beard). Ravil had read many of his books and followed his website, The Russian Academy of Free Travel – hitchhiking, it seemed, was cool in Russia. It transpired that hitchhikers and couchsurfers existed happily in the same Venn diagram, for both financial and philosophical reasons: both ideologies enabled a life – for free – outside the material world.

At 3am, I decided to take cover in the bathroom, multi-tasking with time out, a shower and the chance to change my clothes with modesty. It was a man's bathroom: contents included ten cheap soaps worn down to wafers, and tools for shaving, tooth-brushing and clothes-washing. Waiting minutes for the Siberian water to heat up, I went to brush my teeth – but there was no sink in the bathroom. The apartment's only sink was in the kitchen with a violently wobbly tap. And Russians didn't seem to believe in bathmats, or cleaning, so I was left not knowing where to put my clean feet.

At 4.20am came the surprise announcement, 'Let's sleep'. I silently rejoiced. I'd been dreading staying up all night on the back of ten days' junk sleep, but Ollie and I had both settled into our submissive role in the couchsurfing dynamic. Lack of sleep was the worst thing about couchsurfing. I was supplied with a stained, tobacco-coloured, canvas camp bed ('It's called a *raskladushka* – 'little folding thing''). Ollie took the sleeping mat for his leg, and Ravil – in the grey marl T-shirt he'd been wearing that day and a *tiny* pair of briefs – took to his two half-doors. Somehow, I hadn't thought what sharing a one-bedroom apartment meant: enforced intimacy. Hiding my bare, white turkey drumsticks from view behind an armchair, I tried to persuade myself it was no different to being on the beach together. I then made a dive for my bed, which was so close to Ravil's that we were practically spooning. Sleep would evade me that night.

A voice came from the darkness: 'I have no problem being nude.'

'Are you preparing us for breakfast in the buff?' I joked.

A pause.

'I try to swim nude when I can. My girlfriend and I like to swim nude in the lake.' His words hung in the air as we fell silent. Finally, the darkness afforded us some privacy. So he had a girlfriend – in this cloying proximity, that was a massive relief. Ravil sent late-night texts while I developed an intense hatred for my bed. The head was too high so I slipped down like water, forming a pool of patheticness in the middle, while the metal frame boxed me in like a caged animal. Growl.

21ST OCTOBER

Breakfast was sweet bread and soup supplied by Ravil, and black Earl Grey supplied by us, slurped unselfconsciously noisily by him. We booked in to go to the hospital that evening for Ollie's leg. Ollie rolled up his jeans and we all inspected the lump. Ravil took his history, assumed a grave face and said something about infection. I wasn't worried – I just assumed they'd give him some drugs and he would get better.

By day, Ravil's block was the colour of a Chernobyl sunset. It was built in the 1940s, apparently, quite possibly the last decade it had looked clean. The foot-wide drainpipes that ran straight on to the pavements now spilled shards of ice. We wanted the cold; seeking extremes, this pleased us. We took a tram to check out the city, through those motorway-wide streets, past the city's oppressive Stalinist architecture and numerous industrial cranes. Novosibirsk was a functional, industrial Soviet city, with a population of 1.4 million, a plutonium plant, a civil aviation factory and lots of mining. Novosibirsk – or Rio De Novo, as Ravil so ironically called it – was twinned with Doncaster, no less. But couchsurfing opened up a new prism on unattractive towns: it gave them soul.

On board the tram were passengers of Mongol extraction. We were edging nearer to Russia's autonomous Buryat Republic and, of course, Mongolia. And, yes, both places had couches for us. The Buryatian capital, Ulan-Ude, was our next stop – some 2,300 kilometres east of Novosibirsk. We'd eventually managed to persuade a young Buryatian girl that it didn't matter that her English was bad and that she lived in the suburbs – we had a couch at least.

Back in Novosibirsk, a pattern was establishing itself in our communications:

Me: 'So is … Russia/Siberia/Novosibirsk/couchsurfing …?'

Ravil: [an appropriate answer].

Silence.

Silence.

Silence.

Me: 'So is … Russia/Siberia/Novosibirsk/couchsurfing …?'

Otherwise it was: 'Let's stop and wait for Ollie.'

I spent half my time looking backwards at Ollie, as he lagged behind, beaten by Ravil's turbo pace. Sleep-deprived, I would have preferred not to make conversation, but that was a privilege reserved for better friends. Plus, efforts seemed so unequal – like Polly, Ravil showed little curiosity for us.

'So is there a Siberian flavour to Novosibirsk?'

'All of Russia is the same – no one cares about architecture or art. They just want somewhere to live.'

'So does Siberia want independence?'

'Moscow won't let it. There is a place in Siberia, Yakutia – it's bigger than Kazakhstan – and it pays fifteen per cent of Moscow's taxes from gold, diamonds and brilliants.'

'But does Siberia want independence?'

'The people are too busy to think about it. If you have time, you think, 'I want a car, I want a girl, I want financial independence.''

'So, umm, does everyone get the "clause" treatment?' I said, referring to certain stipulations in his emails.

'Of course,' Ravil said, flatly.

He'd once had five Polish people staying, who'd come back with seven bottles of wine.

'I said to them, did you not read that wine was forbidden?' They had a pretty big dose. I don't want unexpected troubles – it's important to be safe in your house.'

I very quickly determined not to get on the wrong side of

Ravil. The pressure to please this hard-to-please man who had such particular ideas was suffocating.

Ravil was no eager tour guide. We passed by an immense, icily sterile Lenin Square, home to Russia's largest opera house ('I hate opera') and some dwarfingly large constructivist statues of Soviet workers, soldiers and, of course, Lenin. But it wasn't until we returned home that I read in my book we'd crossed the very geographical centre of Russia, honoured by the golden domed Chapel of St Nicholas. Nor that the Arctic-bound Ob River, on the north bank of which we found a deserted skate park, was the world's fourth longest. But I sensed that Ravil wasn't a couch-surfer out of city pride, but for political reasons – he abhorred money. Perhaps he'd always choose to sleep on doors.

At the prescribed hour, 9pm, we went to A&E – not because Ravil assessed it as an emergency, but because this was the most efficient route. Ravil took Ollie behind closed doors, leaving me in a Soviet-era mint-green waiting room and a *tableau vivant* of rather un-*vivant* Russians. A jaundiced miner in leather boots and dungarees covered in a thin film of coal dust was holding a urine sample; another rocked drunkenly, hassling any medic that passed. An hour passed and the jaundiced miner was wheeled past in the recovery position. Ollie wasn't waiting, he was being seen to, so what was taking so long? From beyond, I heard the sound of grown men screaming. What if one of the screams was Ollie?

Standing only in his pants, his hiking boots (covered with blue plastic bootees) and a seeping bandage where the lump had been, Ollie was back, his face waxy and drawn. Ravil was standing at his side, looking solemn. My heart started thudding.

'We have to go home, Fleur. They found puss on my leg and

it could spread to the bone. They collected thirteen millilitres of puss. That's a lot.'

Suddenly it was an emergency. I bit back the tears. Ollie's leg was in serious trouble, so was it wrong to feel sorry for myself? Instantly I was furious with Ollie's London consultant; he should never have been declared fit. And 'go home'? Did I really have to go home after eleven days? There was nothing wrong with me. Or was it because Ollie didn't think it wise for me to travel solo through Russia and China? The marbles had been released on to my path, yet this was Ollie's emergency – we had to sort him out. I was electrified with panic.

In fits and starts, we picked our way back to Ravil's, whose pace, incredibly – or revealingly – still didn't slow for Ollie. We stopped at an all-night pharmacy (it was now midnight) for antibiotics and water.

'Why are you buying water?' Ravil roared.

Ollie and I both cowered.

'You can drink tap water. It's just marketing myth that you can't drink it.'

We found excuses to defend our purchases and hit a wall of silence for the rest of the walk home – no, Ollie couldn't get a taxi. Ravil really had become Siberian, with his intolerance for spoilt, Western softness.

What to do? We were about to book flights home, so I had make a decision, fast. I *hated* travelling alone. I subscribed to the Noah's Ark school of travel – it should be done in pairs. But I, supposedly, was the lucky one – quitting wasn't permitted. I'd waited too long for this adventure. I rearranged my face into one of survival: 'Ollie, I can't come home with you.'

He understood: 'I just thought you'd want to.'

In a way, I did.

At home, Ravil sat down at his computer, slipped on some enormous headphones, and said, 'I'm off to crash cars.'

Ollie's flight home was urgently arranged – there was one to Moscow at 7am. At 4.30am, Ollie and I left for Novosibirsk Airport: I was going to cling on to him for as long as I could. The boys exchanged a brotherly hug and I stuffed a packet of biscuits into my bag – Ollie and I were ravenous, and biscuits were easier than asking Ravil for food. But I still hadn't adjusted to the news. I bolted from our farewell at the airport – an emotional downpour felt imminent.

In total silence, blinking like a pit pony, Ravil let me back in at 6.30am. Well *now* we were in a Pinter-esque tension, an unbearable ache of awkwardness in his too-close-for-comfort bedsit. The camp bed had been put away so, trying to be no trouble, I took to the floor – it couldn't be any less comfortable.

I lay awake, rigid on my mat – even the most microscopic movement would create an abominable rustle. With the feeling that Ollie and I had taken way more than we could give, I resolved to get up early, whether I'd slept or not, and get out. I wanted out. My train to Ulan-Ude was the next night at 1am; I would deal with the day alone. I had to nurse my crumbling emotional land-scape in private. Bereft, lonely, empty, I pined for The Emperor. Ollie's friendship had so persuasively concealed the void within, but now they were both far away, I so craved what I couldn't have. Wanting what was out of reach – it was so predictable.

22ND OCTOBER

A text from Ollie: 'The air stewardess just had to rip a hidden can of beer out of the hands of the man on the plane seat in front of me because he's drinking before take-off. He looks like Rumpelstiltskin and she looks like Sharon off *Eastenders*. Quite a tug of war. Niet. Da. Niet. Da …'

I sat up in bed, stiff like the floorboards responsible for my aches. Behind me, I could hear that Ravil was awake, scrolling through his mobile – it felt strange that he hadn't acknowledged the new day and said good morning. I offered my salutations, and packed up in paranoid silence for a hasty exit. I now felt completely naked.

'Are you hungry? I suppose you are,' Ravil said kindly.

I supposed I was. Breakfast was Mama's cold beef stew and boiled potato. Halfway through, Ravil put his in the microwave without inviting me to follow suit, so I went along with the cold version, as if it were just how I liked it. I found a hair in amongst the potatoes, covered it with another potato and announced myself full. Instead of eating, I mined him for travel tips on Kazakhstan.

'Kazakhstan is extreme,' he said, with finality.

I tried to look unfazed, like a *real* traveller.

'It's extremely hospitable but extremely poor. I only travel with what I need.'

I felt vulnerable.

My sister once locked our new puppy in a room with the old cat, so that they could get to know each other. Couchsurfing's forced friendships reminded me of her experiment. Like cats and dogs, Ravil and I were similarly opposed. As he accompanied me to the station's left luggage hall, he seemed happy in contemplation (or social retirement). I, however, needed to feign some kind of social order, so I babbled away about London life: politics, the underground, Russian oligarchs – wasn't this couchsurfing's cultural exchange? His standard response was an impregnable 'mm-mm'. Sometimes I'd repeat myself, thinking he was saying 'pardon', only to get another 'mm-mm'. But I blundered on, because wasn't it worse to be both needy and mute?

Left luggage passed without incident, and he sent me off in the right direction for a day of organisation in Ravil's preferred Wi-Fi zone, KFC.

'I feel a bit stressed,' I confessed, my voice cracking.

'At least you are stressed,' he replied, wisely.

I forcibly hugged him, squeezing out all of the human contact I could, and turned away quickly. It was time to leave, yet I wasn't ready to be alone. While Ollie was returning to London to look after his limb, I felt like I'd lost one. Like an unfledged chick flung out of the nest, I suddenly felt all alone.

I had the number for Nick, another local couchsurfing host who was, according to his references, 'the coolest dude in Novosibirsk' (Ollie and I had requested his couch, but he wasn't sure if he'd be in town for the 'third decade of October'). I invited him to KFC for a junk-food hit. Meanwhile, I spent the day online, trying to feel connected. I broadcast the news of Ollie's departure to all, and begged for reinstatement of communications with The Emperor. I felt too feeble to try and move on – I needed that lifeline. He wrote straight back, offering to come out, as a friend, as 'whatever'. But couchsurfing wasn't for everyone, and it wasn't for him. He was way too uncompromising and dominant; he was, after all, The Emperor. Right in the middle of KFC, I wept great streams of longing. I wanted to go home, but defeat was inadmissible. It wasn't as if I were the world's first solo explorer. Perhaps couchsurfing would look after me, as I bounced across Asia on lily pads of hospitality, falling into the arms of kind hosts. At least that was the hypothesis.

Ollie, meanwhile, was sending live feeds from London. He'd gone directly to his consultant, who said things weren't as bad as they'd seemed: the abscess would have eventually burst outwards, into the air, rather than inwards, poisoning his blood. Not so bad? That wouldn't have been our response in the Mongolian wilderness. He'd have to have the titanium removed at a later stage, and, for the time being, have consultations every other day. His doctor had found seaweed stuffed into the holes the Russians had made in his leg, a pub gem best known after the event when all is well. Under strict instructions to rest up, Ollie was going to be surfing his own sofa for a while. We were both miserable.

Well, what do you know? Donagh, the Irish architect we'd met in Moscow, walked into KFC as the couchsurfing guest of Nick, a Shrinky-Dinked Russian graphic designer with long blond dreads, a goatee and earrings.

'Ach, you're no more vulnerable here than in real life,' reassured Donagh, once I'd poured my story all over them in one breathless torrent.

I secretly leant on Donagh and Nick, vampirically milking their positivity and wisdom. Donagh had been surfing since Moscow: 'So that people can take me to bars,' he explained, cradling a pint of KFC beer. 'I don't want to stay in alone reading my book – Russia isn't very friendly to outsiders but couchsurfers are leftist enough to open the door.'

Nick was one such specimen. 'I've had thirty or forty people at my place since June,' he said. 'And I'd host someone for long time if they're in a special situation, like trying to get a job.'

There were people who surfed for a whole year, they told me, and there was 'over-couchsurfing'. Donagh recounted how one Russian girl in Moscow extended a two-week stay to a year because she didn't want to pay the capital's high rents. But her host – Russia's legendary Country Ambassador – turned it to his advantage, essentially using her as his PA. This was the alternative economy.

For the first time I felt part of something bigger: the couchsurfing community. We were strangers, yet we had an instant bond: we all shared similar experiences and principles. What's more, Donagh had met Yvonne in Yekaterinburg, and would be in Beijing at the same time as me. I was on a couchsurfing trail! That might devalue the concept for some, but for me, the discovery was a happy one – this was a mobile community. And I saw couchsurfing through other, more experienced, eyes: I realised that Ollie and I had been muddling along in the dark. Nick and Donagh gave me a frame of reference.

For two hours, my loneliness had been suspended. At 11.30pm, Nick and Donagh saw me off to the station. Blessed by serendipity and topped up with kindness, I felt emotionally nourished. My hypothesis was looking promising.

CHAPTER 5

ULAN-UDE: TO HEALTH! TO LOVE! TO VODKA!

A colossal, cabbagey babushka was cradling a potato sack like a baby. The potato sack shook to reveal the wiry, grey head of a small mutt. A defeated and dusty old man – in pitch-perfect Chekhovian tragedy – held his troubled brow in bloodied, swollen hands. A grubby street urchin shamelessly prodded the shoulders of every man, woman and child in his way, holding out his artful hands. I was at Novosibirsk station, waiting for my forty-hour train to Ulan-Ude. Without Ollie, I was *en garde*. Without Ollie, I realised, I was engaged – Russia had come alive. What I found reminded me to count my blessings.

In my cramped cabin, two Russian workers had already claimed the emotional space. Wrung out, I meekly clambered on to the top bunk and attempted to hibernate. My tears seemed to have given me a cold: I sneezed. '*Bud zdorova* [bless you],' said one of the workers, gruffly. I looked down. He was wearing an unconvincing black nylon wig; the other had a heavy Scouser 'tache and kind eyes. 'Chai?' offered the 'tache. And so began a most unlikely friendship, conducted through my increasingly clammy dictionary and sign language. They were truck drivers from Dikson, deep within the Russian Arctic Circle. Was my mother not worried? Did I have a Kazakh dictionary? Have these wafers! No thanks. Have these wafers! Okay! Where was I staying? 'I'm staying with a friend,' I said. I repeated those words in my head: I had a *friend* – of sorts – waiting for me in a new city. That was a powerful feeling.

Clutching an in-case-of-emergency address in Dikson, I turned in at 3.30am, perplexed as to why my berth buddies were happy to share their night and supplies with me. We weren't used to such hospitality in London's individualistic, post-Thatcher society. As I looked at my rations-for-one, I wondered if it were me, unable to think beyond the self, that was uncivilised.

24TH OCTOBER

After a day of hyper-sleep, I was starting to come round from the shock. The Russians had left to drive trucks, and I was alone again. I thought of Ravil – he had given his time, his food, his place and his philosophy. Surely the insight into Russian life would long outlive memories of silly social anxiety.

I found it difficult to look out of the window; the Great Empty Steppe mirrored my sense of isolation. However, out there, edged by lonely firs covered in plump blankets of snow was the oceanic Lake Baikal, the 'blue eye of Siberia'. As the deepest lake on earth, the largest freshwater lake by volume, and – thanks to its self-purifying properties – holder of one-fifth of the world's drinking water, Lake Baikal was, to the Buryatian people, the Sacred Sea. The Buryatians – a traditionalist Mongol people numbering just a million, who practised both Buddhism and Shamanism (despite Soviet efforts) – respected nature like a religion.

I was very pleased with my couchsurfing find in Ulan-Ude, a 25-year-old eastern Buryatian girl called Zhenya. While western Buryats had been 'Russified', dumping nomadism for agriculture, eastern Buryats were more traditional and closer to the Mongols. But I didn't know much about Zhenya – her profile was scant and new – except that her family had, at some stage, swapped nomadism for the suburbs. I was eager for an ersatz Ollie and some shanti love, that beneficent Buddhist practice of forbearance and forgiveness. But having forgotten to get a gift in the 'excitement', and about to arrive with a lot of needs (laundry, tickets to Mongolia and Vladivostok, internet access), it all felt a bit take, take, take. Again.

I was floundering on the platform, lost in a sea of strangers, when Zhenya pulled me to safety. I looked up at her. Tall and beautiful, with long, glossy sable hair, and narrow, Mongol eyes smouldering with kohl, she smiled graciously like a Buryatian goddess. She even had a retinue of three young European males.

'Bernat, Albert, David,' she introduced, in a honeyed Russian accent.

'A-ha!' I exclaimed. 'You must be the Spanish firemen.' News of their journey had preceded them – we were due to share the same Vladivostok host. I was right back on the trail.

We piled into Zhenya's silver Toyota Camry Lumiere. I eyed the Buddhist charm hanging from the rear-view mirror as we tore home, skidding on black ice and dodging pot-holes by veering on to the wrong side of the road. Conversation fell to the three musketeers and me. Actually – as they were quick to point out – they were Catalan, not Spanish, from Barcelona.

'I never wanted a Russian flag,' said Bernat, the self-appointed spokesperson, owing to his superior English. 'But I would like a Buryatian one. We have sympathy for Buryatia under Moscow's centralised control.'

We were so immersed in conversation that both the view and Zhenya's silence were overlooked. Chastened, I tried to chat with her, but after repeating myself and even trying out some Russian (to which she pulled a face of mortal horror), she finally confessed, 'I find your accent difficult.' Zhenya spoke American-English. English-English was niche, it seemed. She dropped her head: 'I need to practise.'

'We can help with that,' I grinned.

'That's why you're here!' she said.

'The suburbs' were the Beverly Hills of Ulan-Ude (well, relatively speaking), at the end of an unprepossessing, three-mile dirt track. We pulled up at a large, detached house. This was my first couch *not* in a Soviet block. The senses were slapped hard. With the distinct aroma of pickled cabbage and charcoal smoke under my nose, I was introduced to her father, a small man of a sensei's build with a beatific smile, and her younger brother, Sasha, who was going mountaineering with his university friends that weekend. In amongst the rush of the family running around, grabbing at ropes and high-tech outdoor equipment, Zhenya showed me my room – my own room! We'd all be going out again in twenty minutes, she told us (it was Friday night), and left to grab at ropes.

My Own Room was large and bare, with a single bed, a computer and, on the walls, two posters of models in bikinis pressed against shiny red Mercedes – the fascinating habitat of a Russian youth. As a matter of emergency, I washed my hair and changed my top (there was no washing or changing on the Trans-Siberian), and chatted to the Catalans who were sleeping in Zhenya's vacated room next door. Worn out, they were all lying on their mattresses. This, too, was their first couchsurfing trip, and we traded tales. Some of their hosts had even met them with name placards, and one of their hosts' boyfriends split for three days because he didn't like couchsurfers. I instantly liked them – but then, I needed them.

We didn't get very far on our drive into town because we were stopped by the police.

'One of you hide!' Zhenya urged dramatically. 'Four in the back is illegal.' We all simultaneously ducked. Wearing a cute leather bomber, an asymmetric black miniskirt and foxy knee-highs, she stepped out of the vehicle.

'She never passed her driving test,' one of the musketeers whispered. 'Apparently Sasha knows the right people.'

Sliding back behind the wheel unscathed, Zhenya purred, 'Sometimes, it's good to be a woman.' The police had been looking for drink-drivers. But the action didn't stop there. After dropping Sasha off, there was then a near miss with a tram, which she avoided by reversing into oncoming traffic. And when trying to parallel park (a group effort), she ripped her tyre on a metal spike.

How many Spanish firefighters does it take to change a wheel? More than three evidently. 'Don't worry!' they rallied. 'We can fix this!' They were quickly pushed aside by a local and we celebrated with a meal in a nearby Chinese café, where Zhenya's Buryatian friends – a cousin, an ad exec, and a well-known opera singer – were waiting. There were no Russians inside – Ulan-Ude was quite the ethnic departure. Its population of 360,000 included Mongolians, Chinese labour migrants (Buryatia was close to the Chinese border), and twenty-one per cent Buryatians.

While waiting for our food, I decided to tell a perfectly relevant joke:

Me: Did you hear about the three Spanish firefighters?

Them: No.

Me: They were called Hose A, Hose B and Hose C.

Them: Oh.

Me: You know – like José! No?

Lost in translation. I distracted the table by switching focus on to Zhenya. The name 'Zhenya' was – like her peers' – a Russian name because they'd been born into the Soviet Union. Despite her strong Buryatian identity, Zhenya couldn't speak Buryatian; her mother, also Buryatian, was a Russian literature and language teacher. But Zhenya knew enough to give me my Buryatian name, *cecek* – 'flower'. I felt like I almost belonged. Zhenya had recently returned to Ulan-Ude to look after her ill father, having been working in Moscow for three years at a Russian high-street fashion chain. 'I miss Moscow,' she said, her perfectly groomed brows knotting. Finding work in Ulan-Ude in the current climate was proving tough, and Ulan-Ude was not cosmopolitan, but, it seemed, the Buryatian sense of family duty took priority. I exhaled – I felt safe, and also excited. I could suspend my guard. That, as I would realise later, would prove dangerous.

'NO!' gasped Zhenya to the musketeers. 'It's not good luck to stick your fork in the bread.'

Sharing-plates of glass noodles, deep-fried pork and chubby knots of steamed bread had arrived. With food to negotiate, conversation fell to the path of least resistance: the Europeans with the Europeans, the Buryatians with the Buryatians. It felt wrong, like I preferred to talk to the firefighters. This was the ex-pat conflict. I wanted to explore new frontiers, but it was hard work. I'd instinctively slipped back into my comfort zone.

Over tea so milky it looked like just milk, the musketeers grumbled about not being able to find a decent coffee. But that was one of couchsurfing's blessings, wasn't it? That it broke the spell of bad habits. I was off the double-shot cappuccinos with caramel drizzle because it just wasn't an option. I was probably kicking all sorts of habits, emotional and physical. That, unfortunately, included sleeping and washing – sometimes they weren't available either.

'Fasten your seatbelts!' the firefighters insisted. We'd ditched Zhenya's car and were in her ad-exec friend Rinchin's gleaming Nissan Presage for a spot of ego-tourism, as he sped, tail-gated and devoured Ulan-Ude's urban sprawl as if driving a tank. The firefighters and I volleyed fearful expletives, but they only seemed to provide the encouragement that Rinchin craved. And the emergency? We needed milk vodka, a Buryatian speciality, to toast new arrivals. Despite losing an hour, plus days off my life, to this perilous and ultimately fruitless quest, it was for the best – we were spared a night on fermented, curdled mare's milk. Couchsurfers couldn't say no – after all, wasn't that why we were here, for the access to traditional delicacies?

Reprieve was short-lived. Russian vodka and balsam (a herbal vodka) would have to do. Rinchin stormed Skin Mountain, a hill studded with Buddhist prayer stones overlooking the city, for the welcome we'd been dreading: the SUV's leather seats were then swivelled around into a cosy circle. 'No, no, I can't drink tonight,' groaned Bernat. Why not? Because exactly the same thing had happened the night before. I could only wait to find out what.

'The first toast is for respect,' said Zhenya, pouring out six shots. Respect – that made it *impossible* to say no. Despite our full bellies, we were instructed to chase with huge *buuzies* (dough-nut-sized, Buryatian dumplings). The boys gritted their teeth and ate their words. Rinchin didn't seem remotely bothered by the drink-driving crackdown. 'What's the penalty?', I asked, in undisguised disapproval. 'A two-year ban, and if you have an accident, nine months in prison,' he said, unmoved. I buttoned my judgment – it felt disrespectful. The toasts kept coming. To health! To love! To friends! To … The fog of forgetfulness soon descended. Suitably tanked up, Rinchin dropped us off at Metro, apparently Ulan-Ude's best club.

I hadn't anticipated a club because I wasn't quite at one with the couchsurfers' motto: Be Prepared for Anything. Despite Face Kontrol not adoring my walking boots, our association to Zhenya – a girl about town with her Moscow credentials – saw us swiftly ushered into the velvet banquettes of the VIP area. Much more vodka was bought, and we were introduced to Zhenya's friends. They'd heard some girls outside trying to remember some Spanish words. News that three macho Spanish guys were in town was out.

It was at about this point that amnesia drew its black curtain. I remembered saying thank you to Zhenya a lot, and clinging to my new ally, David (okay, I was flirting with the unattached one; I didn't want him, I was just feeding my emotional hunger). There were strippers, there were bottle-blonde Buryatian women, there was shameless dancing, there were good times. Apparently.

25TH OCTOBER

Still dressed, still drunk and my mouth desert-dry, I woke up in Sasha's bed, numb from a night on its wooden base – all Russians seemed to like it hard, evidently. But how did I get here? Where was my BlackBerry? Whose was that *chapka* – the Russian fur hat? That camera? And – oh God – did I kiss David or was it a dream? I scrambled to check the photographic evidence: tight embraces, topless boys, boys kissing boys, power punches … worrying. Then I thought about Ollie, and The Emperor, and I realised I hadn't worried about anything since I'd arrived. Getting out of my head had, quite literally, helped me get out of my head.

I could hear that the boys had just woken up and were laughing about the night. I froze, realising that to get out of my room, I had to go through theirs. I drew a deep breath.

'So, boys, I seem to have lost my phone and my memory and gained a camera and a hat …'

I searched David's eyes, but I couldn't find the answer there. I quickly scurried out – I was going to have to ask Zhenya.

'Hungry?' chirped Zhenya, orchestrating the domestics in the kitchen.

'Starving!'

'Sheep soup,' she explained, handing me a large bowl.

Would it be insulting not to eat the solid cubes of fat, the layers of alimentary canal and the tendons swimming like eels? I was the only one eating, so I had no one to copy. Plus, as a couchsurfer, I was learning that you ate what and when you could – the fridge wasn't mine to raid.

'So what do you grow in your kitchen garden?'

With tomatoes, onions, cabbages, cucumbers, apples and potatoes, it was the picture of Siberian self-sufficiency.

Having pointed her attention outside the window, I threw the unspeakables away. And that possible indiscretion? Cowardice struck – I could hear the boys coming. I'd wait to ask Zhenya after they left for Vladistock later that day. Losing one's memory had its hazards, but it was also a face-saver.

Losing my BlackBerry was rather more straightforward – it was lost. Of course, there was the possibility that something more sinister than good times had taken it, but the idea was unthinkable. Hosts had far more to lose.

The day's next excitement was the hypermarket, for the boys to stock up for their three-day train journey. In the car my gaze was conveniently averted outside, to catch, in amongst a constructivist majority, Ulan-Ude's bronze monuments to heroic, mounted Buryatian warriors, and Buddhist buildings with flying eaves. At the supermarket, Zhenya picked up a couple of value tins of horsemeat.

'You need meat,' she said maternally.

'Why?' responded Bernat, with some disdain.

'For the train.'

'No.'

It was useful to see how others – non-Brits – were with their hosts. Bernat wasn't rude, he just didn't want tinned horsemeat. His candour was inspiring.

We hugged the boys goodbye at the station. With them safely out of earshot, I could *finally* ask Zhenya for the missing details.

'You were in the back of my car wearing his *chapka*,' she said, her voice tripping into a laugh. 'And David asked, "Can I kiss you?" You said yes. And then he asked, "Can you kiss me?" and you just started singing.'

(Was it 'Can I kick it?/Yes you can,' I wondered). But did I kiss him?

'Then we got home and you went to bed. When I asked where David was, I found him in your room but you were asleep, and I shouted, "David, go back to bed!" The boys were laughing for thirty minutes.'

As did we. Too bad alcohol took as much as it gave.

✪

My next stop, in two days' time, would be just outside Mongolia's capital Ulan Bator, where I'd be staying in a *ger* – a traditional felted tent. My host, a German woman married to a local, had three negative references – quite a count for couchsurfing. She'd been 'moody', and had pushed her guests into doing her 'maximum price' tours. She responded negatively to one reference, saying the guest had set fire to her house and stolen her phone. It sounded like a cartoon. But she also had plenty of positive references. I was intrigued; it sounded authentic. Maybe Marco from Italy summed it up: 'At Sabina's I had the craziest couchsurfing adventures, she is unique, in both really good and really bad ways, but once you understand Mongolia, you understand Sabina, or vice versa.' It promised some safe danger. I was excited.

'I have to visit my aunt with a broken rib,' Zhenya announced after helping me buy my tickets to Mongolia. 'I'll be back at 10pm [it was now 5pm] – maybe you can go for a walk.'

The apron strings were suddenly severed. I was going to have to be independent again. Placing all emotional needs on my host was an ask too much, I realised, and foolish. So I decided to go and place them on the internet instead.

News from Ollie: he was 'lying very still', under self-imposed house arrest, 'maybe for a whole month', but now that the knife had been at his leg, it was 'nice and flat'. Ollie was such a stoic. I was going to miss his calm crisis management.

10pm suddenly became 7pm – Zhenya was going to come back early. She was waiting outside in her car, with her mother and another cousin, Nastia (short for Anastasia). They screamed when I tried to get in. This was, of course, because I'd got into the wrong car of Buryatian girls. I guess Zhenya saw all of this because I then heard a car horn, presumably to aid my sonar location. But once reunited, no one mentioned it – least of all me in my deep shame. I missed having someone to laugh with.

We dropped Zhenya's divorced mother at home, taking the silent and shy 20-year-old Nastia, a 'customs' student, back with us. Was I hungry? 'A little bit peckish,' I said warily, thinking about sheep entrails. Plus, I'd just eaten half a packet of strawberry sandwich biscuits. Too bad – pancakes, tomato chutney, smetana and Siberian apple jam were promptly laid out on the kitchen table. Nastia and Zhenya folded their pancakes into neat little parcels, so I did too, filling mine with round after round of the most delicious apple jam – crunchy and fresh cherry-sized apples in a tart but sweet sunset-pink apple soup. Zhenya had made it herself; her grandmother did the blackcurrant jam, which they'd mix with cold water for a drink. But that was nothing, her father had built the whole house.

'My father is engineer – he can do everything,' she said, throwing her arms up jubilantly. 'In Russia, we say "golden hands".'

Their house even had a banya. Oh, I'd *love* to have a banya, I gushed. 'I promised the boys a banya for two days,' she laughed, before adding, 'It takes two hours to prepare.' That sounded debt-inducing.

Never mind: the laptop slideshow was good to go. Was this a Russian thing or the tool of smart couchsurfing hosts, equipping themselves with endless conversation prompts? Zhenya opened up a video: a sheep was supine on a table in a field; four men holding down each leg.

'I bought a sheep in the countryside,' Zhenya explained. 'They're very tasty from this area.'

The sheep wriggled – it was *alive*. A man was sawing a knife into its chest. I slowly raised my hand to my mouth.

'My friend killed the sheep by ripping a big artery,' Zhenya continued, matter-of-factly. 'There are less nerves so it's less painful and quite quick. In Buryatia, we don't let blood go on the floor.'

Fortunately, the film finished before the final curtain, but she caught my wide eyes.

'It might not be good but it's what we do,' she apologised.

But it wasn't bad, I said, thrilled by this window on to local life. There wasn't enough respect paid to where the food on our plate came from. I suddenly thought: this morning's breakfast … Yup, from the sacrificial sheep.

Flicking through photos of her family stood around a rainy field being arranged by a wise-looking man in a red-belted black dress and pointy wool hat, Zhenya explained how she'd visited a shaman before going to Moscow, to 'open the road' for her. They'd held a ceremony in her grandfather's village with a totem pole that her brother had to make, and donations to the spirits including money, a sheep, thirteen packets of milk, thirteen bottles of vodka and several kilos of cookies and tea. Like other Buryatians, she would also visit a lama – a Buddhist priest – in times of uncertainty. It would be wrong to extrapolate a general Buryatian character from my one encounter, but it was true that

Zhenya was the gentlest Russian I'd met, possessed of a Buddhist poise and with her ego in check.

'NOOOO!' Zhenya reproved kindly, when I assumed the washing-up position. 'You are a guest – you don't have to.'

Feeling useless, I dragged my feet back to the table. I struggled to adjust to this one-way honour. It was when she described her holiday in Uzbekistan that this strange language of hospitality was finally translated. Zhenya explained how she and a friend had been showered with kindness by a random Uzbek, who even lent them his apartment.

'But didn't you feel indebted?' I asked.

'Maybe not,' she mused, 'because he showed us hospitality.'

That was it – hospitality should be seen as a gift. My thinking was so western, feeling like I was imposing, feeling the need to return the favour. Perhaps us islanders were too accustomed to defending ourselves from foreign invasion to be open-armed to strangers. Perhaps, once I'd hosted in London, I'd relax more as a guest – I'd know what it was to give my hospitality.

Long conversations added up to a long night. Zhenya showed me photos of the firefighters cooking her a Spanish breakfast; I described a traditional British Christmas and New Year, and, in a case of reciprocal disclosure, I found myself saying bad things about Britain because she'd said bad things about Russia. It might have been 2.30am, but Zhenya wasn't going to go to bed – her 84-year-old grandmother was returning from the countryside that night. They were close, like friends, Zhenya said, tenderly. 'Babushka' had always lived in the countryside, but having lost her husband ten years ago, she had moved into the family home. As the youngest son, Zhenya's father was responsible for caring for her.

'There are old people's houses but Buryatian people don't leave old people like this,' Zhenya said.

Abandoning old people was what Britain did. I took myself off to bed, wondering how Britain had ended up being so selfish. Perhaps it was capitalism's fault.

26TH OCTOBER

Like manna from heaven, The Emperor called. We were soon cut off, but the sound of his voice gave me new energy, and I swung right back into 'on' mode, fuelled, or fooled, again by a naive optimism that everything could change between us. I sighed at my indecision. Even out here, I was still caught between being a product of my commitment-phobic generation (we were necessarily indecisive perfection-seekers), and the pressure of my own age (my final decision was due very soon, before the biological clock stopped ticking). Both seemed to pull so hard.

Babushka still hadn't arrived, but the kitchen table had been replenished with bowls of plain, hot rice for Nastia and me, and on the side, Siberian apple jam, and pink rubbery sausage. Zhenya, going about the domesticities with the ease of instinct, was clearly the mother figure, without the slightest hint of resentment.

'Babushka!' Stooped and shrivelled, Zhenya's grandmother shuffled in wearing a folksy, forest-green smock. She looked soulful and handsome, with apple cheeks and walnutty skin and an air of utter indomitability. Privately, I was as excited as Zhenya, but Babushka was in no mood for small talk with strangers. Zhenya and her caught up alone, while Nastia and I settled for watching Paris Hilton on MTV. So far on this trip I'd been blessedly spared much exposure to the fame virus – it never seemed less relevant.

For the afternoon, I was put back into internet day care. I bought a box of chocolates for Zhenya, who then collected me again, along with other friends and family – her mother, Edward the opera singer and his girlfriend Katya. When I pointed out Zhenya's habit of collecting people, she laughed 'I like to have guests in my house – it brings an energy'. She was a natural couch-surfer. Back at home, Zhenya swiftly regifted the chocolates to Babushka, leaving me still indebted to my host.

'Say thank you, Babushka,' Zhenya prompted.

'*Spasiba*,' Babushka obliged, curtly.

But this was good groundwork – I longed to crack Babushka and talk Soviet oppression and rural Buryatian life with her. For now, though, faced with a Russian-speaking majority, I had to assume a dignified silence.

But there was plenty to observe as the family sat down to a dinner of Babushka's raw *omul* (a prized, herring-like fish from Lake Baikal, eaten heads and all) and 'real' smetana (grainy and sour). Manners make one eat the most grim things. Babushka watched over us like an owl, the parents got on like the divorce had never happened, the laptop photo gallery came out, and Edward the opera singer performed rousing Buryatian ballads on his twelve-stringed, acoustic guitar.

Shock news just in by text from Mongolia: my host, Sabina, had absconded. Well, okay, her husband and two young offspring would be around, she wrote, but the safe danger had just broken through its fetters. I felt disconcerted, not least by her woolly instructions to 'walk up an unpaved road until you can't go straight on.' Couchsurfing made me want to believe: if she thought I could find this unpaved road in the dark, then surely I could. Too late to organise anything else, I would have to.

CHAPTER 6

MONGOLIA:
NOMADIC WANDERINGS

27TH OCTOBER

It was a portentous 666 kilometres south to Ulan Bator. The peaceful view belied the omen. A perky sun rose over flatlands of golden grass and distant hills, mystically shielded by mist. Black kites glided majestically above sacred, white-chalked mounds, and smokestacks stood like birthday candles atop old wooden houses. Out here, Buryatia's ancient magic was alive.

After a time, the bus pulled over at a giant felled fir tree. All the ladies dashed towards it, while the men scattered in all directions. Twelve Russians, seven Mongolians and one Brit had a collective toilet break. We had a twelve-hour journey to endure – pragmatism trumped magic.

A Russian student was on her way back to one of Ulan Bator's three Russian universities. At the border, I lent her my pen, and she told me she wanted to travel to Europe. Oh, you should try couchsurfing, I rhapsodised. You will find friends amongst strangers, you will have a place to call home. I sounded like a cult-selling missionary.

Mongolia looked startlingly different to its next-door neighbour. I became hypnotised by the timeless Mongolian Steppe, the stubbly grasses defiantly spiking through a recent snowfall, lonely gers crouching on low hills, and sheep, cows and horses grazing in great, happy gangs while their mounted herders serenely watched on. As a Mongol woman spat on the ground, I began to wonder about Sabina's unnamed husband. Married to this German *frau*, maybe he was worldly and informed (if a little henpecked). I imagined gripping discussions in the cosy, low glow of firelight, his children winsomely duelling in the background.

'Lady, lady – you need hotel?'

We'd arrived in Ulan Bator at 6.30pm to the din of cars beeping, pumped-up policemen whistling, and hawkers swooping in on the obvious foreigner. I flashed my new address around, only to be met by shaking heads. Eventually, my new Russian friend found a taxi driver who said he knew it, and I was off. Some ten kilometres out of town, it appeared he didn't, and he began to ask every passer-by the way. I sent Sabina an urgent text, asking for her husband's telephone number, and began to fret – double time. New couches made me nervous anyway.

We were sent this way and that over long rubble tracks until finally, at 9pm and some eighteen circuitous kilometres from the city, we located the 'unpaved road', lined with fences of corrugated iron, mismatched wood and barbed wire guarding shambolic shacks and gers. Was this Mongolia's slumland? Finally finding the correct house number, I pushed through a dented, rusted steel gate.

A scraggy, dispirited, forty-something man with gnarled, grooved skin was standing behind it in charity-shop clothes.

'Sabina's husband?' No reaction. His far-away, bloodshot

eyes refused to look at me. I detected faint disgust, like how my mother might greet a shabby Mongolian peasant found on her doorstep.

'Couchsurfing?' I said, smile on full-beam, desperation in my voice.

'Mmm,' he grunted.

'Are you sure?'

He tipped his head, as if to say, with much grudge: 'This way'.

Husband apparently spoke no English or German, so we walked through his small dark yard in silence, save the menacing sound of howling dogs all around. And there was the ger: the gently peaked white circular hut with a traditional, decorative door sent a ripple of pleasure through me. He unpadlocked the door, stooped to enter and switched on a bare, forty-watt light bulb. I followed, watching my breath billow out in front of me. On dirty, orange-painted floorboards across a sixteen-foot diameter base stood four, low single beds and one double, covered in a jumble of stained quilts. He stuffed some paper in a central, rusty stove, poured a pail of coal on top, held a match to the paper, and left. The fire fizzled out, and I began to feel like a guard dog left in a kennel. Hadn't couchsurfing promised more than a 'free couch'?

'Knock, knock!' I walked into the cottage: DIY kitchen straight ahead, second room with a desk, computer and a bed next door. While my ger was too cold to carry a smell, the house reeked of horse manure and cigarette smoke.

Kein Feuer, I said, flapping my arms.

Blank face.

I beckoned him to follow me to the ger. On arrival, he struck another match, threw it in the direction of the fire, and left. I slumped on my bed – I'd travelled twelve hours for this? That was the thing about couchsurfing: the host, and not the country, became the destination.

'Knock, knock. Toilet?' He led me into his bedroom and pointed at the wall. Nonplussed, I exaggerated a shrug. He stabbed the air with his finger. I shrugged harder. He picked up a torch and walked outside, so I followed him all around the outside of the house where he then left me in pitch-blackness. I finally spotted a white flapping trail of toilet roll – I was in front of an outdoor long-drop.

Like a stray begging for scraps, I returned to the house. He passed me the phone – it was Sabina. It all spilled out.

'You should have told me your husband speaks no English,' I spat, too cross for manners. 'I didn't come all this way just for a roof over my head, I came for the couchsurfing spirit. I'm miles out of town and there's nothing here. If I'd known, I could have organised something else.'

I suddenly found myself sobbing. Facing the world alone, insubstantial irritations became the biggest thing.

'Calm down, JUST CALM DOWN!' she thundered. 'I am in the Gobi Desert. I have four couchsurfers. They wanted to do a tour.' Her voice softened. 'Jimmy will make you tea and bread in the morning.'

Perhaps I was just being a weak westerner: Mongolians were warriors, after all. Jimmy studiously ignored my leaking emotions. In fact, he was trying to ignore me altogether, but I asked for some tea so he handed me an empty mug and pointed to an old corked thermos flask. He then produced a tub of unnaturally orange Jalapeno Cheese Dip and some rubbery, dry bread and drifted off. Like dogs to meat, his two dirty-faced boys, aged maybe two and five, snatched the bread, dipping it in the 'cheese'.

'*Sprechen sie Deutsch*?' I asked eagerly.

'Mmm.' Then they trundled off.

Like a zombie I sat for two hours in the empty kitchen, while Jimmy played solitaire on his computer and his children slept on the floor. Life-form, even if it snubbed me, was better than the vacuum of the ger. Were Ollie here, all this would be interesting, amusing even. Without him, I craved human contact.

'Internet?' I asked.

Jimmy shook his head, so I hit the panic button, and leant on Ollie to help me. Perhaps, I texted, he could ask the man that we'd seen with the two cows, four children and a ger? He'd looked like a good understudy.

But at least I was witnessing the bare bones of Mongolian life, I thought to myself, as I eventually returned to my ger and dined on the gift I'd brought for the kids. The stuff in my rucksack felt wet with cold, so I climbed into my sleeping bag fully clothed, wondering in the darkness about all those positive references. The system was so self-serving: leave a positive reference, get a positive reference; ditto with negative references. Couchsurfing couldn't work like eBay because, unlike eBay, there wasn't an equal trans-action. I had been so touched by strangers' generosity that I'd fawned all over them. Meanwhile, my mentally composed refer-ence for Sabina just sounded petty. As well as being ungrateful, negative references damaged the writer as well as the receiver.

Feeling empty, I indulged in missing The Emperor – now an easy preoccupation, with our war such a distant event. If long-distance relationships worked, it was because each party idealised the other.

28TH OCTOBER

'Shut up! Stop barking! Shut up, all of you.' I was dreaming I was surrounded by hundreds of baying dogs, closing in with their drooling heads swinging, teeth bared. I woke up at 5am, surrounded by the incessant racket of wrathful dogs, plus the mooing of cows. The fire had gone out and the cold was slowly eating me. I lay, numb of body and mind, until 9am.

Outside, the horizon was blurred by the smoky coughs of Ulan Bator's power plants. A miserable layer of snow barely covered the scratchy, lunar landscape. I knocked for the final time on Sabina's husband's tin-can door, rucksack in hand.

How to get to *zentrum*?

'Mmm.'

I pointed towards the city and did my shrug. With a blackened finger, he motioned some quick lines on a shabby plastic tablecloth. I gave him a pen and paper, but his map was still inscrutable. I pointed at him, pointed at me, and pointed in the direction of the road, staging my walkout. Never before or after did I so smash the sacred veneer of reverence for one's host. But he got it, and led me to the bus stop, pausing briefly to expel mucus from each nostril on to the roadside. I don't think he understood – or cared – that I wasn't coming back. I had nowhere to go, but nothing to stay for. In twelve hours, I'd failed the game, but I had another forty-eight hours to get back in it before leaving for Ulan-Ude.

Feeling winded and grouchy, I cursed this ugly city. Ulan Bator, meaning Red Hero, had, like the rest of the country, been under Soviet 'protection' from Chinese invasion from 1921 until 1990. The dismal Soviet tenement blocks and pompous public buildings of that era had since been bolstered by brash, derivative modern architecture, and a haze of pollution hovered insidiously. With no connection to this place, I felt like an outcast. A bad couchsurfing experience made for a bad city experience.

I found an internet dug-out and climbed into the safety net that Ollie had been organising for me. The man with the cows said yes! I was to meet him between 5 and 6pm, at his workplace, the Ulan Bator Public Library, where his son would guide me home. Saved!

Solo sightseeing was a lonely occupation – a duty, rather than a pleasure. Laden with all my belongings, I trudged round Gandantegchinlen Khid, the decidedly unremarkable national monastery and apparently Ulan Bator's prime sight, but I wasn't open for business. I was homesick.

As the rendezvous neared, I scanned around for young people to ask for directions. They were the most likely to speak English, Zhenya had pointed out.

'Many public libraries!' said an architecture student. He made his suggestion, adding, 'This city bad.'

Why?

'Corruption. No art. No architecture.'

Despite our two-word sentences, it was singularly the most joyful experience so far in Mongolia. And we were agreed on Ulan Bator.

After conducting a quick survey on which public library was *the* Ulan Bator Public Library, I aimed for the winner, only to be told, 'Oh no – you need …'.

So I relocated, and waited, looking invitingly at any newcomers for recognition in their eyes. I was, after all, the only white girl around. After an hour and a half I split to defrost and lick my wounds.

✪

For the first time on this trip, I paid for my accommodation. I took a bed in a one-roomed hostel opposite the wrong public library, which I'd be sharing with two guys, from the UK and the USA. The Mongolian owner lived in the room next door; it was almost a home stay, I persuaded myself. He had internet, so I immediately apologised to the man with the cows. I still had one last chance, so I asked whether 'possibly, if there's any way' I could stay the next night. But perhaps he could give me the street address and phone number.

I explained my predicament to the boys.

'Oh, it's just how Mongolians are – casual about directions,' said the Brit.

Maybe it's the nomadism, I reflected. Perhaps you can just say to a Mongolian, 'Meet me by the crooked spruce when Jupiter is due south,' and they'll be there. I quietly opted out of conversation, relieved not to owe anything.

29TH OCTOBER

'CHRIST, MAN, IF YOU DON'T BACK DOWN, I'LL HIT YOU!'

The veins on the American's neck were bulging; he was clenching his fists and jaw and was standing very close indeed to our gracious, now trembling, hostel owner.

'YOU SAID THIS PLACE CAME WITH A FREE WASH-ING MACHINE.'

✪

'No – there is a sign in the bathroom saying you pay,' said the hapless owner.

'MAN, YOU DO THIS EVERY SINGLE FUCKING TIME. WHAT *IS* YOUR PROBLEM?'

After a time, it began to feel like a case of neglect for me not to step in.

'SHUT UP! IT'S NONE OF YOUR BUSINESS.'

Realising it was like trying to wrestle a steak from a Rottweiler, I retreated. Eventually, American Psycho went to sit on his bed. The owner followed.

'You leave today. You pay now … You have many problems.'

Round two quickly erupted, at which point the owner summoned the police. They arrived instantly. Suddenly, the owner was paid, the police left, and a deafening silence fell. Well, you wouldn't get this couchsurfing, I thought to myself. Hostel owners didn't get to choose.

I left the hostel, bought some traditional purple wool slippers with turned-up toes for Zhenya, Kinder Eggs for the four children and chocolates for the parents, and then spent the day in the National Museum. As I learnt about Mongolian heroes and Communist oppression, tribalism and costumes, traditional music and games, I longed for that ger.

✪

I found the right library. I met the man with the cows, Begzsuren, and his son, the nine-year-old Tuguldur.

'Maybe you find it easier to say Todo,' Begzsuren said kindly.

I instantly knew I was in safe hands. A diminutive, trim thirty-two year old, Begzsuren looked like a wise old man. When he smiled, which he did readily, his eyes were lost entirely to ample, peachy cheeks. Already, moving from Sabina's to Begzsuren's felt like going from black to white.

Begzsuren sat me in his office (a software engineer, he managed the library's computer system) and invited me to use his computer, while he organised around me. Straight ahead, pinned to the wall, was a print-out of his couchsurfing profile:

'We are sorry, we have six mouths, we cannot feed you freely. If our surfer wants that, we can share our tasty dinner and breakfast for 7000 tugriks [$6] per night.'

I had totally forgotten this fact. Perhaps the purpose of seating me here was to remind me.

'My son will take you home by bus,' Begzsuren announced. 'Hold your rucksack in front of you, don't keep anything in your pockets and just follow Todo. I have to collect some other couchsurfers.'

I wondered – was it Donagh and Yvonne?

My smiley nine-year-old guardian led me to the bus stop. He pulled out his English textbook and started singing: 'Hello, how are you? I am fine, I am fine, I am fine.' Obviously, I joined in, until eventually an overloaded bus pulled up and we pushed on. Todo put his arms around a random old man while I contorted myself into various advanced fitness-video positions trying to protect the boy, my possessions and my foothold. The bus continuously lurched and stopped, rattling the passengers like matches in a box. Crushed and pained, we were extreme public-transport surfing.

Finally spat out by the bus, I found myself in a depressingly familiar setting of unpaved roads, corrugated iron fences and cross dogs. Yet, led by this tiny, plucky boy up a long, steep, dirt track, I felt happy – Todo seemed to care.

A godly guiding light shone down upon us from the top of a hill. It was Begzsuren, waiting outside his ger. Inside, it was like walking into a play where all the cast and props were on stage at once. The stove stood at the centre, the galley (basic shelves, metal sink, washing machine) was by the door, the bedding (one quilt on the floor) was on the east edge, and around the back was an old computer, a keyboard and a TV. Begzsuren introduced me to his wife, Mungunsoyombo (whose name I avoided ever after) and his three daughters, aged seven, three and two. Instead of Donagh and Yvonne was a young Danish couple sitting on doll-sized stools at a low table, the girl with dreadlocks and shorn temples, the guy with a buzz cut. They'd been here for two weeks and were leaving after dinner. I wondered how on earth they hadn't overstayed their welcome. And how were seven of us going to sleep in here?

The division of labour was clearly split between the genders: Begzsuren's kitchen-bound wife, smiling generously, handed me a bowl of hot, freshly-squeezed milk (not unpleasant – thin, slightly muddy, slightly nutty) while Begz – as the Danish couple called him – sat with us, working the cultural exchange. As I explained the Ollie drama (since our profile still included him, everyone wanted to know), Begz replied, 'If we break our leg in Mongolia, we drink water with black stuff from the fire.' But not any old soot. It had to be soot made from 'co-pie'.

Co-pie?

'Yes – from the co.' Ah – the cow. Ahhh – cremated cowpats. I telegraphed this immediately to Ollie.

Making a brief break away from the stove, Begz's wife presented us with dinner – stir-fried potatoes, cabbage, carrot and egg. They were vegetarians, Begz explained, for financial, not ethical reasons. But what was baffling me was how Begz – not your average couchsurfer – had got involved.

'I have been doing this since the 8th of July this year,' he declared, proudly. 'That was a very wonderful day.'

Apparently an American Peace Corps volunteer had been asking around to stay with a Mongolian family for two days. Begz was curious, and interviewed him in the library, agreeing 'directly'. The American then introduced him to the website. It was a perfect fit – sharing knowledge about Mongolia clearly made Begz happy.

I glared at the Danish girl with undisguised shock as she licked her plate clean.

'We like to lick our plates,' assured Begz. 'First, it shows a good regard for the cook. Second, it cleans the plate, and third, it's good exercise for the tongue.'

I picked my plate up and placed put my tongue on it, eyeing the others over its rim. I realised I'd been deeply conditioned not to do this – it felt wildly inappropriate. I glanced quickly at Begz, now bare-chested in just a pair of tracksuit bottoms. The message was: relax and be comfortable.

Begz pulled down a visitors' book from the rafters. One Nomadic Ambassador had written, 'Staying with this family was the most amazing travelling experience of my life'. The Danes wrote their loving entry and then warned Begz about the imminent hug-fest. Hugging wasn't popular in Mongolia, Begz explained. He never kissed his wife hello – they'd say it with words, or a shaken hand.

It was an emotional departure: the kids were swung around, bear hugs and back pats were administered, and promises were made: 'Our children will be your children's friends,' pledged the

Danes. I felt foolish for parachuting in for twelve hours. My bus back to Ulan-Ude was at dawn – a one-night stay was not recommended couchsurfing behaviour. But finally I was living Mongolian romanticism, bonding in the intimacy of a ger. Temperatures were sub-zero outside, and yet, with just a wodge of felted wool between us, we were toasty and content. Like camping, it reminded you of all man really needed. As someone much wiser said, 'It is so simple to be happy but so difficult to be simple.' Begz and his family made it look mysteriously easy. There was no bickering, no dramas, no mountains of discarded toys. I smarted at the idea of my own family sharing this tiny space.

Begz's unbidden Mongolian tutorials continued undeterred, now with the assistance of the inevitable slideshow. Initially, I felt grossly inadequate seeing the photos of the Danish couple erecting the ger (it took three hours, apparently – Begz had wanted to move out of his two-room bungalow into more traditional accommodation on the same plot), baking Danish apple cake, a vegetarian meal … Other couchsurfers made sushi, quiche ('French pizza'), Mongolian specialities. I was only contributing with money. Then it struck me: perhaps the others were dodging their dinner debt. Although no one mentioned it, $6 was steep in Mongolia, and it was slightly off-message to charge, though I was happy that this relatively modest sum helped to support such a big-hearted family. But many of their guests stayed for two, even three weeks. Perhaps by making a contribution, financial or edible, people felt more comfortable hanging around: there was more in it for the host, less guilt for the guests.

Meanwhile, the children imperceptibly drew nearer and became more cosy, until I realised I was their climbing frame. This unconditional acceptance was like therapy – these simple pleasures made my heart sing. The children were eventually taken for their sink-baths (there was no shower), and over 'yellow berry' fruit juice ('good for colds'), Begz patiently introduced me to Mongolian games, involving sheep's anklebones used like dice. I learnt about Buddhist haircutting ceremonies, about how to keep a cow, about Mongolia's financial situation (inflation was 30 per cent). I was his captive – and willing – audience till past midnight.

With a pile of my own clothes for a pillow, and a slim roll of felted sheep wool for a mattress, I took to the guest quarters on the west side, with my feet pointing towards the door, as was customary. The younger ones were popped on to their potties and finally, like Charlie Bucket's grandparents, all six of them topped-and-tailed under the quilt. The light was left on for some reason. Was it rude to ask to turn it off? Was it impossible? American Psycho wouldn't fare well here, I mused. I tried to digest the day, silence my heart and forget about the light and the very hard ground, but sleep gave me the slip.

30TH OCTOBER

My cultural awareness programme continued at 6am, and right up until their taxi-driver neighbour drove me away. I was plied with green tea and the finer details of ger etiquette ('leave your weapons outside the ger') and how to greet a Mongolian ('if they are sewing, you say, "Your sewing will be very nice"') and Begz's 'frying' (praying) routine. He would spin his 'frying book', a Tibetan scroll inside a small silver tin, clockwise every morning and chant Om Ma Ni Pad Me Hum. I smiled weakly, not wanting to seem too encouraging – Begz's admirable national pride was all a bit much before sunrise. The perfect balance was so hard to strike.

Slipping on a traditional Mongolian housecoat, Begz tried out his new hugging technique: a genuine, soul-warming good-bye. Outside, snow was falling on to a view that was brand new to me. What had resembled slums at Sabina's now looked like an appealing lifestyle choice – the simple, traditional life, close to Mongolia's nomadic roots. With another couchsurfing couple due to arrive that day, hosting was another lifestyle choice – there were just those who enjoyed having people in their house and sharing their world. I wasn't sure I had that gene. I liked my house to be *my* house, a place where I could leave the world. Too bad! I'd be opening my doors back in London to couchsurfers, putting back in what I'd taken out.

31ST OCTOBER

I was back at Zhenya's, en route to Vladivostok. I gleefully presented my gift of the slippers – a proper present.

'No,' she said, pushing them back into my wilting hands. 'You should give these to my father. Papa!' She called him over and explained. Quite suddenly, he flung his arms around me for a full-body embrace. Surprised, I trod on his toe and whacked my cheek against his. Then he put the slippers on and plodded back to the living room, with his too-large feet falling out of the backs. I was left empty-handed again.

We drove into town. 'Wait here! I have to go to the dentist.' My last chance: I bought flowers and stood outside the dental clinic hiding them behind my back like a creep. She was aghast, but I was relieved. A brief check-in online on Nastia's shaky connection revealed I *still* had no Beijing couch (I'd be there in five days' time, post Vladivostok). Not even the City Ambassador had responded. Begz, on the other hand, had already changed his profile picture to a group shot with the Danes and me. Proof! We'd connected somehow. It was even more moving than the hug.

On the way to the station we conceded a cursory glance at the sights: at the beautiful wooden merchants' houses of the 18th- and 19th-century that the developers wanted to pull down; at the pretty, yellow stuccoed Tsarist trading arcade; and past the fire station where we laughed again about the three musketeers. Couchsurfing, I was learning, was complicated – after three days, we were finally starting to connect, and yet, another day and I'd have outstayed my welcome. Three days was both too short and too long.

My train had pulled into the station and my emotions had risen to the surface. I was about to be alone again, and in Ollie's absence, I'd formed a strong attachment to Zhenya. We hugged and kissed goodbye while I tried not to cry. There was a cruel inevitability in couchsurfing: after building up all that trust and understanding, you'd soon return to being the strangers you always were.

CHAPTER 7

VLADIVOSTOK: THE AMBASSADOR'S RECEPTION

Not only was Mother Russia one very, very large woman indeed, but her trains were also exceedingly slow. I was facing a three-day life-void on board the Vladivostok Express, travelling to the very end of the Trans-Siberian railroad, some 9,289 kilometres from Moscow and 3,649 kilometres on from Ulan-Ude. Vladivostok, meaning 'Ruler of the East', had kept to its name, serving as Russia's eastern defence. Armoured with historic fortresses, it was closed to foreigners until 1992. These days, it was also a sportsman's paradise – my host, Natie, was a windsurfer, skier and boarder. I had the vague, happy anticipation of a seaside holiday in an exotic land on the edge of the world.

On board, I found myself grappling with my Chinese diction-ary prematurely, as my cabin companions were a young Chinese couple. My three new words weren't enough to confirm that they'd become fully literate in Russian hospitality (every time I looked, they offered a boiled egg, some melon, an apple), or whether, in fact, one could also hope for such kindness in China.

They departed in the night. Secretly, I'd been hoping they would. If they had stayed it would mean it was normal to turn on the lights at 4am, chatter loudly, and slurp food like twenty elephants sloshing through a swamp. But I couldn't possibly complain after their charity. If this couple were anything to go by, China would feel like a very different place indeed.

I locked onto the snowy white noise outside and thought about Me. Sustaining conversation for four days was some task *a deux*. Wasn't Zhenya bored? Had I provided what she'd signed up for? Perhaps the real problem was this persistent need to question. Couchsurfing forced the mirror of scrutiny into my hands.

3RD NOVEMBER

Outside, the snow was thawing and the scenery gradually returned to dead, brown forest. Inside, the inevitable butterflies about my next couch struck. Natie would be my very first City Ambassador, a member of couchsurfing's elite (there were also Nomadic Ambassadors, Country Ambassadors and Global Ambassadors – the real goody-goodies). An Ambassador's role was 'to be of service to its members'. Surely I could service my mounting laundry needs at Natie's. And surely – more importantly – her arms would be fully open. After three days of solitary confinement, that gaping, Ollie-shaped absence, and a textual silence from The Emperor (had he forgotten I'd lost my BlackBerry?), I was already feeling primal hug urges.

Showtime.

But somehow showtime passed – my train was still nowhere near the coast or civilisation. Natie called from the station: 'I don't see your train.' That's because, it turned out, I had given her my date, not time, of arrival (the tickets were all in Cyrillic).

'SORRY!' I texted, 'I am so sorry.' I hadn't even arrived and I'd put my host out. By two hours.

'No problem,' she replied, with promising diplomacy. 'I am organising a visit to Vladivostok Fortress for a few couchsurfers this afternoon. Would you care to join?'

Given that my guidebook said that this fortress, built in 1910, was 'really hard to find' and that visiting on your own was 'very difficult', my gratitude was mounting.

Eventually the horizon opened out into the Great Big Blue, with speedboats watching the shimmering waters from their winter sun-terraces, and tiny puffs of white cloud bouncing along a turquoise sky. We'd arrived at Vladi Del Mar.

A sporty orange jacket strode towards me. Inside, was a petite 24-year-old wearing small black spectacles, her shiny black hair in a practical ponytail. I gave her that hungry hug; any British reserve was automatically overridden. She didn't say much, but that's possibly because I launched right into abject apologies.

'Don't worry,' she said in a confident, American accent. 'It gave me the time to get a car.'

We jumped into her windswept friend Alec's Jeep, in amongst his sporting gear, and he drove us through the port city to the north of town.

'Vladivostok is the best city,' said Natie, from the front seat. 'It is small – there are 600,000 people – but it has everything you need. There are lots of opportunities for young people.'

Natie was a magazine journalist, but I'd arrived on a public holiday.

'In Russia,' she tutted, 'there is always holidays and no one knows when or why.'

I was instantly pleased – I was getting the good and the bad.

Inside a 'greige' concrete block, Natie presented me with some pink towelling slippers: 'Slippers are not a Russian tradition – it's just that our streets are so dirty.'

She led me through a murky, narrow hall, past the door to her mother's room and through her eighteen-year-old brother's drab beige bedroom. Given that we had to walk through his bedroom to get to hers, and that it had a sofa for a bed, it was surely the living room. So far, so Soviet.

Directly on the floor of Natie's room, squeezed between her single bed, the wardrobe and the wall, was a waif-wide, bobbled quilt featuring a blue-eyed kitten chasing butterflies.

'Stasya, the other couchsurfer, is sleeping in the other corner.'

I looked over. It was equally tight. What a commitment to the cause, I mavelled, despite feeling shocked by the crowding. And another guest, I cheered inwardly. I had support.

I grabbed my box of chocolates and we adjourned to a pygmy kitchen, where the bin was a saucepan by the sink and the oven was the size of a shoebox.

'This is Stasya from St Petersburg!'

A natural blonde in a lumberjack shirt with ethnic strings and beads adorning her wrists sat at the kitchen table.

'I am hitchhiker,' Stasya declared, like it defined her.

'She is vegetarian too,' added Natie.

Vegetarianism was a third overlapping circle of the couch-surfing/hitchhiking Venn diagram. Natie pointed to the floor, where wonky orange marrows, butternut squashes, carrots and other friends basked like seals on old newspaper.

'We have *lots* of vegetables,' she gesticulated wildly. 'Do you like pumpkin?'

'I love it,' I said helpfully.

'I hate it,' she said, scrunching her nose. 'It tastes of nothing.'

So it did – I was confused. Was it better to be helpful or honest?

Natie took off her jacket, revealing slim arms and a T-shirt that read WINDSURF STAR 2008.

'A prize?' I asked.

'No – we all got one. Actually, I am the best windsurfing girl here but it's a boys' sport. It's *really* windy in Vladivostok.'

I knew I'd adjusted to the Russian manner as I accepted this superlative as truth over conceit. I thought of The Emperor – perhaps this new skill could be applied to understanding his Slavic pride.

With her pale olive skin and dark features, Natie didn't look Russian. She told me that she never knew her father, adding, 'I didn't ask my mother. I just choose the version I like more. Maybe he is a Spanish aviator.' Natie was clearly a survivor.

Stasya would be hitchhiking in China.

How brave, I said.

'Ha!' she nodded wryly. 'Where is the line between courage and loss of the mind?'

Her voice covered two octaves. I looked at her: mild-mannered with an open, soft face and blue eyes, and just twenty-three, she was naive and I was a coward – who was more realistic?

Natie's phone rang: it was time to meet the other couch-surfers – a Czech and a Slovak guy (who'd driven all the way from the Czech Republic in their 1969 Skoda) – and go to the fortress. Natie had agreed to babysit them for the day as their own host's cat was ill. As we waited for them, we sheltered from Vladivostok's sandy winds in an extreme sports superstore and I got the low-down on Natie's job situation. She'd been writing for a magazine, 'somewhere between *Esquire* and *Playboy* with pictures of naked girls', owned by Vladivostok's richest rogue. He also owned all the casinos, so Natie's pay was casino cash. 'Literally dirty money,' she sighed, stroking a new snowboard. When he brought in blonde bimbos as the editor and manager, and they brought in their toyboys, the journalists stopped getting paid, so they quit. It was like a straight-to-video plot.

Sporting a leather pouch attached to his belt, knife creases in his sleeves and deeply bitten nails, another young Russian named Nikolai joined us. Nerdy but nice, he was from the Ural Mountains, and here on some kind of software business that no one had concentrated hard enough on to grasp. He had a hotel room but used the couchsurfing network solely to meet new friends for meals and drinks. It was rather like internet dating – smart and modern, but somehow so clinical.

Finally, a cartoonish Skoda covered in sponsorship stickers pulled up.

'Sorry we are late,' said Martin the Slovak, in a take-it-or-leave-it tone.

'We don't have time. Last week we had an argument about which week it was.'

Outside of the system, time evidently wasn't important – the idea felt rather romantic. Natie effortlessly took charge of logistics, separating the six of us into two shifts to get up to the fortress in the Skoda. Ladies went first. The only way to fit two in the back-seat was if I sat sidesaddle on Stasya. I hadn't washed for three days – I smarted at the ignominy, but, as was couchsurfing's way, I was cornered into getting over myself and my Western preoccupations.

The day immediately changed gear. Mikhail, the young and cute Czech psychologist, was our driver.

'What's your car's name?' I asked.

'Juliana.' He flashed a smile. 'You can't understand her, you just have to love her.'

As the Skoda struggled up a steep rubble lane, he recounted how they'd been burgled en route in Chita, near Baikal. The town was '*very* upset' about it, and the boys were interviewed three times on TV. People would recognise them and ask if they'd had their things returned. In the end, pressured by the publicity, the robber turned himself in. It was but a matter of time before we witnessed the kind of attention that the boys were accustomed to.

'Stop!' The notorious Russian police were suddenly very interested in us. Not, however, in hot pursuit of a bribe, but in the Skoda itself, which they deemed the most hilarious thing in the world ever. So hilarious, in fact, that they all jumped out of their car to film, photograph and laugh at this antique creature.

Off-duty, they were all sideways with beer, drinking from plastic pint glasses. We made use of them for directions to the fortress, but, even better, they invited us to their Police Dog Training Centre nearby and then drove off.

In their drunkenness, they overlooked the fact that this centre was a restricted zone. A plain-clothes policewoman barked at us in Russian, and pushed Mikhail with the full force of her doughy form. We were undeterred, because by now we could see our new drunken friends by the kennels – cage upon cage filled with jumpy German Shepherds. It was the opposite of the controlled image of tourism. In fact, it was a pinch-me moment – two hours earlier I had no friends and an empty brain; now I had a gang, bound by a shared sense of adventure and a will not to be alone, and an uncrushable buzz – that not even the police could touch.

The fortress was appropriately hidden. A guide dressed as a 1910 serviceman in britches and a forked beard showed us round its one-and-a-half kilometres of tunnels and Nikolai dutifully interpreted for me.

Juliana's limitations necessitated a split to get back to Natie's. Stasya and I took the bus – it was far simpler, I realised, to be with fellow couchsurfing guests than with hosts. No matter how sweet, there was always an us-and-them dynamic with hosts; with guests, a solidarity. You could say things to guests that you couldn't to hosts, so there was also the catharsis of off-loading.

But Stasya was also eminently likeable. Was she, like me, homesick, I asked?

'Homesick, what is this?' she said. 'Mmmm, what I miss most are my couchsurfers.'

'Why?'

'Because I like to show them my city, you learn so much about it – it makes me feel …' She emitted a happy squeal. 'Sometimes my guests say, "Where you sleep?" "Wherever I fall down," I say. I sleep in a sleeping bag on the floor,' she chuckled.

I looked at her in awe. She was above physical comfort, and she thought communally – she was born to couchsurf.

Team Skoda and Natie had beaten us. The boys were Skype-ing home on Natie's computer so we piled into the kitchen. Natie dismissed the biscuits that I'd bought for tea: 'I don't like these ones.' I was getting used to this; feeling offended now just felt like a waste of time. Besides, I wanted to ask after the Spanish firefighters.

'Oh yes!' Natie clapped her hands. 'They said, "Don't ask Fleur about that night in Ulan-Ude!"'

My shameful tale enabled a further exchange of confidences. Had Natie ever kissed her guests?

'Of course! I've had over forty guests – they are so nice! Sometimes, I'm looking at them and thinking, okay, when do we start kissing?'

And Stasya?

'No,' she replied, biting her smiling bottom lip.

'All the girls are in the kitchen,' said Mikhail cheekily. 'Can I help? I can do anything – *anything* at all.' He raised his eyebrows suggestively. This boy had been on the road for too long. No one responded. Natie's mother entered to pick up a tin of fish livers. I watched for signs of irritation, but, as she physically stepped over those of us in her way, she seemed genuinely pleased about it all.

'We will make *vareniki* – it's *pelmeni* for vegetarians!' announced Natie, clearing the decks. She started making the dough with flour and water, and I begged for her to let me help.

'To not help is to be helpful,' she responded matriarchally. But eventually, we were conscripted: 'It's like a ceremony – we need four people.'

Natie handed me little dough balls, which I rolled out and passed on to Mikhail to fill with a potato and mushroom mix that Stasya was making. Natie was good at couchsurfing management.

'Did the Spanish boys cook for you?' I asked. I was wondering – was everyone cooking for their hosts?

'No! Some of my guests even promised they would.' Natie spoke rapidly, like it had been building up. 'I don't know why not. Tell me what I can do to make them cook!'

The gauntlet had been thrown.

The little pockets of *vareniki* were boiled for a few minutes like tortellini, and served up in sampler-sized portions with smetana and soy sauce. It didn't seem nearly enough for my first meal since breakfast. Led by Martin, also a journalist, the foreigners tackled the questionable appropriateness of Russia's continued Soviet glory. Why did every town square have to contain a Lenin statue?

'Lenin is not a hero,' retorted Natie. 'But you don't need to ruin history – for us, it's just some letters together; it's meaningless and now when you want to find the centre, you head to Lenin Square.'

'But if I went to Berlin and saw Hitler Street, it would be the same thing,' said Martin.

'That's absurd,' she laughed.

'It's absurd because Russia is acclimatised to this name but it shocks us that there is no apology.'

Natie then described a national competition to choose the greatest Russian – Lenin was in the top ten but Pushkin would probably win. The results, announced in December 2008, actually saw Prince Nevsky win, and Pushkin come after Stalin, who came third. Perhaps the results were fiddled.

'No one trusts the government,' Natie said, frowning darkly. 'We have corruption at all levels. Even the president. If you want it to stop, let's start here. We have corruption in kindergartens even – there is a price for everything. Here, it's the first economy.'

As if to prevent any national superiority surfacing, Mikhail looked at me intently, and asked: 'Do you know what Continental Europe thinks of Britain?'

'Err, no.'

'The joke is that you are all inbred because you are an island and you keep out foreigners. In Europe, you know, we have been having this great party. You missed a big one!'

It was funny how I felt more British away from Britain. I stood out more here.

At 9.30, Team Skoda returned to their own host. They'd be taking the ferry to South Korea the next day.

'Pliz,' said Stasya, 'Pliz write me "work is shit" in Czech – I collect in all languages.'

When they'd left, Stasya, Natie and I went our separate ways, to the computer, to shower, to bed. Online, surrounded by her brother's empty beer cans, ashtrays and glamour-model pin-ups, I found a solution for Beijing. Well, you don't turn down an offer to stay in the three-week-old, five-star Park Hyatt for free. Being a journalist had its perks. I'd ease myself into China gently. The hotel seemed like a (very) comfortable compromise. But I'd still couchsurf, the Nikolai way – I was going to test-run the instant social life.

It was also time to reinstate another test. The Emperor and I hadn't communicated for a week, and I was beginning to adjust to the absence of texts and attention. So I emailed, suggesting a total embargo of communications again, to try what we'd tried before Ollie left. I was starting to distrust myself in love at such distances: it wasn't real life – away from our battleground, The Emperor had gradually been lionised.

In the bathroom I witnessed a curious Russian ritual – the toilet raid. I was performing my bedtime ablutions, when first the doorbell went (which I ignored), then followed by a knock on the bathroom door. I unlocked it and Natie's mother rushed in, wearing a very short nightie. She locked the door and sat on the toilet. I thought she might be hiding, but the sound effects quickly revealed otherwise. I turned my back and 'busied myself' to save her modesty and muffle my smirks. Then up she got, flushed the toilet and left. I noticed the bath was full of clothes as if it *was* the washing machine – laundry would have to wait till Beijing.

I hurled myself into 'bed' with wet hair. Natie had been asleep for an hour so blowdrying it would be a major imposition. My feet touched the wardrobe, my hands the wall, and my head rested upon a thin, lumpy pillow that smelled 'vintage'. Natie's bed was so claustrophobically close to me, I could hear her breathing. I didn't feel at all sleepy, and I was *starving* – just the usual couchsurfing hazards.

4TH NOVEMBER

I woke to a seagulls' dawn chorus, with pins and needles from the hard floor. I surveyed the room properly: decorating the pale blue walls was a wetsuit, a snowboard and a world map (which all the best couchsurfers had). Planted upon it was the sticker: WHERE ON EARTH IS PERTH? Couchsurfing always left a trail, but this Perth couchsurfer had ingeniously left physical memories. My boxes of chocolates weren't going to do that.

We rose at nine for a breakfast of green tea, bread, sausage and Russian cheese. Natie's mother strolled into the kitchen and picked at our bread as if nothing had happened the night before.

'Tonight, Stasya and I will cook dinner for you!' I pronounced cheerily.

'No,' Natie said decisively. 'We should go to a cafe – it's easier.'

But I was resolute.

We continued to carb-load at leisure around the kitchen table.

'Guys, you are too relaxed,' said Natie, deadpan.

How glad I was to share the affront – having a collaborator

made it funny. And it was true, we were both immobilised by the comfort zone. Ever the Ambassador, Natie suggested we meet up with Nikolai and take the boat to Russky Island. Nine miles off the mainland, it was once a closed naval base. Now inhabited by just 5,000 Russians, it was something of a forgotten land, but Putin was putting it back on the international map as the site of the 2012 boring-but-important Pacific Countries Economic Forum.

Under a brilliant blue sky, we met Nikolai in the harbour, home to Russia's daunting Pacific Fleet. Our fellow travellers, old, drunk, disfavoured Russians, did not suggest a prestigious destination. Nor did the bus which, upon our arrival at Russky Island, was in such a hurry to move on that we missed it. Instead, we wandered through a forlorn housing estate and on to an interminable ghostly dirt road – the bus route to somewhere. 'Let's hitch!' I ventured.

Now that I could, I mentioned the previous night's toilet raid.

'Is this normal?' I wanted to know.

'Mmmm, it's not so normal,' said Stasya. 'But many Russians have to share their bathroom and toilet between a whole family.'

And now, couchsurfers. Had Stasya ever had any problems hitchhiking?

'No!' she said, her face lighting up. 'Sometimes, Russians let me stay in their house, or they called their friend to stay me. I had all different drivers – directors of corporations to lorry drivers. Some drivers say they only drive when they drunk,' she laughed. 'It's easy as a girl because people want to care for you.'

From her bag, she produced an orange balloon and started blowing it up – it was her hitching aid. But Britain didn't trust hitchhikers.

'No,' Stasya agreed. 'I hear only Poles and Slovakians pick up hitchhikers in Great Britain.'

Great Britain?

The occasional car sped past, kicking up the dust. At the next distant rumble, Stasya calmly stepped out into the road and, with the technical skill of a policeman, flagged the vehicle down. It was a truck, driven by the sinister-looking, camo-sporting Alexei, who'd lived on Russky Island all his life and who carted sand around construction sites. He drove the three of us past a whole lot of nothing, and dropped us off by the military academy. The hitch was remarkable in its unremarkableness. But I wasn't so sure about doing it alone.

We bought a peculiar picnic of dried, chewy calamari, yoghurt and salty doughnuts from a tiny, isolated shop and looked out to the Sea of Japan. So what did they know about Russky Island?

'There is a contemporary Russian writer,' said Nikolai with characteristic precision. 'Yevgeni Grishkovetz. He was unlucky – he was conscripted to the Navy for three years and he wrote about his impressions there; he is a very emotional writer. The book is entitled *How Did I Eat a Dog*. It means to know something inside out.'

There wasn't much to know on this island.

'And you, Nikolai – what about your military training?'

He'd spent one day a week in army training for two years at university, he told us, then did a PhD to get out of doing the rest. The university dodge was apparently pretty standard.

Stasya was staring out to sea: 'I would like to swim.'

'But it's freezing!'

'Oh not so cold!' she said blithely. 'I have only two conditions: blue sky and empty sea.'

But to our disappointment, she didn't: she decided the inlet didn't qualify as sea. So on one side I had a free spirit who liked swimming naked, on the other I had a software expert with a PhD – I was a strict compartmentalist at home, but those boundaries didn't apply in the couchsurfing club. There were other things we all agreed on.

We returned to the motherland for sunset, said goodbye to Nikolai, and bought ingredients for a veggie-pleasing cauliflower cheese. Natie had again turned her apartment into Couchsurfing Central, hosting a tea party for four local hosts. We caught the tail-end: one girl, Marina, told us how her mother had joined couchsurfing when Marina left for Japan for a year, because now she had a spare room and was very 'boring' (bored). That was the exciting thing about couchsurfing – it attracted the adventurous.

So how did one become an Ambassador? I asked.

'First,' Natie explained, 'you send a request to the couchsurfing team. You need to have had more than ten experiences, and to be verified to level three or vouched for by another City Ambassador.'

And what was she expected to do?

Nothing specific, 'maybe organise a few local meetings'.

It was seen, rather casually, as a matter of trial and error – if it didn't work out, the honour could be removed. But Natie, like Max, Zhenya and Begz, was an instinctive diplomat.

Other patterns were emerging: couchsurfing hosts were informed, progressive and irrepressibly energetic. They were over-achievers who built their own homes, gathered people, span a lot of plates. They often had the manner of a head prefect – charming yet sensible. I didn't share many of those characteristics. And there were types within the type – some were hippies, some were early adopters, some were ex-pats. And their phones all rang a lot.

It wasn't my fault that I served up dinner at 11pm. The powwow didn't stop till past 9pm. I made a right meal of it; curdled and burnt the white sauce, producing a lumpy and watery anaemia. When the hob only knew two settings, under-powered and over-powered, cooking in a stranger's kitchen was harder than expected. Natie was very sweet about things, giving the cauliflower cheese a pretty name that it didn't deserve: 'White Trees'. Whichever, this was a milestone. I'd brought Britain into Natie's kitchen, producing a vaguely edible classic. And as I perspired and fussed over my offering, I'd given her the gift of free time. It was much more satisfying than giving chocolates.

5TH NOVEMBER

5.20am: Natie woke up in time to make me tea before my flight to Beijing. Too drowsy to feel emotional, we had a big, easy hug. Ambassadors might have been self-selecting, but, I realised, this was the way to locate the naturals. I'd be looking them up more often. And I'd try to avoid one-on-one couchsurfing – the very prison of politeness. I could be more myself when there were others to contribute to the delicate art of conversation with strangers. It felt less contrived, less intense. How I cursed the mountain that had tripped up Ollie.

CHAPTER 8

BEIJING: CARRY ON COUCHSURFING

It was as if I'd swallowed the contents of the 'DRINK ME' bottle. Out of the window, silver birches had been replaced with dizzying, attention-seeking, silver skyscrapers. My chin was practically upside-down when I looked up at the 249.9 metre-high Park Hyatt, Beijing. Just below Beijing's legal limit of 250 metres, it was currently its second-tallest building.

I threw off all my clothes (inside my suite, of course) and emptied my bag all over the floor. I had a 'rain-cloud' shower. I made myself three espressos. 'Is that housekeeping – could you collect my laundry?' I was in private; I was *free*. I could be naked, messy, demanding. I was also cheating, but hey, I was wayworn. I'd had nine hours' floor-grade sleep in the last three days and my body was battered. I'd started to acquire some new face furniture and was looking and feeling like I'd been beaten up. Emotionally, I was drowning. My secret self had so much to off-load, and I had no time to vent. I had to put my head above the water. Plus, my organisational skills had expired. With Russia's internet limitations, I'd been seriously paddling to stay afloat.

I looked down upon the world from my window. Tall buildings, elevating their occupiers from the crowds below, were designed to provide ego trips. It gave me vertigo. I wasn't used to this – staying in people's homes was an exercise in humility. That *couldn't* be bad for you. I ate a complimentary Asian pear, then hesitated before placing the core neatly in the vase-like bin. I was contaminating this pristine environment; it was the opposite of what I'd experienced when couchsurfing. I wasn't sure which made me feel more uncomfortable.

'SECURITY ALERT! It is possible that someone may be trying to intercept your communication.'

Big Brother's all-seeing eye was on me as soon as I logged on. My heart sped up. I swept my eyes suspiciously across the room. How close were they? What did they know? My blog was completely blocked, so I turned to couchsearch China.

Good news: the French/Taiwanese couple in Beijing, François and Xinxin, could host me for two nights after my hotel stay. My natives-only rule had had to be shelved in China. Most hosts were ex-pats (hosting strangers was, quite reasonably, anathema to the Chinese). The mixed couple seemed like a good compromise, plus, I reasoned, there'd be an inkling of maternal instinct there; maybe they'd feel protective towards me (plus we'd be three – no dreaded one-on-one). And perhaps the propaganda-shunning ex-pats would have a more honest perspective.

The rest of my plans for China were precarious. I decided against a stop at the Silk Road City of Lanzhou in north-west China where a student with just two references promised a room with his random friend. In my next stop, Xi'an, – home to the Terracotta Army and 1,200 kilometres south-west of Beijing my Chinese host would accomodate me in this hostel for free. There was nothing, not even someone to meet for a drink, in Tibet, and very little further west, the route to Kazakhstan. It felt like the crouching tiger was waiting to pounce on me.

But I wasn't really alone – there was a whole community out there to help, apparently. I experimented by joining the China couchsurfing group and posted a thread asking for advice. In the Beijing group, I posted a thread Desperately Seeking Great Wall Allies. Who'd have thought I would be posting for friends on forums? Perhaps my London snobbishness was finally loosening its grip.

I sent a message to Stefanie, the City Ambassador for Beijing and a Swiss-American teacher – she responded with a summons to tea.

'Wow – is this typical?'

I was in shock from the luxury and size (and spotlessness) of Stefanie's place.

'Oh, this is normal,' Stefanie said coolly, wearing an Obama-Biden T-shirt (Obama had been declared President Elect earlier that day). 'Though it's not typical for a Chinese person.'

On a 3rd-grade teacher's salary, this single mum had a deluxe three-bed apartment with a living room twice the size of most of my Russian couches. We settled down on her mammoth L-shaped sofa.

With a seventeen-month-old daughter, Stefanie no longer hosted. She was essentially a forum marshal.

'There have been a few issues with people saying things they shouldn't,' she said, righteously. 'One woman called her host a sexual predator.'

'Oh yes?'

'I stepped in. He didn't do anything dangerous. Then some-one wrote me hate mail saying I was a controlling Nazi. I called an emergency Ambassador meeting and we sat here for five hours making a formal statement.'

'But what actually happened?'

'Right. There's a host here who trawls the travellers in Beijing for single women and invites them to stay. He'll say, 'You can either sleep in my bed or on the floor,' but the floor is filthy. One girl due to stay felt uncomfortable and decided to spend the night in an internet café. He denied saying that she had nice breasts. Plus, when she was expected at his, he'd asked her to stay away for a time, because, she'd deduced, he was having sex with his girlfriend. A guest shouldn't have to know you're having sex.' I bit hard on my lip to avoid laughing. It was inevitable that miscommunication over sex was a minefield in couchsurfing, what with cultural differences, linguistic mix-ups and dangerous levels of politeness. Not that I'd seen any of it.

Stefanie's work, I realised, was about office politics. It all seemed rather distanced from the point of couchsurfing.

'Do you like being an Ambassador?' I asked. It suddenly didn't sound so cool.

'It's a blessing and a curse,' she said, tucking her hair behind her ears. 'People want to be friends with us so they can be vouched for; it's not about you, but your status. But you get to meet more people, and you get more responsibilities.' Stefanie was a total school-prefect type.

Other sins were 'mooching' (freeloaders eating the food her maid made), being ungrateful (a couple who'd been travelling for years were so burnt-out they were totally unappreciative), 'Oh, and just awkward people that I don't click with,' she said dismissively. I smiled harder. 'And during the Olympics, my God, we got so many requests, like a year ahead because the hotels were so strained.' Some couches were even charging apparently. And plenty of hosts had to couchsurf in their own city, after being kicked out by greedy landlords who quadrupled the rent.

So what kind of characteristics did she notice amongst guests?

Stefanie fetched a colour-coded spreadsheet of all her guests, their age, nationality and sex: Germany, she said, was the biggest group.

'Err, what about personality?' I asked.

'Oh, just grassroots people, environmentally conscious, keen to better the world, idealists.'

My heart soared. And did people ever keep their promise of visiting their guests?

She didn't really sell it: 'I stayed in Shanghai with an old guest, but it isn't quite the same: you don't have the magic of the unknown.'

I was unsure we'd clicked, so I made my excuses. She sent me on my way with a Great Wall day-tour tip and a word of caution: 'I hope you don't bump into Tiny Tang: he charges Chinese people who want to practise their English to come to dinner with his surfers.'

I left her ivory tower and headed back to my own, somewhat unfulfilled. My phone rang on the way back: it was Yvonne who I'd met in Moscow. I played it cool. She was up for going to the Great Wall. And the Forbidden City. I was tempted – it was better than going solo. Now finding myself in an unlit road at midnight, I realised there was too much authority in China for danger to thrive. Late-night Hackney was a far worse prospect.

I switched on the DO NOT DISTURB light and dived into my king-size bed, my body uniformly supported by an expensive mattress, my first sprung mattress since London. Lightly covered by a cloud-like down duvet, and at 200 metres up, I felt like I was in heaven. But after eating dinner alone in my room and having no one to say goodnight to, I found myself deeply lonely. This place was dead inside.

6TH NOVEMBER

After a curiosity-fed-the-cat breakfast of black rice pudding and pork floss that resembled orange bouclé wool, I headed to Tiananmen Square to meet Yvonne. At the metro, I was queue-barged out of line by a bumpkin with a sack of rice on his shoulders. With a population of 1.3 billion, the Chinese believed that if they waited their turn, they'd be waiting forever. Yvonne was looking like a proper traveller. Her hair was even more matted and dirty.

Was it a sign of my loneliness, or my new-found tolerance? Whichever, it was joyous, energising even, to see Yvonne – though there were times when I had to ask her to stop talking as we wandered around the dynastic microcosm of the Forbidden City. I felt ashamed of my impatience with her in Moscow – I'd not stopped to think that this lone traveller might have been lonely. Now I, so loquacious, was in a similar position. We shared our experiences. Yvonne told me how her host in Tomsk, in south-west Siberia, had supplied her with a picnic for her train journey, fretted she hadn't shown her enough sights, and cried when Yvonne missed her train. This was Perfect Host Syndrome. To a degree, I'd experienced the same thing in Ulan-Ude – we'd both found it hard simply to accept.

Amongst all the Chinese tourists outside the Forbidden City, we'd become something of a tourist attraction ourselves, so we escaped from an impromptu photo call and made tentative plans to meet later for a salsa night that we'd both seen on the Beijing group forum.

☆

For buttering-up purposes, the Public Relations Manager treated me to a Park Hyatt dinner of spiny lobster with garlic butter, sushi, sashimi, pot stickers, Alaskan king-crab cocktail and peach pudding.

'How are you finding the x/y/z?'

'Oh, amazing, superlative, don't think I've ever had better x/y/z.'

My facial muscles were straining from the performance. I left the top-floor restaurant feeling giddy from the fuss – physically, at least, I'd become low-maintenance.

Drugged up on gastronomy, I lay on my bed. Yvonne texted to say she wasn't going to salsa. I tried to work some motivational techniques on myself. Could I go alone? Not when I didn't have to. I would be returning to couchsurfing the next afternoon, so I decided to embrace the isolation. Besides, I had unlimited Wi-Fi – never had my computer been a source of such comfort.

The Emperor had broken the ban. Which made me happy. Whatever geographical perspective I had out here was completely thrown by the emotional confusion of couchsurfing. I wasn't capable of making the Decision. Perhaps, I relayed to The Emperor, we would understand what to do after this three-month separation. Or perhaps we'd never come to a conclusion.

7TH NOVEMBER

All change: my next host, François, had phoned, instructing me to go to the West Gate of Peking University for 7pm. I was looking forward to getting involved again. So far, it was as if I'd been looking at Beijing through a straw. I met up with Yvonne to buy Great Wall tickets, and by some serendipity, Donagh called, having seen my post. He was in Beijing! I bought him a ticket. Our gang was growing.

I was surprised to find myself sad about leaving my luxury shelter. But I had been cosseted: concierge and housekeeping didn't come with couchsurfing. The PR manager gave me an ornament the size and weight of a sewing machine – the very symbol, it seemed, of our mismatch – and bade me well on my hour-long journey to Beijing's 'burbs.

Such was the magnitude of Beijing, it turned out, of course, that there were two West Gates. I eventually got myself into position, and savoured the view. Pacing about under the lamppost was a tall, slim man, wearing a tweed overcoat – so noir. This heroically handsome academic was waiting for *me*: high cheekbones, dark stubble, plenty of neat black hair, luscious French accent. François and I kissed on both cheeks, he took my rucksack, and we walked to their apartment. He stamped the ground, and then again, harder – the stairwell light came on.

'*Alors*, welcome at our apartment!'

We walked into a dark, cosy lounge: flatscreen TV, laminate wooden floor, fresh vanilla walls, a tomato and cream chunky sofa.

'You're lucky,' he said, as we slipped off our shoes (mercifully, no second-hand slippers). 'Zthe centralised 'eating as come on. Our first couchsurfer, in October, ad no 'eating. Ear is ze kitchen – zthis is my place!'

His phone rang. It must have been Xinxin: 'Okay, I wait you here,' he said.

The tour resumed: 'Zthis is ze bathroom – we don't trust the gaz 'eater, so to shower, you ave to turn on ze gaz in ze kitchen.'

It looked like a small toilet; he had to point out a showerhead fixed to the wall like a coat hook before I recognised it as a bathroom. Its basin and bathmat were in the lounge.

I bent over to pick up a spot of rubbish.

'No!' he cried out. 'Don't! It's a cockroach trap.'

Fortunately, I was distracted by the introduction to *my own room*. Under the ugly glare of fluorescent lighting lay a black hospital-esque bed with three caged sides, a navy towel for a curtain, and a Taiwanese flag in the window. Tour over, we settled on the sofa, where François explained the plan – we would wait for Xinxin to finish work and then go for a local meal. François seemed to be conscious of others' needs – it was the making of a good host.

An open laptop on the coffee table reminded me – my 'Security Alert'. Was I being paranoid? I'd been too paranoid to ask in the hotel.

'Oh sure, you are being watched,' François said, gravely.

My eyes widened.

'Zere are somesing like one million government guards watching us in Beijing. But you are okay – you will leave soon. If you are Chinese, you will be in jail or zthe working camp.'

No PR director would have admitted this.

François explained how words like 'Taiwanese independence' were filtered, never arriving at their digital destination but were instead stored in a huge database. Even his rugby team's website in France was blocked. As if to illustrate what it felt like, he typed

'England' into Google Images. Just a couple of pages appeared, many images refusing to load.

'So Chinese people don't know anuzzer life,' he said, heating up. 'Zey don't imagine.'

His thoughts had evidently been bottled up for some time. He continued. 'Ze government don't have to do any propaganda, zey are all so indoctrinated. Zey don't trust foreigners – we are ze mean invaders of ze 19th century. I tried to talk to Chinese students but it's like talking to a wall. Zey ave stereotyped answers to everyzing.'

There were even Chinese bloggers paid, he said, to write good things about China. He'd been looking at a website, How to Survive in Beijing. 'If you are a foreigner, it says you 'ave to be with foreigners.'

That, I guessed, was where couchsurfing came in.

His phone rang. 'Okay, okay, we come.'

We stepped out to a nearby restaurant. I exhaled: I felt protected, excited – and also sorry for them – neither seemed happy in Beijing. It was 8.30, which was 'very late to eat in China,' explained François, attentively. 'Zey have lunch at 11.30, and dinner at 6.30.'

Xinxin, a plain-looking office girl with spectacles and a ponytail, was sitting alone in an empty restaurant. I'd either missed it or she really didn't smile at me. Xinxin deployed her Alpha Female routine, coyly stroking François ('I'm not your pet,' he smiled cynically), leaning her head on his, and venting, often facetiously, about terrible China.

'The Chinese are too stupid to understand credit cards. They don't trust people, they don't trust each other. They don't know how to respect people. They are disgusting – they spit on the floor in restaurants.'

Startled, I didn't know what to say, so I didn't reply. But I needed Xinxin to like me. While Xinxin gnawed at beef on the bone, François backed her up, explaining that when spitting on the pavement was banned during the Olympics, people just spat in the gutter instead. Apparently phlegm contained the devil. A ruckus in another room erupted – the staff were tucking in: 'The Chinese are only happy if they are very noisy and very busy,' explained François, reading my astonishment. But why were François and Xinxin in Beijing, if they hated it so much? Xinxin pointed at François, François pointed at Xinxin. It was, they said, the compromise – a geographical middle ground with a relatively smooth visa situation.

Another grievance from Xinxin: 'Foreigners can't stay in cheap hotels in China.'

' Why?' I asked.

'They want to steal your money,' she scowled. 'They want you to go to expensive hotels. And unmarried Chinese couples can't stay in hotels – they think you're a prostitute.'

Again, François substantiated her bluster: 'It's 'ard to be sexual couple in China.'

I examined my pork mince intently.

'They're very conservative,' he continued. 'You hardly even see people kissing.'

I thought about behind-closed-doors and carnal needs. Couples and couchsurfing – I had my doubts.

I don't even remember how it started; the conversation began innocuously enough. We were back on the sofa, and I'd presented them with Prosecco, courtesy of the Park Hyatt. Suddenly, Xinxin erupted:

'Open-minded? The English? They're too arrogant, like the French. They think they're the best.' Her lip was fixed in a curl.

Needless to say, I couldn't agree – perhaps, I thought to myself, she was bitter about my comparatively easy ride. I tried, humbly, to defend my nation, but quickly stopped – I didn't want to get carried away.

Feeling like the enemy, I took a toilet break. As in – snap! – I broke the toilet seat.

'Don't break our toilet!' François teased from the lounge.

I flinched – they could hear everything.

'Don't worry,' he soothed, after I'd grovelled. 'It was about to break anyway.'

I didn't covet François, but I did find myself wishing for the one-on-one over Xinxin's presence.

'Next, I want a black boyfriend,' she said. 'I've already had two French boyfriends. I'd like to try something else. I want to collect them all.' She threw her nose in the air.

François stepped in: 'Actually, no, we are getting married.'

'Oh. How wonderful,' I said, thinly.

'I want to be protected by the French government,' Xinxin explained, now giving herself a head massage. 'Taiwan is controlled by China – it can't protect me. If someone wants to put me in the jail, it's very easy. My office say they can get a reward for reporting me for talking about Taiwan independence.' She removed her socks, dropping them to the floor.

'You should just shut your mouth,' said François, picking up her socks.

Yes, that would solve everything. I was getting too much perspective.

My Hyatt reserves had been all but drained and I had to get up at 5am the next day to walk the Great Wall. I left them to themselves and lay on my wooden mattress. Was it personal with Xinxin? Was she a demanding only child? Or was she a frustrated, disenfranchised woman trying to be heard while her nation was being submerged? How I took for granted my British rights. Perhaps she was entitled to resent me for dropping by, dangling my freedom under her nose.

8TH NOVEMBER

'Now I know what they mean by breathtaking views,' said one fellow climber, 800 metres up. For others, 'The Great Fall of China' would have been more appropriate, as we scrambled on all fours over the more neglected parts. Meanwhile, as this virile wall snaked out deep into the horizon, Yvonne, Donagh and I got on to the topic of sex.

Given that couchsurfing comprised a twenty-something majority having sleepovers on an extended holiday, it was inevitably a fertile hunting ground. Yvonne and I listened, rapt, while Donagh recounted how a Polish girl staying in Paris returned from a daytrip to find her host trying to seduce her with romantic candles. We laughed, but couchsurfing was hard enough without being caught in that sort of corner.

But worse, surely, was knowing your host was having sex, in the same room as you. Donagh had been there: 'I just had to pretend to be asleep,' he said. 'I was so conscious of my every breath. And then it happened again in the morning. When it was all over, I feigned waking up, with a big yawn and a stretch. It was pretty awful.'

And what about when couples couchsurfed? Did they?

'No,' said Donagh (he'd had first-hand experience). 'You just don't feel like it. Even with your own room. The conditions just aren't optimal.'

These words were to be heeded – no love tours, and no couples in one-room apartments. The jury was out on couples.

Over lunch, the Frenchman and Israeli in our group lingered in the conversational shadows. I realised how accustomed we had become to socialising with strangers. We compared couch notes on the bus back. Donagh had stayed with Begz on my recommendation.

'I almost didn't though,' he chuckled.

Begz had wanted to interview Donagh first, after Donagh's predictive texting had written that he'd 'love to fist him in the library'. Donagh's profile picture, in which he held two fingers to his head like a gun, didn't help. But there was a point – making judgement calls on a profile wasn't an exact science.

'Sometimes, when I haven't got on so well with my hosts,' Yvonne said, 'I realise I should have spent longer looking at their profile.'

I was thinking the same about François and Xinxin. But really, it was only in hindsight that profiles – incomplete and indirect – made sense. Donagh, something of an advanced couch-surfer, had started looking for more like-minded, creative people for better conversations. I, however, was drawn to opposites – the ger-dwellers, the shaman fans, the gunmen – that promised a bigger leap. But less common-ground inevitably meant harder work.

✪

Donagh had a couchsurfing house party that night. I wangled an invite, but first I had to give host-love. News had come in that they were both ill, and when I got home, there was indeed a chill in the air – blowing from Xinxin's direction. I asked after their condition – Xinxin had a headache from having felt cold outside and hot inside. Hard work was going to get harder.

Over another local dinner, Xinxin was working hard to ignore me, while François worked twice as hard to ignore the tension. She became forensically fascinated with her nails, the tablecloth, the middle distance – anything but us. François mediated, attempting a business-as-usual conversation, while I became increasingly needled by neuroses. The debacle illustrated what a fragile relationship the couchsurfing bond was. François was an accomplished host, but with Xinxin sabotaging it, he crumbled.

It certainly made going to the party easier – in fact, it was almost my duty to leave. It was the twenty-fifth birthday of 'Sustainable John', an American guy who worked for a British renewable energy company in Beijing. Chic, ruby walls were sexed up with black-and-white photography and a giant projection of Obama. A dreadlocked Chinese guy nodded studiously to the Junior Boys. Before long, I was lured into the orbit of Fabby, a flamboyant homosexual ex-pat.

'So may I ask you a personal question?' Fabby said, camping up the coyness.

'Umm, okay'.

'Have you ever laid any of your hosts?'

'Young man! No, thank you very much.'

'I have,' he volunteered. 'I've even had a couple of straight guys. I just say to guests, "If you are comfortable, you can have half my bed if you'd rather not sleep on the floor." I don't like to say no to surfers, ha ha ha,' he squealed.

Politics, economics, the environment and China were all discussed at length, but eventually it was time to go home.

'When are you leaving?' said Mike, an American businessman who'd talked about his hope to bring the world together. 'Couchsurfing is bottom-up,' he'd said, 'I also want to do it top-down, with foreign investments.'

'Tomorrow.' I was taking the night train to Xi'an.

'That,' he said, lifting his hands grandly to the skies, 'is both the miracle and the tragedy of couchsurfing. You meet these people, and then they leave town.'

9TH NOVEMBER

Silence. Outside my window, an old Chinese man was practising Tai Chi in the courtyard. Showering in the toilet required a similar form of contortion. Even still, I drowned the toilet roll and drenched the toilet. I then positioned myself on the sofa and psyched myself for our morning reunion.

The unfathomable mood had unfathomably faded: Xinxin re-engaged eye contact and 'normal' conversation resumed while a melodramatic Chinese soap opera blared from the TV.

'I prefer Hong Kong soaps,' Xinxin said, still unsmiling. 'Chinese soaps are so boring. They only ever portray the military, or how to respect your boss.'

Chinese soaps were used as parables, it appeared. François was going to the market: 'Maybe you would like to see?'

Bien sur!

As we passed radioactively large mushrooms, radishes like cricket balls and trucks of ducks en route to Peking, François patiently translated China's mores for me.

'Ze Chinese don't say please, zank you or sorry, so when you say please to zem, zey are so pleasantly surprised,' he explained.

This was to become my secret weapon in China. In return, I taught him English idioms, and we briefly experienced that couchsurfing 'moment'. With two complicit halves, it was so simple.

Back home, in one cunning move, attention was simultaneously being sought whilst excluding me: Xinxin was running around in her knickers, playing out a soft love performance, with kissing and giggling, so I retreated to my room to save her modesty, packed up and checked in with Donagh. I was going for an architect's view on Herzog & de Meuron's Olympic Nest and Koolhaus's CCTV Tower. I was going to miss Donagh – sharp, informed, sympathetic and bitingly funny, our relationship never needed 'work'. Surely a friend in absolute terms, not borne out of traveller desperation.

Oh, but François and Xinxin were going to lunch – would I like to come? I hesitated. Not really – but I had time … Okay! I'd saved face. We walked to a Korean restaurant ('They eat dogs,' said Xinxin, sensationally). I was glad I stayed around and invested in the relationship – we passed a perfectly pleasant hour.

It was time to say *adieu*. It was stiff and mechanical and I was glad to be free. Maybe staying with couples wasn't such a good idea – if it wasn't love, it was war.

CHAPTER 9

XI'AN: MY GOD, THEY REALLY CAN DRINK!

All aboard the Xi'an Express. Soft sleepers – the Chinese four-berth railways carriages – were for soft people like me. The options got a lot less soft, with hard seats in fourth class. 'Soft' didn't stretch to space, silence or smoothness, but I harnessed the down-time by lying vegetatively on my bunk in my train cabin. I was all thrilled out. A trickle of relief entered my consciousness as I anticipated Xi'an. Actually, a hostel would be perfect. There'd be other travellers there: reinforcements. That would give me some kind of freedom. They'd pester me to take their tours, but apparently, that was the easiest way of seeing the Terracotta Army – the 8,000 clay soldiers commissioned by the megalomaniacal First Emperor in 210BC to guard him in the afterlife. Safety in numbers. I slept for a record eight hours.

10TH NOVEMBER

'When you arrive, you can take bus 603 to Bell Tower then you can call me. I can pick you up there.'

'Sorry, the subscriber is not reachable.' It was 9am and I'd arrived in Xi'an and made my phonecall, only to hear this recorded response. Undeterred, I did a spot of sleuthing and found the Bell Tower Youth Hostel, presenting myself with all the entitlement in the world.

'Hi, I'm the couchsurfer. I'm here to see John.'

'Excuse me?'

There was no John.

'Couchsurfing? No? Errrm, could I use your computer?' I felt my face warming; my smugness melted away.

Hubris was waiting for me and my sense of entitlement.

I received a text message: 'John forget phone. He went old hometown. He maybe tomorrow come back.' It was closure. So my couch had fallen through. This was the matter-of-time catastrophe I'd been expecting, but I was surprisingly unruffled. The scab of Ollie's departure must have healed. Of course, I could just quit – temporarily – and stay in this hostel; after all, I had no idea where John's hostel was. Besides, my id was yearning to befriend three Brits in the lounge. Staying would be so easy. But for all couchsurfing's challenges, stepping down on to the tourist trail and off the couchsurfing one would be like switching to black-and-white from colour. I'd rather take on the perils of couchsurfing than lose that again.

I was starting to suss it out. One way to find active hosts was to join the local group. Luck was back – they were having their free-for-all monthly dinner *that* night. I RSVPed, mentioning that my host had disappeared, and sent a couple of last-minute couch requests.

The couchsurfing community was nothing if not a friend in a crisis. All three last-minute requests responded, but all too late – the City Ambassador, Gareth, had already rescued me.

28-year-old Gareth lived with his Canadian girlfriend, Beth. What was it I was saying about couples? Losers couldn't be choosers. Besides, I was going to be in *Ambassadors'* hands. Even if they were self-appointed.

So now I had company for dinner, a couch (plus reserves), and a break from couchsurfing till the evening. The Brits were still kicking around – they were going to see the Terracotta Army the next day, and no, they didn't mind if I came along.

One of China's oldest cities, Xi'an was not only the capital of Shaanxi province, but China's on-off capital since 220BC. It had long since burst forth from its perfectly preserved 14th-century, fifteen metre-thick city walls, but the old town had all a visitor could ask for. Xi'an was also the eastern terminus of the Silk Road. As Middle Eastern merchants colonised the city from the 8th century onwards, so Islam took root, spawning a Muslim quarter. A Chinese mosque, I discovered, looked pretty much like a Buddhist temple, with pagodas and flying eaves, except there were also wispy-bearded Chinese men wearing white skullcaps.

I was high on my own creed – with couchsurfing, I was alone yet protected. So I was a little surprised to find myself feeling meek on arrival at the rendezvous point for the local group, KFC. I hid behind some fauxliage to compose myself. Before me was an alarmingly large, 600-cover eaterie. I wasn't even sure what I was looking for. White people? I spotted one, with two young Chinese people, but surely I couldn't make that assumption. I was stuck.

'Are you here for the couchsurfing meeting?' It was Romeo, a Ken-like, Californian airline pilot whose couch I'd also requested.

'Hello Romeo!' (I enjoyed saying that.)

'Do you know if this is the right KFC?' he asked, pointing to another KFC directly opposite. This was a Chinese hazard – so big, everything came in duplicate.

Suddenly Romeo and I *were* the couchsurfing meeting, and the mixed group I'd spotted earlier – Jeff, an American bespoke tour operator; Maria, a Chinese student and City Ambassador; and Thomas, a Chinese student – gravitated towards us to meld into one thoroughly 'normal' collection of strangers. None of us had met before, yet any awkwardness was overshadowed by a need to share stories. It didn't seem at all tragic, just modern – this dynamic would take months to achieve naturally.

'Oh, I think you're my host!' I said, waving casually across the Colonel's table at a girl wearing a hoodie and a silver nose ring. Not one to fuss over hair or make-up, or, it seemed, female neuroses, Beth had a ready laugh and a healthy appetite. She looked over, smiled – eyes and all – and said hi; it was the most laid back host encounter ever. I was just part of the gang – it was at once relaxing and distancing. The diffused attention was a relief, and, with kinetic conversation all around, thoughts of The Emperor, loneliness and exhaustion were all suspended, and the night, as it so often did, ran away with itself.

A few more surfers drifted in, and we went to dinner. Beth took charge, ordering the beers and shared plates. As she talked into her phone (couchsurfers were never islands), I chit-chatted with the eighteen-year-old Maria who was studying English and who'd couchsurfed around Europe on bread and generosity. Faultlessly genial, she was perfect school-prefect material, but she didn't host because she slept six to a dorm.

My, what a very English accent you have, I observed.

'Oh, thank you,' she said, with the shock and grace of a Miss

World crown acceptance. 'That's very important to me.' She placed her hand on her heart. 'I love your history and your Royal Family. I think you should keep them.'

I sat up straight and tidied my hands away under the table.

'So,' she inquired politely, 'have you stayed with any single guys?'

I hadn't. I probably could make an entire trip of single guys, and maybe many did. That would be some odyssey, but it wasn't for me. Emperor or no Emperor, I'd be hopeless with the 'what if'.

A small window with Beth popped up and I learned that she and Gareth were English teachers for the private language college, English First, and that she was going to have to wake up at 10.30 the next morning to play in a college badminton tournament. I was either in for a bender of a night, or welcome lazy days. These nights were like waiting in goal, unsure which way to dive.

'Do you fancy some karaoke?' Beth was meeting some of her colleagues at KTV, a karaoke bar.

We piled out, and at the bottleneck at the door, I overheard a soft cockney accent, 'So, which one's Fleur?' It was Gareth, a roly-poly Brit wearing a cream blazer (never the wisest colour for the carefree) and thick, long-sighted glasses. He had mousey, mussed-up hair brushed forward from his crown. He looked like a teacher.

'Hello Gareth!' It was another laid back meeting.

Pouring, spilling and slamming the Absolut Vodka was a fifteen-strong coterie of western and Chinese twenty-somethings in KTV's VIP suite.

'I know it's a Monday night,' said Beth loudly over the music, 'but because it's a private school, we work weekends. Tomorrow's my day off.'

My mind was resisting being pushed into Saturday night gear. Too bad.

'Which school do you teach at?' someone asked.

'Oh, I'm not a teacher, I'm a couchsurfer,' I said. I had defined myself by couchsurfing. I didn't mind that – couch-surfers came with some pretty positive characteristics.

Suddenly, a giant, amplified belch boxed my ears. Aghast, I turned to the girl holding of the microphone. It was Beth.

'Oh, that's Beth for you,' said Gareth, noting my horror.

Whilst the westerners slurred away without the protection of inhibition, the Chinese sang ceremony-standard Chinese pop.

'I've heard, like, two bad singers in the two years I've been in China,' Beth said, in one of our little exchanges snatched throughout the evening.

I tried to sink into the background, but eventually obliged Beth with a duet on Janet Jackson's *Again*, while Gareth performed a very British rendition of *Big Girls are Beautiful*.

'We're booked in till 6am,' Gareth shouted gleefully.

'Oh, I see,' I faltered. It was already 2am, and by now I was the damp log in the fire. 'That might be a bit difficult,' I said, my head bowed.

Good news: Beth had vanished.

'Oh that's Beth for you,' said Gareth.

It was good because, according to Gareth, she'd probably be homeward-bound. In fact, she was just outside, chowing on a sausage sandwich and thick in an altercation with some locals. They'd laughed at her for being a foreigner.

'Oh, I need to collect my bags from the youth hostel,' I said, contritely.

'You can collect them tomorrow.'

'But I need them – they have everything in them.'

'It's too far.'

'It's like twenty metres up the road, at the Bell Tower – it's the very centre of town.' I shocked myself, but my impatience was out of its box.

'I don't know where that is.'

'Okay. We are going there. I will pay for it. It's really no detour.'

I checked myself – I'd just overruled my host. Anyway, she capitulated.

'Sorry,' she said, shaking her head. 'I'm being drunk and bullish.'

We set off, only for Beth to demand a detour to McDonalds (the sausage sandwich was long forgotten) which thankfully was shut. Couchsurfing was calling upon every social tool in my box to preserve relations. Still, at least I got out of staying up until 6am.

In a street the size of a whole town, some way beyond the city walls, our taxi pulled up at a Sino-Soviet block even more horrible and miserable than the Soviet version. Blood-like rust streaks ran off the cages around every window, on to the concrete walls. It looked like a communist asylum.

'Wooffff, wooffff!' We were mown down by a small, flaxen dog with an acute case of cabin fever. Gumpa – a suspected Chihuahua cross named after Forest Gump and a Chinese beer – yapped, bounced and tore around in circles in seeming perpetuity. I'd left one ruckus for another.

In an apartment set over some 150 metres squared, there was space to run. We stood in the lived-in, but modern, living room (bra on the glass dining table, large, loaded ashtrays, and expectant duvets on two diner-style red-and-cream leather sofas). But they weren't waiting for me; I'd be sleeping in the spare room, Beth said. These were Gareth and Beth's day beds – and night beds, when they were too lazy to get up. Beth crashed on one to watch *The Wedding Crashers* at full volume, and I went to my room.

It could have been Tracey Emin's bed. Strewn across my double room was a knot of polyester thread for a pillow (no case, just a large, matted, cloud-like mess), dirty socks on the laminate pine flooring, a carrier bag full of rubbish on the door handle and a puzzling collecting of weaponry: a samurai sword, two daggers, a hunting knife, a replica (I hoped) Heckler & Koch sub-machine gun and some nunchucks. I calmly put it down to the male condition and made my peace with the room. I had stayed in a lot worse.

A virulent tom-cat trail wafted out of the bathroom. There was no shower curtain, a loose toilet brush was resting on the tiled floor, and there was an apparent grudge match over who cleaned the toilet. I got out as quickly as possible, and crashed into my rude-smelling bed. Unyielding, it was like lying on an operating table.

Even with my door shut, the Wedding Crashers were still making mischief at the top of their voices. It was now 3.30am, and I was exasperated. Maybe Beth had passed out. Then I'd be doing *her* a favour to turn it off. I tried to gauge the situation through the crack in my door, but it revealed nothing. I zigzagged across the living room with the weak pretext of 'tidying my boots', stole a look, and went in for the kill – she was out of it. I slumped back into bed, wondering, had Gareth and Beth come to be Chinese-style 'noisy and busy', or were they just conveniently aligned? In any case, the chaos of couchsurfing nomadism, added to chaotic hosts, was a chaos too much. I was desperate for calm.

11TH NOVEMBER

I was awoken by the sound of an untraceable dripping tap. Opening my bedroom door led to a deluge of dog barking and ankle chasing. Being conscious here was like having tinnitus. As I left to meet the Brit boys for our trip to the Terracotta Army, Beth hollered useful instructions from the sofa.

'What's your address?' I asked, forward-planning my return.

'I don't know – just call when you get back.'

I slipped seamlessly into being a tourist. As we wandered round the colossal mausoleum – the result of one man's pathological fear of loneliness – I explained my night to the boys. Only as the words came out of my mouth did I feel a little mad for accepting it as normal. Unlike them, I was staying out of town, compromised and exhausted. But at the same time, I felt proud I was couchsurfing: I'd been on a local night out; I'd sung Chinese karaoke; I'd seen inside a Xi'an apartment. I had mixed feelings, but that was the point – couchsurfing was a double-edged sword.

✪

It was tracksuit-and-telly time at home. Gareth and Beth were swaddled in duvets on their respective sofas, so, after presenting them with a trusty box of chocolates, I eased myself into the matching armchair. *Family Guy* was on the box, and Gumpa was administering dog therapy to all interested parties. We all got out our laptops. We chatted. Sometimes we were silent.

'Having the ability to be part of the furniture,' said Gareth, lighting up a Chinese cigarette, 'that's the best kind of couchsurfer.'

It was, I guessed, somewhere in between being relaxed and invisible. Or perhaps being relaxed about being invisible.

A night in – this was the most exciting event thus far. It took a certain host not to feel the need to provide constant entertainment. As it did to excuse a boyfriend who'd staggered in at 10.30am – as Gareth had that morning. I admired that. Someone mentioned popping out for a bite to eat, but I was willing it away – right here was perfect.

I caught up on my couchsurfing correspondence. I'd be leaving the day after next for Urumqi, 2,568 kilometres north-west of here, and the capital of Xinjiang, an autonomous region in furthest north-west China, where the Muslim Uighurs (pronounced 'weeghurs') of Turkic origin were the ethnic majority. My last stop before Kazakhstan, it was considered something of a frontier land – poor, undeveloped and one of China's few regions with a Han *minority*. Fittingly, the couchsurfing possibilities looked a little wobbly. I'd originally organised a Uighur host but after an ambiguous message ('Everything is changing, so if u cant stay here, i take u to a hostel'), I played safe with an ex-pat teacher, Peter, in his late fifties, where 'safe' was one previous recorded guest. He'd messaged back, mentioning my 'husband' and that I'd be arriving in the dead of winter, when people hardly ever went outside. I had my misgivings, but frankly, I was lucky to persuade him. I'd devised a new strategy – I'd approach those listed as 'maybes', and then work harder on the message. Now with half a dozen positive references, I had a little more currency.

Finally, there were stirrings: Gumpa was put on a lead and we stepped out into the neighbourhood. It was like walking through town with the Mayor and First Lady. We couldn't get past their friend's street stall until we'd sat down, tried every colour of her unnaturally colourful 'meat' balls and greeted the entire family. She refused our money: 'It's considered prestigious to have western friends,' Beth explained, aside. 'Sometimes you know you're just a little sideshow for them to show off.'

A commotion was blowing up in the street. Some Chinese Muslims in skullcaps had seen us and were shouting. Hands were thrown in the air triumphantly and backs were patted fondly. We were given a hero's welcome, and seated on the pavement outside their kebab shop.

'The police try and stop people eating outside,' said Gareth, with the assurance of a well-settled resident. 'They think it's not modern or western, which is a shame because it's the best thing.'

After three failed attempts to order myself some tea ('*cha*'), Beth took over, yelling '*CHA!*'

She turned to me: 'Sometimes they don't understand unless you shout.'

Gareth and Beth were in no ex-pat bubble; they were the bridge to local life that I craved. I had a rush of host-love. I described my Beijing couch.

'I don't understand ex-pats who just complain,' said Gareth, clinking glasses with Beth, downing a shot of fortified Korean rice wine, and rinsing with a slug of beer. 'If you don't like it, go home. I know ex-pats who have been here for two years and know as many words.'

The same couldn't be said of Gareth and Beth, who'd learnt their impressive language skills in the streets. Gareth could say some really rude things, but, added Beth, the Chinese didn't swear in casual conversation: 'When you swear, you really mean it – unlike in English.' I looked into my lap, feeling a little coarse.

Gareth and Beth seemed much more excited than me by the

arrival of tiny, skewered scraps of salted, spiced lamb, heart and chicken wings. I asked if they felt aligned to the Chinese attitude.

'I love it,' said Gareth, gnawing vigorously on a bone. 'I can't spend any longer than six months in the UK. The political correctness just oppresses me. I'm a very physical teacher – I like to hug the kids if they're upset, or if they're playing up, I pick them up and put them outside. Okay, so people can't vote, but there's a certain freedom here.'

Beth wiped the grease from Gareth's chops, adding, 'Of course, you get bad China days when all the shouting gets to you.'

Like the previous night – with the ex-pats.

Censorship was an inevitable topic. The 'Three Ts' – Tiananmen, Tibet and Taiwan – were to be avoided, they explained.

'I play dumb with my students,' said Beth, feeding Gumpa leftovers. 'They'll say, "Don't you know about Tibet?" and I'll pretend not to so they tell me what they think.'

'And?'

'That it's a Chinese, not a world, issue,' she shrugged. 'We have assistants who say they'd fight to the death in a war against Taiwanese independence.'

'And the thing about Tibet,' said Gareth, 'is that, before China intervened, they used to have slaves. They still use knives to settle traffic arguments. I'm not saying they're bad people, but they're just people. I can't stand Hollywood types who climb aboard the Tibet bandwagon because it's fashionable.'

I realised I only knew the Richard Gere angle. Gareth and Beth were clearly sympathetic to China, and I was factually ill-equipped. Taking on the issue would at best give a Pyrrhic victory, so I left it, swiftly returning to the issue of school. Now *there* was access – ever since discovering they were teachers, I'd privately harboured the notion of visiting a Chinese school.

'Umm, if there was one thing I could do in Xi'an ...'

My request was noted – it shouldn't be a problem.

It seemed appropriate to shout them the £4.60 dinner (double what it used to be, apparently). The Korean wine now drained, Beth disappeared down a dark alley.

'Has she gone to the toilet?' I asked primly.

'Oh yes, everybody does it.'

Walking home together, I thought about my polite, cautious approach.

'It doesn't do to be too reserved,' I reflected out loud.

'Well,' said Beth, 'I can't be anything else but myself.'

My 'good night' to the hosts was always accompanied with, 'So what are your plans for tomorrow?' It was the way to avoid nasty surprises. I was going to climb the Taoist mountain, Huashan, the next day, but for my final night in Xi'an there didn't seem to be any plans. Gareth was taking his business English students to KTV (was karaoke good for business English?), but that would finish early and Beth wasn't doing anything. I turned in for the night, feeling like, given the right conditions, this social experiment was working.

12TH NOVEMBER

I was mistaken in thinking a visit to the Chinese mountains would be some kind of spiritual quest. I'd been expecting a day of contemplation and meditation alongside the physical trial of climbing to 2,000 metres. Instead, there was the constant accompaniment of Chinese tourists shouting and trying to hear their own echo – no sooner had one shouted, than another drowned out his echo with more shouting. I scuttled back to town, keen to pick up where we'd left off the night before. I dropped Gareth and Beth a text saying I'd be back by 7pm.

I didn't hear back until 8.30, when Beth called to say that she was going to karaoke with Gareth. They'd be back at 10.30. 'Oh,' she added, as an afterthought, 'would you like to come?' I'd got up at 6.30am and really didn't feel like raucousness, so I said I'd see them later.

'Wooffff, woofff!' Gumpa was very pleased to see me. I was kind of pleased to see her. I hadn't wanted to be home alone for my last night – was I allowed to begrudge not being told as much until 8.30, now too late to organise anything else? As the evening crawled by, past 10.30, past midnight, and still no sign, I recalled Gareth's words: 'part of the furniture – that's the best.' It would have helped were I a hardcore hedonist. I re-read their profile – the words 'beer', 'drinking', 'partying' and 'up all night' jumped out. Last-minute rescues didn't have the luxury of being good matches. And perhaps I'd been spoilt by Russian hospitality. Maybe ex-pats just didn't have the drive of national pride.

And so, with that other little pile of abandonment, Gumpa, I shivered on the sofa. It was freezing and there were no more clothes I could put on – it was November and 5°C outside. 'The government says when it's hot and when it's cold,' Gareth had explained. I got up to shut the French windows, only to realise that they had to stay open; scattered with long, skinny dog-logs, the balcony was Gumpa's litter tray.

I reached out to Ollie. He'd been out and about again and had found an unexpected benefit to his crutches – strangers were offering to carry his drinks.

'Whoever said London isn't friendly?' he emailed. 'You just need the right props.'

Meanwhile, The Emperor and I were exchanging anodyne updates – serious discussions had been frozen until my return to London. It didn't stop the serious thoughts. I was thoroughly confused. With all the surface clutter blown away, I was left with deep love, yet deep doubt. It was too complex to comprehend. Feeling depleted, I went to sleep fully-clothed.

13TH NOVEMBER

Rigid with fatigue, I woke at 9am, listlessly listening to someone padding about. A thought suddenly propelled me out of bed – I was leaving that afternoon. If they were teaching all day, I'd miss them forever. I found Beth, just on her way to private kindergarten. 'Oh, shit, I totally forgot to tell you,' she said, whirring around the apartment. Gareth was still asleep so I held out, tucking into a breakfast of crisps from my supplies.

Gareth and I met on the sofa, his naked form wrapped – almost – in his duvet. He told me about his and Beth's tour company, Young Pioneer Tours, which made government-guided trips to North Korea (as was the only way). He gave me a mint 100 Won note – it felt rather like school prize-giving; like I'd passed. But Gareth had a meeting, so – once he was fully dressed – he gave me a big, genuine squeeze goodbye.

At which point Beth returned. Provided at least one of these guys was around, this was a great couch – there was no tension, no games. Beth explained about 'Special KTV' – karaoke bars that doubled up as brothels. They'd once been befriended by a sozzled Communist party leader, who took them to a Special

KTV, went 'to wet his whistle' (it was a status thing to have women on the side, apparently) and then returned to drink more *baijiu* (or 'white liquor'). 'My God, they can really drink,' she said. I could only begin to imagine.

It was that time again. Beth and I bid each other farewell: 'You were super low maintenance,' she said warmly. Oh. Perhaps I should have demanded more attention.

CHAPTER 10

URUMQI: UNACCUSTOMED AS I AM

It was easy to spot the correct rail platform for Urumqi – I just followed the procession of white skullcaps and darker, more defined faces with larger eyes, longer, bridged noses and so many luxuriant moustaches. These were the Uighurs. The forty-hour ride to Urumqi, with nothing but the lifeless, rocky backdrops of Inner Mongolia and the Tibetan Plateau to look at, gave me time and space enough to anticipate my next host. Peter was my first single male and my first generation gap. I was trying to go with the avuncular idea – he'd written that he liked to cook, enjoyed a glass of wine and hung out at the English Club with his local Chinese and Uighur friends. I was trying to relax into the promise of the more mature man's finely-honed quality of life. But I had my reservations. Not least of which was the fact that my last three missives had gone unanswered.

Had he gone off the idea? Had I got the wrong number? The train pulled into a still-dark Urumqi where a seething, shadowy crowd blocked the exit, heckling and shoving. I'd stepped foot into Xinjiang, meaning 'new frontier', it was the furthest place in the world from the sea. One-sixth of China's territory, it bordered Kazakhstan, Kyrgyzstan, Tajikistan, Afghanistan, Pakistan, India, Mongolia and Russia and was home to nearly fifty ethnic groups. Overwhelmed, I sought refuge until sunrise in an internet café, where a fight between two adolescents broke out, a woman stood reading over my shoulder for an hour and my catatonic neighbour used his keyboard for a pillow. All this was becoming very hard work. It was, as Alain de Botton put it, 'the peculiar activity of travelling for pleasure.'

But I was the lucky one, wasn't I? I was *travelling*, just like I'd wanted to. I felt conflicted. I wanted to be here, but I longed for home. I'd place all hope in my couchsurfers, then crave my departure. I wanted The Emperor, then I didn't. I couldn't get away from the grass is greener cliché. Perhaps that was what I needed to come to terms with – to respect my side of the fence more. I had to stop wanting to flee whenever there was a pause in the pleasure. I had to stop seeking perfection.

As the sun kissed the snowy Tian Shan mountains into a glowing pink heaven, I made for the ticket office. I had to buy my ticket to Almaty, Kazakhstan's largest city, erstwhile capital and optimistic answer to New York, which lay 1,374 kilometres west of Urumqi. I'd be taking the midnight train in two days' time. I felt weary even at the thought of travelling again.

Nestled in the queue were a couple of American girls. I was surprised to see white faces out here. It wasn't long before we broke the ice. Lindsay and Cayce were from Maine, and were also headed for Almaty.

'Let's share a cabin,' one suggested. 'It will lessen the chances of spitting and farting.'

Hello luck, my old friend. Lindsay and Cayce were travelling indefinitely, they said. I was a *couchsurfer*, I said. So were they!

Peter called. He had a new phone and couldn't read his texts. He sounded kind but serious – not someone to muck around. I leapt into action: 'I'm on my way,' I promised.

'Okay, I'll go outside and wait,' he said, softly.

The spit of Clive James but with a longer face, Peter was waiting by the roadside under a concrete flyover, wearing a heavy, khaki parka. A substantial man, he had the languid gait of someone who'd been there since I'd hung up.

'Give me your rucksack,' he intoned.

His face, like his voice, was impassive. He led me through the cold, iron gates of the school compound, past fallen leaves and gaunt trees, and into ashen high-rise homogeneity.

'This is your room,' Peter said phlegmatically. A pillowy airbed lay beneath a lonely ethnic wall hanging. It was the kind of living room you might expect a school to supply a teacher with – adequately, but not cosily, furnished. Beyond the presence of the bed, the room went about its normal business: Woody Allen box set on the 'mahogany'-painted coffee-table, Indian cotton drape on the sofa, guppies by the bookshelf.

'Because the heating is on, you shouldn't need extra covers.'

Heating was a good sign.

I dumped my bags and followed him into the kitchen, which was also the hall. We hovered around a small, busy kitchen table: two chairs, paperwork, condiments.

'There's a line through China,' he continued, slowly. 'Above, it is heated; below, it isn't. Urumqi is heated by huge coal plants, so it's one of the twenty most polluted cities in the world.'

A chilling Mozart concerto started up from the living room.

'Have you had breakfast?' he asked.

'Oh, I had some biscuits on the train,' I said, as if giving a statement. I couldn't get past the idea that I was in my headmaster's office.

'I made some soup – would you like some?'

'Are *you* going to have some?'

That wasn't the answer to the question, it was me trying not to be any trouble. Peter wasn't hungry, but two varieties of soup – a thick, busy bean-and-potato, and a chicken broth were served with white sliced bread, butter, and, if I wanted, Vegemite. I ate my soup with great efficiency, then dashed to my bags to retrieve my gift, a non-fiction book that he had requested in response to my offer, and an unopened packet of biscuits. It was a clumsy attempt at paying him back.

Peter methodically ran through his plans for the day: an hour-and-a-half head, shoulder and foot massage, then lunch at a local Uighur restaurant, followed by a walk in the park, then an ex-pat bar, then the English Speaking Club, followed by dinner nearby.

'It sounds wonderful,' I enthused. 'What a relaxation programme you've lined up! I'd love to accompany you, if that's okay with you, of course.'

This being quite possibly the most generous welcome yet, I was disconcerted. It wasn't that I was getting mixed messages, but that I was getting none at all. I saw not a single smile. His voice withheld all emotion – every word was delivered in the same minor key. Peter was here but so distant.

I cautiously inquired a little more of my host as we took a taxi to the massage parlour. He'd come to Urumqi four years ago because it was 'remote, isolated and full of history'. Peter, it struck me, was like an old elephant, carrying a great sadness in his core. He was running away from something, for sure. Most teachers didn't bother coming here, he explained, they all headed to the East Coast. He used to hang out with ex-pats but he got 'bored' of them being so cliquey, so he joined the English Speaking Club. It didn't quite add up, these twin missions for isolation and company, but it matched my confusion – I felt both in the way and required to entertain.

As Peter and I lay side-by-side on our respective massage tables, I, like a Victorian child, spoke when I was spoken to. At least the pain in my couchsurfer's neck, from all those planks for mattresses, was finally being relieved.

Peter paid. 'I'll get lunch,' I said quickly. Which was a heavy, sweet lamb *plov* and rose-petal tea in a simple restaurant (no menu). Shadowing Peter in a bald attempt to adapt, I thought of Beth: I was finding it very hard to be myself. But with no feedback from him, it was impossible to know what was working. I paced his high-speed eating and then followed him outside, where he lit a cigarette and pointed out Red Mountain, a symbolic, terracotta-coloured inner-city mountain. It was another immovable rock.

'I want to go to the toilet,' Peter announced.

'Okay,' I said, 'I'll just wait here and look at this hilarious wedding shop.'

But Peter crossed the road into the park.

'Or maybe I'll wait in the park.' I trotted after him.

'I'm going for a wander,' he said. 'I'll meet you in Fubar, it's just over there.'

'Sure! I can hang out here,' I said cheerily. 'How long will you be?'

'Thirty minutes? Or longer if you like. An hour – I don't mind. I have some things I want to discuss with someone at the bar.'

My body was all unwound from the massage, but my mind was a knot. Why was Peter so unhappy? Had he heard bad news? Was he uncomfortable with this unlikely coupling? Sitting obediently in the park, I bade my time before reuniting.

'I thought you'd got lost,' Peter said, with dramatic irony – I was lost in tension. Fubar was a cosy, hip bar with slouchy leather sofas and exposed brickwork. 'They have good collection of *Time* magazines,' he said.

I took it as an instruction, and grabbed one, flicking through it perfunctorily. I was looking forward to some social back-up at the English Speaking Club. Would Peter be like this with his friends, I wondered.

'You should try and find someone to take you to Turpan,' he advised.

Some 150 kilometres away, the oasis town of Turpan was a key Silk Road stopover and Uighur stronghold.

'Tomorrow would be a convenient day for you to go, as I have plans.' I nodded – he *really* didn't want me around.

'Actually,' I blurted, 'if there was one thing I'd really like to do here, it would be to see your school – if that's at all possible.'

'Okay, I'll think about it.'

We went to the English Speaking Club, which met every Saturday afternoon in the damp basement of a large bookshop. Seated at café-style tables were twenty-five Chinese men and women aged between twenty and forty, and one American woman. Peter set me up with a few introductions to businessmen, teachers, entrepreneurs and students – all without smiling.

A psychiatrist told me that incidences of bipolar disorder, depression and schizophrenia were higher now, because 'people are very busy and there are no jobs.' Someone gave me a tincture of Chinese herbal medicine to drink with my thimble of jasmine tea. 'Urumqi,' said a businessman, pushing back his shoulders, 'is a city built like London. The paths of the animals became the roads – it is not a planned city.'

I was surprised to see Peter approaching me, but in fact it was just to say that he was going home – not feeling well, he said. The departure may have fed my paranoia, but frankly, I was relieved. Losing his protective wing wasn't a problem; he was as much of a stranger as anyone.

'Fleur is going to make a speech for us!' It was Walter, one of the Chinese regulars.

'A speech? On what? I don't have a speech!'

'Yes, yes – come on. Stand over here, that's right.' Walter jostled me into position. 'Ladies and gentlemen, we are very lucky today …'

How very *39 Steps*. However, thanks to couchsurfing, I had a ready-made story. I galloped through its principles and my itinerary, and quickly sat down – only to be surrounded by as many people as could fit around one table, with a second tier of schoolchildren, the hapless charges of a local teacher: 'Excuse me, may I ask a question please ..?' Eventually, I managed to move the subject back to China.

I heard the truth about China's single-child policy – one of the older ones present who had a brother reckoned China's youth were too dominant and selfish.

'A nation of princes and princesses will gradually be a social problem,' he said gloomily.

An overly made-up teacher tutted at him: 'Be careful what you say!'

Predictably, a rosier view-point swiftly followed: thanks to nutritional improvements, the younger generations had higher IQs and much more 'power of creation'. The Chinese were 'diligent and hardworking'.

It was true – the English Speaking Club was a case in point. Not having native English speakers didn't deter them from practising their English – they'd still meet and talk amongst themselves. An economics student buttonholed me, and I seized my opportunity, 'inviting' him to Turpan. It was hard to understand him and he looked at me excitedly, like I might be edible, but I was lucky to find anyone happy to make a six-hour round trip with me. I couldn't afford standards.

'Fleur will be our guest of honour at dinner!' This attention was the antidote to Peter's sangfroid. I was escorted to a restaurant called Fabulous Guest, and was seated with my back to the wall, as was appropriate for the guest of honour. As I looked around the table, I realised this was my first real Chinese experience. It wasn't what I'd been warned of – I was surrounded by interested, warm, sentient beings, all amply hospitable and generous, not least to the foreigner. Muslim-spun Chinese food piled in: deep-fried naan, spicy noodles, spicy tofu, spicy chicken, and a whole, impassable pumpkin. As guest of honour, it was me to go first at the pumpkin. I dishonourably asked for help.

Across the table the American, an archeologist, said, 'Fleur, you're very lucky – you're in the best place in Urumqi right now. You are with its most intelligent people.'

I had to agree, I said.

She continued: 'And people here are so kind. In Beijing and the east, they're polite, but they're not kind.'

A businessman who owned a BMW said, 'They're more westernised, ha ha ha.'

Touché.

'What about the financial crisis?' I asked.

'Yes we feel it,' said an entrepreneur, who'd profited from SARS by making an anti-viral cleaner. 'Property prices are going down, food prices are going up. We are relatively safe but we are just a village – we shut the door, but the wind still blows.'

After a dramatic pause, someone pointed out: 'Fleur has a very sharp nose!'

It made me feel quite distinguished.

Then someone added, 'We call foreigners *da bi zi*. That means 'big noses' – the Russians especially are *da bi zi*.'

At least we were all connected by laughter – even that I wouldn't take for granted after my experience with Peter.

16TH NOVEMBER

It was at Turpan that I discovered that couchsurfing had me under some kind of spell – a patience spell that quickly wore off when not in the company of one's host. I felt for the economics student who'd agreed to accompany me, but to be fair, it was a trying day – that six-hour journey, plus long walks around dry, historic sites, all to the relentless accompaniment of: 'So, in Britain, what do you eat for breakfast? Tell me about British history. What do you do in your spare time? So, in Britain …?'

When I fixed my gaze through the bus window, he'd say: 'Are you meditating?'

And at the remarkable 13th-century desert city of Jiaohe, he started shouting to hear his own echo. Maybe I was witnessing the social problems of an only child.

But it wasn't all bad. We heard snake-charmer pipe music,

distant drums, donkeys braying. We saw sequinned headscarves, dusty grapes, gambling in the streets, Arabic script and sandy, mud- and straw-built houses and mosques. It was more Egypt than China. And I was lucky enough to gain a Han Chinese economics student's perspective. His parents had come to Xinjiang from Sichuan under the government's 1999 Western Development Policy – the cause of much Uighur resentment towards the Han Chinese. In Sichuan, he said, there was only one acre per person; now his parents had a one hundred-acre tomato farm. Xinjiang also had vast natural resources, especially oil and gas.

'But the government doesn't really invest in Xinjiang,' he said. 'If you want to be developed, you need the sea.'

This twenty-year-old had never seen the sea.

I escaped into his English notebook on our return journey, spending longer than necessary reading a meticulously inked copy of Bertrand Russell's *What I Have Lived For*.

'I have sought love, first, because it brings ecstasy – ecstasy so great that I would often have sacrificed all the rest of life for a few hours of this joy. I have sought it, next, because it relieves loneliness – that terrible loneliness in which one shivering consciousness looks over the rim of the world into the cold unfathomable lifeless abyss. I have sought it, finally, because in the union of love I have seen, in a mystic miniature, the prefiguring vision of the heaven that saints and poets have imagined. This is what I sought, and though it might seem too good for human life, this is what – at last – I have found.'

I *knew* that place! And that was such a privilege. I should respect it more. Perhaps it was all connected – this lack of respect for love, the refusal to accept the rough with the smooth, and the extended play of a western thirty-something. Love had a hefty price tag, and rightly so.

Like a loyal dog, Peter was waiting outside for me. How was he feeling?

'Not well, actually,' he said. 'I've been in bed today.'

And yet, 'Some friends came round for a late lunch and beers this afternoon.'

So, like, very ill. He set me up with soup, his computer, his DVD collection, breakfast for the next day (my last), and hand-written instructions in Mandarin for getting to Xinjiang's state museum. A school visit was looking promising too.

Peter retired at 9pm – I was past fretting whether he wanted to be with me or not. The answer was obvious, but it didn't negate his kindness.

17TH NOVEMBER

Good news – school was on. As Peter led me through the huge campus for 5,000 students, he explained lethargically that he taught fourteen 17-year-old 'rich kids' preparing for international study. Peter was lucky – most classes had thirty to fifty students, and in villages, lessons could be for whole schools of 1,500 pupils. His salary was 3,000 quai a month (quai was slang for yuan; 3,000 quai was about £300). Chinese teachers earned 2,000–3,000 quai.

'Parents are prepared to spend a lot of money on their children's education,' he explained, 'as they'll return and look after them – they see it as an investment.'

At every door, a neat row of stationed students kowtowed us as we passed through. We wended our way through a long maze of undecorated concrete walls to Peter's classroom, and as we walked past a couple of students beatboxing, he revealed that he'd asked his students to prepare questions for me. That moved me from the observer to contributor – it gave me butterflies.

The students completely ignored us when we walked in, instead continuing to talk, tear pieces of paper into tiny squares or sleep on their desks. Some were in uniform – shiny navy and white tracksuits with the slogan SWIFTER, HIGHER, STRONGER on the back.

'Can someone clean the board?' Peter asked. He repeated himself until a boy reluctantly co-operated. There were two blackboards – the one at the back, featuring the words, 'I love China!' and with a portrait of President Hu propped against it – was left preserved.

'Every three weeks, the students have to draw a new positive picture of China there,' Peter explained. His manner in the class-room was exactly as it was at home – grudging, if a little shorter in patience. We took to our positions behind his desk.

'Emily, what's your question for Fleur?'

'Where do you come from?'

'I thought I told you all this morning,' he moaned. Emily tried again, and Peter went to sit on the sofa at the back, leaving me alone.

'Please tell us about this couchsurfing … Can you speak Chinese? … Will you be volunteering for the London Olympics? … Do you like China? … Do you pray for designer fashion?' (A hint?)

I earnestly answered their questions, but Peter called out: 'You're not supposed to just listen to her. You're meant to inter-act. Think about what she's said and ask something back. You see, Fleur,' he said, turning to me, 'they're taught by the lecture method; they're not used to engaging'.

Eventually, a kind of conversation ensued – albeit mostly with Timmy. With his pink shirt, hairdresser's hairdo and fascination with *Sex and the City* ('You are so Carrie Bradshaw!' he'd giggled), Timmy left no doubt as to his sexuality.

The questions continued, and I got to ask my own questions back:

'What hours are you in school?'

'9am till 10pm.'

'What happens if you're late?'

'A fine – five yuan (fifty pence) the first time, then ten, then fifteen …'

'What about extra-curricular activities?'

Peter stepped in: 'There aren't really any. Their life is very different to what you know back home. They're not allowed boyfriends or girlfriends.'

They weren't even allowed to sit close to the opposite sex. On Sundays, their day off, they slept.

'What about uniforms?'

Compulsory: 'They don't want us to compare ourselves to each other.'

But once in the classroom, they'd show off their own clothes underneath.

A strangely hypnotic, polyphonic melody started – the school bell. English was out – I'd taken the whole double lesson, and I was euphoric. It was a serious contender for the highlight of my trip. It was worth the price of strained relations.

CHAPTER 11

ALMATY: FORCE 10 FIGHTS AND COLD COMFORTS

'It's crap – Cayce had her bag stolen.'

The two American girls I was expecting had become one. Lindsay, a luscious olive-skinned brunette with tamed, strong brows and an angular jaw looked understandably tense as she arrived in Urumqi station's waiting hall.

'Just after we met you, walking through the station. Her passport, tickets, visas, money – everything.'

Crap indeed.

'She's had to travel 1,000 kilometres back east to fix it. And my Chinese visa was about to expire so I had to keep going.'

As the unwashed masses barged past with bulging cardboard boxes and Chinatown-check holdalls loaded with cheap Chinese wares, we warily pulled our bags to our chests.

It was just as well our journey to Almaty was thirty hours long – Lindsay and I had much to discuss. Both with companion-sized gaps to fill, we connected like cup and saucer. It was looking like weeks before Lindsay – a 24-year-old beerologist (not in fact a heavy drinker, but a beer expert) with Russian-Jewish origins – would be reunited with Cayce. While couchsurfing protected you from some amount of loneliness, the undiscussables – ie, the host, their home and their habits – all ate away at the lone surfer. More than just providing a welcome ear, Lindsay was wise, witty and honest, and had a far-sighted perspective. I felt a surge of new-friend affection.

But she hadn't sorted a couch in Almaty.

'It's like trying to get a job without any experience,' she said, sketching in her art book. 'If you don't have any experience, you can't get the job, but without a job you can't get any experience. I mean, is it all about a couchsurfing elite?'

She'd made contact with one partied-out South African who'd just arrived in Almaty and couldn't handle hosting, and a local woman who'd talked of 'appointments' to go skiing and making full itineraries. Lindsay suspected she was a tour opera-tor. And if not, she said, it would probably cost loads to keep up with her.

I was by no means 'in' – the couchsurfing scene was pretty embryonic in Kazakhstan. There wasn't a single local group, Ambassador or even ethnic Kazakh signed up, and of its 124 couches, barely any remained once the flakes, the can't-offer-sofas and those in apparent need of psychiatric assistance (as found the world over) had been weeded out. I'd settled for the last resort: a couple's bedroom floor, whose two references were dated 2007.

'Okay, I'm just going to come right out and say it,' Lindsay said, her deep chocolate eyes avoiding mine. 'Do you think I could stay with your couchsurfer?'

Well, it was good news for me, but my host had stated one surfer maximum – would two people for three nights be a liberty too far? I texted the guy, Dmitri. 'Okay. You are welcome,' he responded. I suddenly got that holiday feeling again.

18TH NOVEMBER

A quantum leap into the 'Glorious Nation of Kazakhstan' put us into the world's ninth-largest country. Outside the train, the planet petered out into the brown-earth nothingness of steppeland, while inside the fun was just beginning. Two Kazakh guys entered our carriage for their own amusement. They didn't look like Borat. Of Turkic and Mongol extraction, our friendly companions were heavy-set and weathered (even the young one), with slanted, Mongol eyes, bridged, oriental noses and expansive, ruddy faces. The Soviet diet of vodka and carbs had clearly taken effect.

'Chelsea Futbol!' cheered the older one, flashing his gold grill teeth. This was what Britain seemed to be known for nowadays; at least with random drunk men met on trains across Asia. The Premiership was globalisation in action.

'Kazakhstan is boring!' he cried. He couldn't understand what we'd want here. His English wasn't up to explaining why, but I had an idea. With a population of sixteen million (and just six people per square kilometre), this former Soviet Republic wasn't exactly paradise. To Moscow, it was a dumping ground and a blank slate for experiment. From 1949 until 1989, a whopping 456 nuclear tests were conducted in Semey, north-east Kazakhstan. The local cancer and leukaemia rates were still grossly inflated there. From the 1930s onwards, Moscow collectivised Kazakhstan's agriculture, annihilating its nomadic farming and killing millions through starvation. The Aral Sea was barely a sea any longer after the grand Soviet irrigation projects of the 1960s diverted the rivers that fed it. By 2007, it had shrunk to one-tenth of its original size, destroying its eco-system and fishing industry, and leaving widespread unemployment, disease and destitution.

But the episode that most shaped Kazakhstan's modern history was Stalin's deportation of political prisoners to its open spaces. While many died, and others returned to their country of origin after independence from the Soviet Union in 1991, a huge ethnic and religious mix remained – in addition to the fifty-nine per cent Muslim Kazakh majority and twenty-six per cent Orthodox Russians were over one hundred other ethnic groups, including Ukrainians, Uzbeks, Germans, Koreans, Uighurs, Tatars and Greeks.

Nowadays, Kazakhstan was run by the Kazakh, Nursultan Nazarbayev, the country's first president since independence. The stories were rife: he was one of the world's richest men; he'd given Air Astana, the national airline, to his mistress; he controlled the media through his eldest daughter, who ran TV and radio stations and newspapers. But the people loved him: every school and business proudly hung his portrait, and news reports would close by giving thanks to him. 'He's like the king,' international commentators said.

Boring? Tragic, complex, and known for temperatures hitting -40°C, Kazakhstan didn't sound boring. Besides, after China and all its control and efficiency, I was looking forward to a more heady sense of romance and passion.

19TH NOVEMBER

Our first drama in Almaty was a drunken, pre-dawn brawl between two Kazakhs at the station. Our second was at the police station, where we were swiftly cornered into paying a backhander to register as tourists. I thought of Ravil: 'Kazakhstan is extreme.' Our as-yet unknown third drama was closer than we anticipated.

Right: Cheerleading grins for our couchsurfing profile picture. Ollie's the one on the right.

Left: Savour it: one of Ollie's few photos – his couch at Olga's in Moscow.

Above: Pick a block, any block: trying to locate Max's apartment in Moscow.

Left: The ratpack: Polly and DouDou in Yekaterinburg. Taken by Ollie.

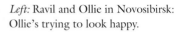

Left: Ravil and Ollie in Novosibirsk: Ollie's trying to look happy.

Below: My truckdriver friends aboard the Trans-Siberian – the wig was no lie.

Right: Grandmother knows best: Zhenya and Babushka in Ulan-Ude.

Below: The reality of romance. My first ger in Ulan Bator.

Right: Head to the ground in Vladivostok: my couch.

Below: Team Skoda takes on Vladivostok: from left, Nikolai, Stasya and Natie.

Right: Ever decreasing smiles (from left: Driver, Stasya, Fleur) – someone was happy about hitching a lift on Russky Island.

Left: What was meant by breath-taking views: Yvonne, then Donagh, scaling the Great Wall.

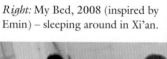

Right: My Bed, 2008 (inspired by Emin) – sleeping around in Xi'an.

Above: Pay attention, class! Trying to follow Confucian teachings in Urumqi.

Left: Raising the odds: street gambling in Turpan.

Below: Meet Lindsay. Meet random Kazakh. Lindsay, meet random Kazakh.

Right: Love in a Cold Climate: Gulnara tells her story in Almaty.

Above: Dinner in Shymkent: everything looked better in the dark (from left: Lindsay, Vicente).

Right: Looking on the bright side in Shymkent: home sweet home.

Below: The slow movement: Mary horse-riding in Korgalzhyn, near Astana

Above: A picture of resourcefulness: our home stay host, Tonya, in Korgalzhyn.

Below: Sleeping on the wild side: my tiger-print couch in Karaganda.

Above: Trying to pull Oleg off his computers in Karaganda.

Right: My two-dimensional bed in Chengdu.

Left: On the shelf: the hard-sleeper to Kunming.

Below: The Norwegian fisherman look in Kunming.

Left: Oh beer! Who drank all the supplies in Guilin?

Below: A very rare sight in China – no people. Only ghostly hills in Xingping

Above: Playing ball: a Chinese ping-pong table (and Axiang) in Xingping.

Left: Learning the hard way at Zhuo Yue English College in Yangshuo.

Below: That's all, folks! A Chinese Christmas.

Above: Rupert crying on Manfred's shoulder in Shanghai.

Almaty was apparently a beautiful city in the summer, with its tree-lined boulevards, lush parks and dry, sunny skies. Now it was barren, flat and heavy with pollution. With its bleak Soviet architecture, it looked remarkably like Russia. We decided to cheer ourselves up in a café, where it became obvious that money was going to be an issue: firstly, Almaty was very expensive, and secondly, Lindsay and I were on different budgets. I bought one coffee – Lindsay abstained – that would last me over two hours.

When he finally arrived, the 27-year-old Dmitri looked like a Russian golfer: his ferrety, vitamin-starved features encased in a *sportif* beige zip-up cardigan. Was he shy, anxious or irritated? Hard to say, but for sure he was frozen and reticent.

'Can I buy you a coffee?' I said, flicking all switches to 'charm'.

'No, no,' he said aloofly, and went and bought his own.

'We drive in my car – I have job to do.'

'No problem!'

We piled into his black Toyota estate and drove through Almaty's grimy avenues, shadowed by a crane-filled skyline. We worked on warming him up; Lindsay and I were an instant team.

He was born in Almaty, he told us, he worked with his dad, he liked Russian rock, Russian football, and he spoke enough Kazakh to be polite.

'How is it to be Russian here? We'd heard it could be hard.'

'We were some difficulties,' he said, swerving through the traffic like a real man, 'but now they left us alone. Country needs professionals – being Russian is not a reason to say 'Go out!' The government wants to encourage English, Russian and Kazakh – we need all of them to be competitive.'

We told him about our brush with the law.

'Oh! You got good deal!'

The mentality here was that it was just easier to pay.

I was starting to feel the familiar sense of excitement that came with the eventual thaw. With back-up, it happened so much more quickly – with two of us protecting this fragile relationship, you could take more risks and be more cheeky. We flirted with him. We were Dmitri's ninth hosting experience, he said – so why, I wondered, did he only have two references?

He pulled up at the post office, apologising for making so many stops (previously at the bank, the bus station, the beer shop). By now we'd been in the car for over two hours. Lindsay needed the loo: 'Couchsurfing is the greatest affirmation that you are human and not just a dollar sign,' she said, fidgeting in her seat, 'but it also removes all your human rights. Or you remove them yourself.'

✪

It seemed there was very little variation between Russian, Chinese and Kazakh Soviet apartment blocks. Now marooned on the western outskirts, in front of us was a sombre sprawl of identical towers and dead-looking trees. As we stood under each other's noses in the tiniest lift, we were all slightly awkward, but Dmitri seemed nervous.

Clutching a large, pink, stripy stuffed cat was Dmitri's glowering girlfriend, Anya. She had a thing for pink: she was wearing pink chenille tracksuit bottoms and pink piggy novelty slippers. She even had strawberry pink hair. She said she was going to bed – it was 5pm. Oh dear, was she ill, we asked with concern. No, she sniffed, tired. And a princess, it seemed.

The kitchen was the familiar tight, MFI-calibre space I'd seen before, in Russia. The cats – and the acrid smell of ammonia

– drifted in. A skittish kitten went for my shoelaces while the Siamese looked on disapprovingly. We ate insipid homemade borscht (more water than ingredient) and dry bread off a glass-topped table filled with foreign bank notes.

'Did all your couchsurfers give you these?' I asked.

'Actually, yes,' said Dmitri.

'I have the perfect thing,' I said, eagerly handing over my mint North Korean note. Regrettable? Maybe, but it felt like an appropriate gesture; besides, I wasn't attached to it yet. I also re-gifted the Park Hyatt statuette I'd been lugging around since Beijing – I wasn't sorry to see that go.

'Dmitri!' Anya called from the bedroom. He went to her. Lindsay and I whispered and played with the cats until the distinct sound of sobbing became impossible to ignore. We exchanged a look of panic. Eventually Dmitri returned.

'Is everything okay?' we asked.

'Oh yes, it's nothing,' he said, his icy eyes transfixed on a point at the end of his nose. 'It's just autumn … how do you say …? Moods?'

If true, it was quite a case. We had our doubts. It would take the utmost in resilience not to think we were in part responsible. I reappraised the kitchen – it was definitely too small for us to sleep in.

As if playing a game of tennis for one, Dmitri began a perpet-ual cycle of to-ing and fro-ing, while we were incarcerated in the kitchen. The bedroom – and our rucksacks – was Anya's for now. Conversation was inevitably limited. We did manage to elicit that Dmitri was apparently 'unusual' to have 'this kind of apart-ment' at his age. He was lucky, he said, and got it for $25,000 before the boom. He suggested a good Kazakh restaurant for

'sheeps' and horsemeat ('it's a special taste') and told us the difference between Russians and Russian-Kazakhstanis: in Kazakhstan,
they were more friendly and more open-minded, given the many
races here.

'Dmitri!'

He jumped to attention. He was so good to her, we agreed,
so tolerant.

But suddenly 'A Scene' was upon us: screaming, yelling,
sobbing and the sound of hitting – we could only hope it was a
hand slapping the bed. Continuing for a good (or very bad)
twenty minutes, Lindsay and I put our hands to our mouths. I
was in conflict: I was relieved Lindsay was here, I felt guilty for
subjecting her to this, but wondered if it was *her* presence that
had sparked the fire. Whichever, I felt silly for having to endure
it with such devout patience. Romance and passion? Take it back.

Entering stage right, out of nowhere and into the Kafkaesque
spectacle was Dmitri's goofy Russian friend Ivan, a Goa-loving,
authority-hating hippy in an Indian pillbox hat. Why invite more
guests to a domestic? To babysit for us, we suspected. We could
only presume that Dmitri had called Ivan, but – of course – we
were the last to know. While crisis talks went on in the bedroom,
Ivan diverted us, sharing with us his stoner tattoo, his motorbike
crash scabs and his brand new Indian philosophies.

Eventually, the spider of the web slinked into the kitchen,
puffy eyed in a pink-and-white polka-dot dressing gown. Dmitri
trotted in after her. She sat on Ivan's lap, giggling coquettishly
with her head cocked and finger in her mouth. At one point she
tried to say something in English, but we didn't understand, so
she ran sobbing into the bathroom. Inevitably, the kitchen soon
divorced into English and Russian factions, but our attention was

undisguisedly on their corner, where complicated plans were clearly being devised for us.

'You can meet Ivan at 8.30am tomorrow,' Dmitri announced.

'We don't need to meet so early,' I smiled sweetly. 'How about lunch?'

I was missing the point: we *had* to leave the house by 8.30am. What's more, given that the plan ran from morning to midnight, we realised that they were trying to remove us from this kitchen-sink drama entirely. We hastily got out of it.

'No, no, don't worry – we'll look after ourselves.'

It was now past midnight, and Lindsay and I cautiously followed them into the bedroom. A blanket was on the floor for us. I shot into the space furthest from their bed, and into insomniac shock. A silent tension took hold of the room, magnifying every sound. Were we about to witness the, ahem, 'kiss 'n' make-up'? As I tried to stifle my coughs and stop the kitten clawing my toes, I thought, wasn't this the truth that I'd wanted from couchsurfing? The real deal wasn't always pretty.

20TH NOVEMBER

Breakfast was stale jam cakes and black tea in the dark, with cricked necks and brittle small talk on the side. Anya would take us to the bus stop, Dmitri told us. I bristled – didn't she hate us? She polished her black patent-leather knee-highs, pulled on a wolf-fur jacket and led us out, while we attempted to flatter her into accepting us. On the bus, at last alone, Lindsay and I tried to comprehend the situation. Hormones? A threat to her throne? The Russian temperament?

We worked through the previous evening until it was almost off our chests. We bought Kazakhstan's hallowed Alport apples, which Kazakhs claimed were the grandaddy of the fruit. We strolled through Panfilov Park, past its 53 metre-high, wedding-cake style Russian Orthodox Cathedral of the Holy Ascension (one of the world's highest wooden buildings) and lucked out with a private recital in the Museum of Folk Musical Instruments. With company for sightseeing, that holiday feeling was back on.

'I'm going to kidnap you,' I said to Lindsay. I was off to Shymkent in two days' time to stay with an American Peace Corps Volunteer. The Peace Corps was a group of over-achieving American graduates on community development projects, and made up practically half of Kazakhstan's couchsurfing popula-tion. Actually, I didn't want to go to Shymkent – a rough-sound-ing town 610 kilometres away in South Kazakhstan. I'd wanted to go to Turkestan, some 150 kilometres further west, and home to Kazakhstan's most important building, the sacred Mausoleum of Sufi mystic Khodja Akhmed Yasaui. Shymkent was the nearest couch I could find. Alone, I was hypersensitive to the nuances of couchsurfing; as a pair, I realised, the bad bits were much more bearable. My captive agreed to come willingly. Besides it was her twenty-fifth birthday in a few days' time.

Dmitri called. 'Is it okay if you leave tomorrow? My sister is coming to stay.'

We were due to stay two more nights, but we couldn't very well say no.

'I can help you find a hotel,' he added.

Since Kazakhstan's Noughties oil boom, very ordinary rooms were very expensive. Maybe it was worth revisiting

Lindsay's early couchsurfing legwork. She put in a call to the South African, Marisa, and explained the situation.

'Okay,' Marisa agreed. 'But you must arrive at 7pm and you'll have to be flexible.'

Fine! The anticipation of yet another new host began.

We owed ourselves a little comfort, so we shared a meagre omelette at RVS, a Soviet-themed restaurant with red necker-chiefed Young Pioneers waiting on us. As we discussed this perverse glorification of Soviet might, which had been responsi-ble for the deaths of millions, Lindsay revealed her anxiety at being recognised as Jewish. It categorically wasn't part of her identity, she said, but an inescapable part of her look. I felt fortu-nate – Britain didn't have so many sworn enemies. How much of my couchsurfing luck was down to being British, I wondered. That nationality was simply inherited and not chosen made it all the more arbitrary.

Ivan wanted to meet up. Or did he? He was proving excep-tionally hard work when he and I hooked up in a café (Lindsay had gone online to check Cayce's progress). Slumped adoles-cently in his chair, his limp hand resting on a bored chin, he seemed to be there against his will.

'Why do you want to buy me a drink?' he said testily. He eventually melted but was I glad to see Lindsay, if now rather down because there was no progress with Cayce.

Ivan then outsourced, taking us to see his friend who spoke good English. I doubt Ivan had predicted that we would be witness to a surreal and privately hilarious courtship between her – a university administrator – and a slimy Iranian-American professor, who persistently professed his love to her, in front of us, in the fluoro-lit confines of her office. 'I scream in ecstasy the depth of my love and emotion for you,' he read to her (it was by Rumi, the 13th-century Persian poet). Love, like sex, was one of those easy common ground topics, and finally, Ivan and I bonded. He had pushed away the love of his life, he told us – they had been as one, an island, a universe, but he wanted to know other loves.

'Other loves? Other than the one? You have to respect love!' I implored. 'Love is rare! What else do you expect to find?' I paused – I could do with heeding that.

After a street dinner of crisps and two bread rolls, we were eventually returned to Dmitri's at 11.30pm. I had entirely lost the will to please our hosts. I had just one question: how far away did his sister live? 'Oh, not so far.' I didn't believe his sister was the reason we'd been asked to leave. At midnight, the bedroom light went out, but Lindsay and I stayed up in the kitchen, resisting the lair, necessarily processing the day. Plus, I wanted my North Korean banknote – since the contract had been broken, I stole it right back.

21ST NOVEMBER

'So, couchsurfing's experiment in idealism,' said Lindsay, as we sat naked, watching porridgey Russian women beat each other with oak sprigs in Almaty's green-domed Arasan Baths. 'A success or a failure?'

'Well, it depends how you define a success,' I said, generously. I couldn't admit defeat. Observing hyper-real anthropology within the species' natural habitat was priceless, surely. The opportunity to have a little control – and a few more rights – was something that I could happily pay for. Couchsurfing was exhausting, but good experiences could energise you into forgetting your fatigue. A bad time was a total comedown. Like now – I had emotionally flat-lined, and I totally resented having to maintain a public face.

But the hapless Ivan was on babysitting duty again. We met in a café – he was going to help us buy our tickets to Shymkent.

'So, Ivan, now that all this is history,' I ventured, 'please tell us: what really was the problem?'

'Dmitri didn't tell Anya you were coming.'

'What?!'

'He is owner of his place. She just lives there. He is Russian man – he is in charge.' Ivan's voice was accented with right, not apology. We'd got it all wrong. It was the sexist male Russian temperament we'd been dealing with, not the female.

There was no sign of any sister back at Dmitri's when we collected our bags that evening, and certainly no apology. The negative reference started writing itself in my head, but the situation had been so personal, I just sounded curmudgeonly. Largely, references were just thank-you letters for the gift of hospitality – if you didn't receive it, then you didn't write.

✪

'Come in!' invited Marisa, our new host, as we panted outside her fifth-floor apartment. She was beautiful and young, with sleek black hair framing her cheeks. Her open-plan apartment was clean and modern and had an expensive view of the Tian Shan mountains. The sleeping arrangements were immediately apparent: just one double sofa-bed. Someone could share it with her, she said in a crisp English accent. I had my sleeping mat – I volunteered to take the floor.

There was little with which to cold-read Marisa, just some 'foreign fashion' heels in the hallway and dragon-blood red polish on her perfect short nails. She made us Twinings lemon and ginger tea and we sat around the kitchen table.

'So why on *earth* did you come to Kazakhstan?' she asked, as if we'd made one very large mistake.

'Oh, you know, the remoteness, the mystique, the size, the Steppe, *Borat* …. So why did you come?' I asked.

'Big skies,' she smiled enigmatically. 'Do you speak Russian?'

'Well, we get by with our comic combination of spoken, sketched and performed.'

'Hmmm.' She studied me with narrowed eyes.

'So you speak Russian?'

'No, but it doesn't matter – I have a finely tuned instinct for knowing exactly what people mean. Don't you find it funny that Ollie broke his leg?'

'Err, not really, actually.'

'Oh – I think it's hilarious. Don't you?'

She changed the subject again. Twisting and turning in conversation, Marisa evidently wanted to throw us off her scent.

'Let's go to dinner – are you hungry?'

Marisa took us to Kishlak, a cheery Uzbek restaurant where the local Kazakh girls were exercising their elbows on the dance floor. Lindsay messaged the tour operator, who'd been clamouring to take us up a mountain, and asked her to join us – we could make up our minds on neutral territory.

'Aren't you tempted to give yourselves a fictional identity when couchsurfing?' Marisa asked, pouring herself a green tea.

'Umm, not really. Wouldn't it be betraying the principle of couchsurfing, by not being what you said you were?'

She didn't seem convinced.

'By the way,' I continued, 'I can't detect any South African in your accent.'

'Well,' she said, batting her lashes, 'you adapt, don't you? So venn I am tokking viz mein Deutsch freunds, I speak viz a German accent, ja? Let's dance! Come on!'

Lindsay and I followed her, rocking woodenly with grim smiles as Marisa put on a seamless, hip-swinging performance.

Thankfully, we were safely seated again when the 'tour operator', Gulnara, arrived. Table topography left me closest to her, so while Lindsay chatted to Marisa, I was left to screen Gulnara, admittedly feeling decidedly hostile. However, it soon transpired that Gulnara was no operator, but an enthusiastic Uighur girl who'd just joined couchsurfing. Exotic, bright and full of local knowledge, I soon devoted all my energies to her – *this* was what I wanted from couchsurfing. She analysed our situation at Dmitri's – it was very unusual in Kazakhstan for random girls to stay with random boys, she said. Jealousy was very common. And the Russians were cold.

Marisa went off to dance alone and Lindsay and I listened, rapt, to Gulnara while grazing on Uzbek lamb dumplings. She was twenty-six, single, and – she said – considered 'past it'. Perhaps there was a connection between these western-looking Asian girls and their deferral of marriage; maybe they were more modern than past it.

Gulnara lived with her mother and sister; it was usual to live at home until marriage. Her last job was working for an international marriage agency, connecting western men to Kazakh women.

'I had thought it was a very nice job,' she said, tucking her blonde-highlighted black hair into place. 'Here, a woman's first dream is to get married.'

But, she discovered, the women just wanted money and a ticket to America, and the men wanted young girls. She'd once introduced a 72-year-old to a sixteen-year-old Russian, and they later married.

Had she heard of Christopher Robbins' travelogue, *In Search of Kazakhstan*, I asked. We described it to her: it opened on a chance encounter with an American off to Almaty to meet his Kazakh internet bride.

'It's strange,' Gulnara said, after hearing the details. 'That this Almaty woman doesn't want to leave Kazakhstan.'

Gulnara had recently returned from her very first trip abroad, to Europe. The Italians hadn't heard of Kazakhstan, and thought she was saying she was Korean. It was also there that she realised she didn't know how to use a map. I was struck with a longing to host her; with the right attitude, differences were such positives.

'So, what's the plan, guys?' Marisa asked, looking twitchy. It was midnight. 'Clubbing?' she suggested.

Err, we were shattered. Marisa wasn't. She gave us her keys, and we arranged to go to ice-skating with Gulnara the next day. Lindsay and I strolled home, past the glittering, frozen leaves and the oil barons' Hummers and Dodge Rams, to execute the day's post-mortem.

Lindsay had extracted a little more information from Marisa: her parents had had a very messy break-up, she didn't have a home base and had pointedly worked around the world. And, she'd said, she couldn't bear the idea of being bracketed together with another person. So this girl was pathologically closed – she didn't want anyone getting close to her.

'It's as if she's wearing an Edo mask,' said Lindsay, as we slouched in Marisa's bare living room. 'We only saw the white side, but it worries me that there's a really scary dark side. I guess the nth degree of her unpredictability is that we can't rely on her. I mean what if ...'

'What if' was a paranoia too far, but I was secretly glad for Lindsay's reaction. Couchsurfing was always a guessing game. What are they thinking? Am I doing the right thing? And – ultimately – who is this person? With Lindsay's input, I was (darkly) reassured that it wasn't just me over-reading a situation.

22ND NOVEMBER

'What time is it?' Marisa asked. It was 8am. 'Oh fuck!'

She showered and rushed out. Marisa was the shark that died when it stopped moving. She returned an hour later, disguised as Perfect Host, with Kazakh breakfast pastries variously filled with apricot, poppy seeds and lamb (notably not for herself, owing to a wheat intolerance). As I rubbed my neck, sore from sleeping on the floor, Marisa offered a shiatsu neck massage, which I accepted. And we *chatted*. Was she happy here? we asked.

'No bad experiences,' she said, spooning the flesh out of a kiwi fruit. 'But it's a very international, corporate experience: everybody is professionally friendly. So far it's just been hanging out with father figures at five-star hotels and ex-pat pubs.'

I mentioned I still had no couch in Astana – Kazakhstan's capital, no less. Marisa gave me the number of her British colleague, Mary, who'd just moved there. I liked the 'professionally friendly' Perfect Host a lot.

✪

Medeu, the Olympic-sized ice-skating rink some 1,500 metres up the Tian Shan mountains, was closed for renovations in preparation of the 2011 Asian Winter Games. But with the loss of ice-skating we gained time for a proper conversation. We inhaled the clear air and discussed horse-riding: Gulnara wanted to learn, but her family tried to stop her – it wasn't for girls. But there was one traditional horse game where a girl was needed: 'girl-chasing'. If the horseman caught the girl, he could kiss her; if he failed, she could whip him. Another entailed two teams fighting for possession of a headless goat. Such were the ancient games from the land that first domesticated the horse 5,000 years ago.

Another festive restaurant saw us dining under bamboo trellises and hanging vines for lunch. It was festive, Gulnara explained, because Uighurs loved to dance: 'too much even'. At weddings, they would eat for five minutes and then dance for four hours, but 'with really serious faces – like they are doing a job.' She ordered *lagman*, a spicy, hand-pulled noodle dish and milky tea for us – in Russian. That's what she spoke at home. That was the influence of city life.

Gulnara was too shy to host, she told us, because she didn't have a western-style bathroom but a Kazakh set-up: a toilet and a banya. And while she had a guest room – since her sister, mother and she all slept in one room – she always had so many relatives visiting (or 'inviting themselves'), that she never knew when it would be free. It sounded like madness, but then maybe it was us who were mad for letting our communities disintegrate.

It was time to start our twelve-hour overnight journey to Shymkent, so we hugged goodbye. This had been my purest couchsurfing experience since Russia. She might not have hosted us but that didn't explain all the difference. Perhaps it was about being Muslim, as – like most Uighurs – Gulnara was. Hospitality was fundamental to Muslims, even more so than to the Russians. How was my first American host going to compare?

CHAPTER 12

SHYMKENT: NO ONE EVER CHOOSES TO COME HERE

'A wild and lawless place,' said the guidebook of Shymkent. 'Just a road,' Ivan had called it, 'somewhere to stop for petrol.' No doubt we were fresh blood for our socially-deprived host, Vicente, who on his profile had written that he enjoyed conversations about 'moral philosophy and macro-economics' and liked 'wearing a pirate hat while sipping quality rum.' He was cool about Lindsay coming; in a place like this, maybe bringing birthday cheer had more clout. And his 'couch'? – a real couch in the living room: 'privacy is not really an option.'

In Shymkent, neither was choice.

We shared our carriage with two Kazakh women: a TV journalist in full make-up and an economist wearing sparkling, knock-off Moschino.

'Try our national bread, *bausak*,' they said with Asian insistence.

It was like naked deep-fried pizza. I tried to tell them about couchsurfing: 'You should do a story on it!' I said to the journalist.

Lindsay admonished me: 'It sounds like you're advertising couchsurfing, Fleur.'

I cringed and buttoned up.

I made contact with Marisa's friend, Mary, who I'd be staying with after a couple of days in Shymkent (I wasn't sure about Lindsay's plans). She texted back with exemplary British politesse: 'You are most welcome. Couchsurfing sounds like a very good idea.'

There would be no safety checks, no dodgy references to dodge, and no clue as to what I'd be getting, but two facts reassured me: *she* was British. And, of course, she had to trust me more than I had to trust her. The idea of going off-piste thrilled me, and when information stopped, my imagination took over – we'd surely have an implicit cultural understanding. This one, I thought, would be easy.

23RD NOVEMBER

The steppe eventually surrendered to the insidious advance of corrugated-iron dwellings and western 'Muthafuka' graffiti. This was my stage-hand's 'two minutes' – without fail, my nerves were activated. My knowledge of macro-economics was rusty. Plus the success of this next couch was on *my* head, and I was one down.

'Passport!' The policeman immediately latched on to our wealthy foreign faces as we stepped into the station. But, after protractedly examining us and our documents, he found no cause to extract a bribe from us, and we determined to avoid eye contact with the police for the rest of our stay. Outside the station, a dozen black-clad Kazakhs seemed to think that if they gnashed at us like stray dogs for long enough, we'd eventually agree to pay them for a ride in their conked out Ladas.

'Everything is about money in Kazakhstan,' Gulnara had said. Even hitchhiking was impossible because all drivers expected payment. An old woman barked at the men to leave us alone, adding: 'You need room?'

We spotted Vicente who was wearing a black paddock jacket, black jeans and a black New York Mets baseball cap, like one of the locals. He led us to his flat, anticipating the route with a practical 'We're going left here ... right there'. 'Vissentay' was a 'Dutcho-Rican' New Yorker, he explained – Dutch mother, Puerto Rican father. Evidence of his Puerto Rican hirsuteness was trying to escape from around his cuffs.

We impatiently quizzed him on his work in Kazakhstan. He was half-way through his 27-month posting, he explained, helping to relocate the inhabitants of the Aral Sea area to South Kazakhstan, where there was more hope of work, running water, and survival. A vague sense of futility lingered in his voice.

Still, given the Peace Corps' gruelling selection process (nine months-plus, including the production of an 'aspiration statement', undertaking dental examinations and more), it seemed safe to assume we had an accountable, intelligent and morally lovely host. However, any personal details were completely eclipsed by what he had to say about Shymkent and Kazakhstan.

'Shymkent is known as the Texas of Kazakhstan.'

Oh?

'Yuh – you don't want to walk alone at night.'

Shymkent, he continued, was the heart of Kazakh nationalism (the most recent group to feel it was the Kurds, who'd fled after their houses had been burned down). It was also the first city over the border to receive Afghanistan's opium, creating a needles-in-stairwells situation, but in any case, villages grew their own. No couchsurfer ever came *for* Shymkent – they were only ever passing through.

We quickened our pace down a couple of broken, busy roads and into a joyless, low-rise estate. Through a solid steel door ('all Volunteers must have a steel door'), we arrived at the unofficial base-camp of South Kazakhstan's Peace Corps Division. All the local Volunteers had keys and an open invitation to hang out and read from Vicente's alphabetically-ordered library (mostly bequeathed by former Volunteers). Pack-animal behaviour seemed sensible in Shymkent.

It wasn't exactly spacious. The fridge was in the living room on account of the size of the kitchen. We handed over the mandatory chocolates and, in return, were supplied with the kind of information you'd never find in a guidebook. Vicente had seen a lot of shit here, and, it seemed, he needed to get rid of it.

Like bride-napping. We gasped: bride-napping?

'I'd just arrived here, it was about 1am, and outside my window I could see a woman screaming bloody murder inside a smart, parked car. The engine was on and a nervous-looking guy was standing outside it, shouting at the driver. After ten minutes the guy outside got in, told the girl to shut up and they drove off.' Vicente dragged his fingers through his collar-length hair. 'It's so they don't pay the dowry,' he continued. 'It works because once the bride is taken, her reputation is ruined. She couldn't marry again.'

He'd heard of a couple of western girls being bride-napped in Kyrgyzstan.

'It happens more in villages, but actually, when you see it, you hope they *are* marrying her – it's an atrocity, but it's the best it could be.'

Prostitution was rife. Two of his Volunteer friends were presumed gay because they didn't visit prostitutes in their South Kazakhstan village. Condoms were expensive and only available in certain supermarkets, and AIDS awareness was shocking – he'd been asked by students if HIV could be caught off toilet seats and glasses.

Corruption was – surprise, surprise – a major problem: 'Teachers, doctors and police – they're the most crooked,' Vicente said solemnly.

Well, we knew about the police (Vicente had even been mugged and offered prostitutes by them), but doctors and teachers?

'The doctors get paid very little. Anyone with any intelligence goes into business not medicine – they can make more money selling apples. The doctors diagnose problems that you don't have, and then make you pay for medicine. One Volunteer went to three clinics, and her tests came back with two positives and one negative. She went back and got two negatives and one positive. It's terrifying.'

And teachers? Educational qualifications were seen as commodities – students' grades depended on how much their parents paid, and Volunteer teachers weren't allowed to do final grades because it was 'too political'. Vicente ran an English-speaking club at one of the universities and his students had asked him about bribery in the US.

'I had to explain that, if that happened, students would be expelled and tutors would be struck off. They just said, "There'd be no more teachers and no more students if that were the case in Kazakhstan."'

The culture-shock was huge and I was speechless. I had a little sit-down on the threadbare, burgundy-wool sofa – mine and Lindsay's bed for the night.

Vicente read my mind: 'You can't know Kazakhstan from visiting Almaty – it's much more cosmopolitan and developed. This is the reality. There's a phrase here: "Roads get paved when Nazarbaev [Kazakhstan's president] comes."' No Volunteer ever chooses to come to Kazakhstan,' he said, enjoying the drama a little.

Vicente had arranged lunch with two Volunteers, both English teachers in a nearby village. We pushed open the door of the building to find ourselves in – *in* – a funeral, right on Vicente's doorstep, shoulder to shoulder with twenty or so mourners paying their respects to a lifeless, yellowish-grey old man. It was Vicente's neighbour, lying in burial robes in an open coffin. A Russian Orthodox priest sang litanies while the crowd crossed their chests. We backed out like guilty children and hurried up to the road.

The Americans were excited about their burgers and chips. Village life was much tougher than life in Shymkent, apparently. Clarissa, a timid 22-year-old from New England, had just been sworn in: she seemed understandably shaken.

'The boys suck,' she said, neatening her Alice band. 'It's impossible to teach them. If they're not being rude, they're breaking out into fights. Before I started, some Volunteers said I'd need Prozac, others said I'd have an amazing experience. I just don't know what to make of it so far.'

Kazakhstan aside, the Peace Corps programme was itself pretty demanding. The first three months was spent learning either Russian or Kazakh (Russian was more useful, Kazakh more impressive) and living with a host family. Then they'd be placed with a local NGO for twenty-four months, and spend the first six months living with another host family.

Eric, a young Berkeley graduate with spectacles and tidy, flattened hair, had extended his six months' stay with his Uzbek hosts: the grandmother, father, mother, aunt and five daughters, aged between two and twenty. He did at least have his own room, a requirement for all Volunteers.

'It's usual to keep having daughters until a son arrives,' he said, seeing our little 'o'-shaped mouths. Eric was considered their American son.

Uzbeks were plentiful in Kazakhstan, given its comparative wealth and freedom, he explained, but were much more conservative and religious. 'So in Uzbek schools, they have two different-coloured teapots – one full of vodka.' Well, conservative and religious, so long as alcohol could still be worshipped. Kazakhs were much more open about drinking.

Vicente nodded vigorously: 'They drink because it's February, they drink to the president, they use any excuse.'

Life expectancy for Kazakh men was sixty-two – the same as retirement age. Birthplace was such a lottery, I thought. What had I done to deserve London?

Sexism was rife – Eric was forbidden to help around the house.

'There's nothing that's inappropriate for a man to say to a woman here,' he said resignedly.

But even with the men, only an authoritarian approach seemed to work.

'The first time I got my organisation to listen,' said Vicente, 'was when I stood up, said, "You're wasting my time," and walked out. That's left over from Soviet times.'

With my lack of appropriate stories to reciprocate, and their need to discuss, I felt increasingly useless in my silence. We returned to base-camp, the funeral at least, having passed, and slammed the steel door behind us. Vicente's place – classic student digs, with its ethnic drapes, curry smells and cigarette burns on the old mud-coloured rug – now resembled relative luxury, after all we'd heard.

Vicente picked up his phone and stared at it. Was he waiting for a call?

'Maybe a date tonight,' he half-smiled. 'With a Kazakh girl.'

He was wary though – the possibility that they were after a Green Card, plus the threat of being beaten up by the girl's male family members (as friends had been) put him off. Plus Kazakh girls tended to be socially immature and uninformed. But this girl was 'completely abnormal' – she had a career and a car and went on business trips. They'd met at aerobics.

Lindsay and I laughed, but social snobbery was futile out here.

'My personal life is in shambles,' he sighed.

But they did have something to look forward to: Vicente's Thanksgiving dinner on Saturday (though I'd be long gone). The Volunteers discussed what dish to bring and then it was time for Eric and Clarissa to return to their village before nightfall. We wished Clarissa good luck.

'Thanks,' she said. 'Only twenty-three months and two weeks to go.'

✪

'So – I hear it's your birthday,' said Vicente.

'Yup, Lindsay replied sardonically. 'I'm now officially over the hill for Kazakhstan.'

Vicente suggested an outing to the year-old 'Mega Center' shopping mall to buy celebratory drinks. The pride of Shymkent, this was where the kids posed for their Facebook photos (but here, the Russian version, *In Kontakt*) – a mall was as good as it got in a town that was 'just a road'. We splashed out on cheap champanski – Kazakhstan's answer to bubbly.

The Kazakh girl never did call. This was to our advantage, of course. Vicente didn't seem surprised. Their usual line was, 'I don't think you'll marry me and take me to the USA so I can't date you', he said.

Instead, we went to Karavan, a themed restaurant with concrete camels, cream *caravanserai* tents and sand-coloured walls – it was deserted. It being Lindsay's birthday, we could avoid Kazakhstan's most festive dish, *beshbarmak*, no more. Meaning 'five fingers', as cutlery could be overlooked on this special occasion, it comprised slabs of handmade pasta and lumps of mutton or horsemeat. It was standard fare at weddings, as was boiled sheep's head (Vicente had tried the cheek and nibbled on an ear) and fights.

'They *all* end in fights,' Vicente announced matter-of-factly. 'But I try not to go because you have to give money to the parents, who seem to pocket it.'

'Tell us something positive about Kazakhstan!' we begged. Was everything violent, immoral, retrograde? But Vicente wasn't a bitter ex-pat; he was a pragmatic observer – there just seemed to be a lot to complain about.

All Turkic culture was outwardly rough but, he conceded, 'personal interaction with Kazakhs is very positive – though you need to be here for a while for that.'

The fancy themed restaurant had its advantages – our *beshbarmak* arrived with cutlery and thin, sanitised strips of meat. Usually, Vicente explained, it came in great hunks that the alpha male would rip into more manageable pieces. It was horse all right – I tried to rationalise it, but I couldn't continue past a little taste (tender, sweet and beefy), though leaving it felt wrong, too. I was confused – here, horse was fine to eat, pig wasn't.

A grubby gypsy boy lingered at our table peddling red roses. Vicente bought one for Lindsay – with intent? Possibly, not least since Lindsay was very cute, very smart and, as fellow Americans, they had an 'understanding'. But Lindsay, I was starting to realise, was too pessimistic to fall for romance.

We ordered Shymkent beer (apparently Kazakhstan's best) and vodka by the gram and tried to make merry but somehow I wasn't feeling it. Was it the cheerless Kazakh Phil Collins crooning dismally in a shiny silver suit, was it the depressive effect of 'Kazakhstan's Texas', or was it because conversation had fallen into a deep rut of American sports? I took time out. Perhaps Vicente was used to couchsurfers running out of steam; after all, no one ever came fresh to Shymkent.

We survived the walk home, guided up Vicente's inky black stairwell by the short, dim glow of his mobile phone. 'We used to put new light bulbs in,' he said, 'but someone would always take them.'

I admired Vicente's resilience – he had another twelve months of compromises and concessions to make.

A new object of fascination presented itself back at basecamp, in the shape of Vicente's 21-year-old room-mate, Kanat. His spirited Mongol eyes, strong, noble nose and diamond-facet chiselling were held together with the poise of Gandhi. As brave, smart and honourable as Vicente was, he couldn't bring the buzz that a local could.

Kanat was Vicente's pet project. He was studying agricultural engineering on an academic scholarship (a subject which he hated, but without bribe-paying parents, this was his only way in). Vicente was in the process of raising funds for Kanat to study abroad in summer 2009.

'If I achieved just that, my time here would be a success,' he said, looking at Kanat paternally.

The smell of raw garlic was very, very close. It was Kanat's hot lemon, garlic and honey drink. 'My mother says it's good for colds,' he said, his long, lean feet falling out of too-short slippers.

Lindsay and I, meanwhile, were sipping champanski through pursed lips – sweet, flat and weak, it was rather like our celebration. Wisely nursing a cognac, Vicente told us how a couple of Volunteers had ended up with nerve damage in their ears from bad alcohol. Our champanski party was aborted. But the Kazakh material never dried up. The formula of the evening went like so: we'd ask Kanat about life, he would answer, and Vicente – his muse, teacher and father figure – would offer clarifications and additional notes. It was touching.

Us: 'Do you feel free?'

Kanat: 'Sometimes I'm afraid to share my ideas. They will kick you out from university for disagreeing. It's still – how do you say – totalitarian. Even our journalists only write pro-government news.'

Vicente: 'The one thing the government won't stop you doing is studying abroad.'

There was a government-run international studies programme (called *bolashak,* meaning 'future') for the country's best students, but they had to put their house up for collateral. If they didn't have a house, they'd have to buy one. And if they didn't return, they'd lose it. Vicente was keen for Kanat to travel independently of this programme.

Kanat even started to sound like Gandhi: 'I love my country,' he said, clenching his fists passionately. 'It's my mother. I would like to change the Kazakh view of life. We will die for our future generations' freedom.'

His inspiration, he said, was Vicente – and couchsurfing. Meeting so many foreigners changed his view about accepting facts.

It's possible the earnestness was all too much for Lindsay, who'd fallen asleep on a dining chair, so we all retired. Lindsay and I top-to-toed on the narrow couch – it felt strangely comforting to sleep close to my ally. We had an early start the next day, to make our pilgrimage to Turkestan – to Kazakhs, three visits here were considered as holy as one to Mecca.

24TH NOVEMBER

The freezing trickle of the shower was like Chinese water-torture.

'Ah, I failed to tell you – there's a trick to getting hot water,' said Vicente, brewing fresh coffee in the kitchen. The trick being – of course – to turn on the kitchen tap first. Tooth-brushing was more like target practice – with no basin in the dimly-lit bathroom, it was a long, dark aim for the bath's plughole.

Vicente did, however, give us precise directions to Turkestan. A UNESCO World Heritage site, the immense, turquoise-domed, sandy-brick building was built (and left unfinished) in the 14th century. Under the watchful eye of the Almighty, Kazakh hospitality came to us, as the free ('*free?*' we asked in disbelief) guide invited us to her staff restaurant for *plov*. Lindsay and I re-aligned, mucking about in the market, catching up on our impressions. Things were looking up. Then Vicente texted: 'Bad day, going to the gym tonight. You can use the kitchen to cook, or I'll make dinner when I get home.'

We were in the dark about details, but we did know that it should be us – good day, indebted – doing the right thing. We returned to Shymkent, bought a random assortment of ingredients, and set about cooking up potluck – from rice, peppers, cauliflower, onions, garlic and a good pinch of couchsurfer love. In a kitchen too small for a fridge, Lindsay and I washed and chopped. There wasn't an inch of surface space yet the cupboards were empty (save a mortar and pestle). A halo of missed shots circled the bin – this kitchen belonged to a man. And to the cockroaches.

'Crap.'

We were suddenly in total darkness. We'd overloaded the electrical system by – wait for it – putting on the kettle. This was life in Kazakhstan. Doing the right thing had suddenly gone very wrong, and Vicente's day was about to get a lot worse.

Vicente was in a baaaad mood. He'd been asked to leave his project a whole year early due to differences with his director, the Shymkent manager of the Aral Sea rehabilitation project. Plus, it was *very* complicated to fix the power cut. There was a Russian alcoholic in the block who understood the system (last time he'd been bribed with a bottle of vodka, though he'd been too drunk to do the work). But Vicente's Russian was 'horrible'. I felt rather in the way.

Still, blackened cauliflower and rice so heat-damaged it had fused into one single lump looked a lot better in the dark. We ate around the living room table; illuminated by one short-range candle, our disembodied voices jumped about in the darkness. I was happy to be invisible.

'Kazakhstan is one of the most difficult places to work,' Vicente said morosely. He had a full head of steam to let off. 'What can you do if people refuse to modernise, when they think their way is the best? I'm not a lazy person but there's only so much you can do here.'

'Pour yourself a cognac,' Lindsay ordered, dryly. We managed to prop up the evening discussing his options, but in couchsurfing's tight grip, moods were contagious. I was a reactive, and here, I struggled to find the tools to lighten his mood. I fell silent, leaning on Lindsay to pick up the slack. She'd decided to stay in Shymkent for Thanksgiving so I was feeling mildly surplus. Plus, not being intimate with Boston, or baseball, or Berkeley politics excluded me from the American club – I was surprised by our cultural distance.

I'd already started looking forward to the social vacuum of the 27-hour train journey 1,000 kilometres north to Astana the next day. I craved solitude, despite having been so happy to find Lindsay. I had been on the road for six weeks, and I was missing what I knew – home. I grounded myself by thinking about The Emperor. It was rather like talking to God, being nourished by this abstract, one-sided love.

25TH NOVEMBER

Vicente got the money shot that morning. It was at my expense, but it served as a useful recovery tool. After a candlelit shower (not romantic, just hopelessly dark), I decided to dress in the living room. Using my towel as a curtain, my concealed back faced into the flat, while my exposed front just faced a balcony with nothing beyond. Except Vicente, of course, having a cigarette. Like a gentleman, he said he saw nothing, but we laughed at least. Humiliation – like dancing in Almaty and karaoke in Xi'an – did at least dissolve barriers, however small. Vicente had a round of interviews to attend, so Lindsay and I arranged to meet him in the afternoon for his weekly English-speaking club.

✪

Underneath enough American flags to launch an election campaign, Vicente, flanked by two Volunteers, was holding court in 'The American Corner'. Here we were to practise English – so why, I wondered, was it promoting America? But so what? There were thirteen Kazakh students (including Kanat) and three Russians all ready and willing to share with us. I was psyched.

'So does everyone remember what we're here to talk about today?'

'Technology!'

'That's right!'

They were blogging, social networking and researching, they said, though their parents had no idea how to use the internet.

Was there censorship?

'Yes,' said a Russian girl who wanted to become an interpreter. 'Any emails with the words 'drugs', 'kidnapping' and 'Nazarbaev' are intercepted.'

And then what happens?

'Nothing.' But, they said, journalists had been imprisoned for speaking out, and there was 'of course' the death penalty, though no one, apparently, was on Death Row.

Unlike in the States, of course.

And then I mentioned the B-word. A student had asked, 'Is Kazakhstan becoming a popular destination?' Well, who could deny *Borat's* impact? The students were clearly still smarting. One of the Volunteers delivered the stock western apology: the real joke was on Small Town America.

They disagreed: 'At the MTV Awards, Borat kissed the feet of an actor playing our president, as if he is our king, as if Kazakhstan is a dictatorship.'

Hmmm. Nazarbaev had changed the constitution so he could be in power forever, while previous presidents could only have two terms. And at the last election, in 2005, the independent election monitor OSCE reported opposition harassment, pressure on voters, and media bias and confiscation of opposition publications (despite their exit polls showing a eighty-three per cent majority for Nazarbaev). The president had even banned *Borat*. Borat himself, meanwhile – sexist, prostitute-loving and wife-abducting – was unquestionably alive and well in Shymkent. This time, however, it wasn't so funny.

After ninety minutes it was time to leave American hegemony and youthful optimism to return to base-camp for the final time before going it alone.

Lindsay was feeling volcanic: 'I was *so* uncomfortable walking into that room full of tacky decorations. It's like, "We're American, and we'll solve all your problems". Isn't this about colonisation, not charity?'

I could have cheered.

Vicente explained, evenly, that the American Corner was a US government-backed project (there were a dozen in Kazakhstan); the nationalistic festoonery was their idea. But he'd gone with it – after all, he was here for the government too. It was widely accepted that the Peace Corps was politically motivated. Even the Aral Sea project funding – $15 million from the States – was negotiated as part of a $150 million aid package in return for Kazakhstan's surrender of nuclear weapons.

'And we'll throw in some college kids,' said Lindsay, cynically.

It was time to leave – literally, and psychologically. My good-bye with Vicente was perfunctory. Something had stood between us, and I think it was Kazakhstan. I now knew a few of its grim realities, but I didn't know much about him, and he even less about me. In Lindsay, I was leaving a real friend and a confidante. And there wasn't much chance of us crossing paths again.

But now I had Mary to look forward to. Such was couchsurfing – replacements were always waiting in the wings. One hoped.

CHAPTER 13

ASTANA: OFF-PISTE COUCHSURFING

Meaning 'capital', Astana took over as the first city in 1997. Opinions differed as to why, when many still believed that Kazakhstan's cultural, financial and symbolic heart remained in the much more populous Almaty. Perhaps it was to develop another city, some said. Or to escape imminent earthquake danger. Or demonstrate Kazakhstan's new-found, oil-money confidence. Or, perhaps, as some believed, it was to start over with a clean political slate, where opinions weren't so disillusioned. Two days didn't seem enough time to draw any conclusions.

26TH NOVEMBER

Like climbing a mountain, the route to the world's second-coldest capital became steadily snowier. My cabin companions, two Russian women, were keeping in winter shape by eating enough food to run a restaurant (including a whole chicken, eaten with their hands). They invited me to join them – being a lone female came with special privileges – but I said I needed to sleep. I was rebelling against being social property while I could.

The large ladies got off at Karaganda, patting my arm with fond concern. I should have got up to look at it because, after Astana, it was to be my final stop in Kazakhstan – but I was indulging an urge to do absolutely nothing at all. Just for a bit.

Meanwhile, Mary and I were caught in a charmingly British anti-power struggle by text:

'Hope your journey's going okay. Just going to the supermarket, is there anything you particularly fancy? Will do my best to locate if so!'

'How kind – but please don't go any trouble! I eat everything, apart from those salty, sour cheese balls.'

'Would you like to go out tonight – maybe you'll feel like stretching your legs after so long on the train.'

'A stretch on a sofa would be lovely too. My needs are minimal – just a conversation in real English.'

Our merry dance pulled me right out of my stupor, and I was comforted already by this grandmotherly behaviour. But what if we were trapped forever in eternal deference? Someone was going to have to dominate eventually.

My train pulled into Astana at 10pm, and I made my way through the empty city, twinkling with Vegas-style lights, to Mary's gleaming, green-glowing block. I was looking a mess, but I didn't mind – it felt like I was coming home.

As two British girls, we didn't need to kiss or shake hands, but Mary's ready laugh instantly warmed the atmosphere. She seemed younger than me, and was dressed as if in Sunday mufti: a brown scoop-neck sweater and clean blue jeans. Her sensible chestnut hair brushed her shoulders and framed a naturally pretty, permanently smiling face. As she swiped a smartcard in the lift (yes, even the lift cost money), I realised her laugh was nervous. Of course – this was completely alien to her.

'I must apologise again, for the bedding on the radiator,' she said gently, in Received English but for a soft Derbyshire burr. We were standing in 'my room' – her living room – a large, soulless rectangle dominated by a velour, zebra-print three-piece suite. It was easy enough to list the room's contents – a large TV (which Mary 'hardly ever watched'), and a glass coffee-table on which rested a small cuddly camel – as this was the sum total. Mary had moved in just two weeks ago. I grabbed the 'French' Merci chocolates I had bought for her, and we settled in her modern, featureless and spacious kitchen to drink flower tea made from carefully boiled mineral water.

It struck me that there was a particular couchsurfing characteristic that I'd thus far taken for granted: confidence. Mary, unused to the situation, shifted in her seat, wrung her hands, fiddled with an imaginary ring and clasped her chest – I'd thrown her right out of her comfort zone, just when I thought I'd be returning to mine. At thirty-two, she was older than I'd guessed: submissiveness was a genius anti-ager. I found myself talking about me and my adventures a lot, in an attempt to relax her and encourage trust. Only now did I realise how normal couchsurfing had become to me. Yet all the while here was the most attentive, interested host I'd had – the roles had reversed into a dom/sub relationship.

We ate late, at 11pm. Methodical and precise, Mary prepared some 'vodka' carbonara for us: rigatoni with cream, onions, garlic and sausage with a nominal splash of Russian vodka.

'I used to be a vegetarian,' she said, sucking her teeth at her own disappointment, 'but I just felt so culturally arrogant.' She added, quickly: 'That's not to say I would think someone arrogant for sticking to their principles – I just didn't want to make a fuss.'

Taking manners too far was reassuringly British, but, I wondered, how on earth did she cope in 'extreme' Kazakhstan?

Mary explained that she taught business-English to employees of Air Astana, and I tried to imagine her taking a class. Her last job was in a cement factory in Volga, she said, giggling with embarrassment, as she was prone. It was 'a long and boring story', but she'd originally followed her Russian-studying ex-boyfriend to St Petersburg. They'd split up, he left and she stayed.

'Maybe there was something a little masochistic about learning a difficult language and enduring the Russian climate,' she said, revealingly.

Had she made any discoveries in Astana? Seen inside anyone's house? Did she notice any racism? Had she been to any clubs?

No, she apologised, she hadn't been very adventurous. An acquaintance had taken her out sightseeing once, but she felt shy about getting in touch again, 'like I'd be inconveniencing him'. In the meantime, she'd been teaching herself chess on Wikipedia. But wasn't she lonely? Homesick? She didn't really have a home anymore, she explained. She'd been with her ex-boyfriend for nine years, so she was enjoying the space: 'It's absolutely brilliant,' she said, in that way of not wanting to trouble anyone with negativity. And, she said, she felt safe in Astana.

Soon it was 1.30am and Mary had to be up at 7.30 for work (she never mentioned until I asked, of course). There was porridge and bread and Marmite for breakfast, and she would be back at 11.30am.

Maybe she'd be up for some sightseeing afterwards? I asked – she would. And I would do the washing-up, I insisted. No 'nos' about it. But it was a quick job: the kitchen was immaculate. The bathroom too – even the toilet seat was kept politely closed.

27TH NOVEMBER

Breakfast had been laid out for me, B&B-style. I skipped out into the city – it was frozen both physically (the temperature was -5°C) and metaphorically. I understood now why Mary's flat was soulless; Astana felt the same. Clean, synthetic and empty, it was like a city waiting for its people to come. Built to house 1.5 million people, there were currently 600,000 inhabitants. But a wave of mild euphoria stroked me – there was none of the weight of Shymkent here. Astana's only undercurrent so far was a benign aversion to offend. I wanted to spend longer than two days here. I wanted to tip the emotional balance away from Shymkent. I wanted to explore the countryside. I'd have to ask Mary, but I knew the answer. Mary's armour was a nut of niceness.

Mary was, predictably, preternaturally patient when I was one-and-a-half hours late from my exploration. My excuse: my 'cabbie', an out-of-work construction worker, was extorted for money by a policeman, right in front of me.

'Possibly the only crime in Astana is committed by the police,' Mary explained. 'No one else would dare because most people here are government officials; there aren't many ex-pats like in Almaty.'

She'd been advised not to carry more cash than she could afford in bribes, and had looked into getting her driving licence out here: it cost $50.

Like a theme park where the theme was 'This Is A Capital', Astana was full of derivatives: sub-Dubai golden skyscrapers; a sub-Louvre glass pyramid (by Lord Foster); offices modelled on Moscow's Seven Sisters; and, right at Astana's symbolic heart, a White House-esque presidential palace. Apart from construction workers, we were the only people around – a 'children's football coach', who was parked outside the government buildings in a Toyota Land Cruiser, asked if we were journalists. We felt watched.

Mary didn't mind at all going up the Baiterek Tower again. Like a giant World Cup trophy, it rose some ninety-seven metres off the ground in honour of Astana's birth date, 1997. Up here, it became apparent that the very small Astana was closely surrounded by empty steppe. So why all the skyscrapers? The Towers of Babel sprang to mind. Our gaze was lured out on to the open horizon – maybe, I said, we could indulge a call of the wild?

Yes!

Had she been to the countryside?

No!

It was no doubt a cart-pushing-the-horse situation, but Mary said she was up for me hanging out for a bit longer. Maybe after a few days, I would even make her cross. But really my ambition was to get her to relax.

For now, I was still stuck in Mary's treacly outer layers, baffled as to her real motive for being in Kazakhstan. Like trying to tame a wild deer, I gently prised it out of her over a long afternoon wandering through Astana's sights, buying each other's tickets and drinks tit-for-tat. As the sun was setting, she revealed, finally, that 'maybe' this was a chance to prove herself as she never had in the UK. Always held back by her lack of confidence, she'd spent her twenties in underachieving jobs that 'you'd never plan to do', like processing grant admission forms at Heriot Watt University. Really, she hoped to do an anthropological PhD on Kazakhstan, but was ashamed of her lack of focus. It turned out that someone so down on their abilities was actually an Oxford graduate (which, naturally, she tried to conceal). It was impossible not to be endeared.

✪

I'd organised a dinner for us that night with a young Russian couchsurfing couple, Sergey and Yelena. They could no longer host because they'd had to move in with Sergey's parents after Sergey, an MBA graduate, lost his job in the credit crisis. It was hard to ignore the difficulty of four strangers slipping into perfectly natural conversation when we sat down to supper in their bedroom. Having a third party – Mary, the non-couch-surfer – made me all the more aware of those shy beginnings. Even with four of us working at it, it was still difficult. I felt protective over Mary and vaguely bad for having involved her.

But, as was so often the way, it was worth persevering. Yelena served an indoor picnic of dried calamari, halva, 'potato' cakes (so-called for their look, not ingredients), aubergine 'caviar' (which neither resembled, nor contained, caviar), bittersweet apricot kernels and sunflower seeds, which she proceeded to shell expertly in her teeth, creating a small mountain of husks. Perched on a tiny wooden stool next to her, Sergey did the talking.

'There is no future for "Europeans" in Kazakhstan,' he said, clutching his brow. 'During the USSR, there was no nationalism, but they changed our history – now they teach us that Russians were invaders. Many Russians have come back to Russia. It's not good now.' Sure, they had Kazakh friends, he explained, but the problem was the government. They feared a more pro-Kazakh state. Sergey and Yelena wanted to emigrate to Canada, where there was no nationality. They planned to leave, with their parents, in two or three years. I felt bad for my own good fortune which somehow I managed to make so complicated.

The wedding photos were duly presented on one of their matching laptops, Yelena sporting the obligatory bouffant bridal gown with a pearlescent sheen, Sergey in a cream suit and, tellingly, a bold stars-and-stripes tie. They pointed out their French couchsurfer in the crowds – they'd only met him that week, and he'd stayed for the duration with Sergey's 'angry' parents. That must have been one double-edged sword.

Would I go couchsurfing for my honeymoon? Sergey and Yelena did, only to be detained by Uzbek customs for seven hours. Couchsurfing was technically illegal in Uzbekistan, but Sergey and Yelena hadn't even made it in yet. They'd been presumed Christian missionaries for carrying bibles and religious newspapers.

'There are no human rights in Kazakhstan,' explained Sergey, ' but there are more than in Uzbekistan.'

My eyebrows were left somewhat raised by all these revelations – I loved couchsurfing for introducing me to ideas so far from my own experiences.

It was impossible to leave without seeing – or signing – Sergey's couchsurfing wall of fame on their bedroom door, a poster of signatures by all his beloved guests (in his prime, he told us, he'd had six people in his room). One poignant comment read: 'Sergey without guests is like a bird without wings'.

We left, Mary now with two friends in Astana. I felt rather proud of couchsurfing.

28TH NOVEMBER

Might Mary be interested in accompanying me to the Museum in Memory of the Victims of Repression, some thiry-four kilometres out of town and on the site of Stalin's notorious Gulag, ALZHIR (the Akmola Camp for the Wives of Betrayers of the Homeland)?

We set out to the Gulag site, now called Malinovka (meaning Little Raspberries, after the fruit planted by the prisoners). Despite one man's heartening efforts to ask every other person at the bus stop if they wanted to share transport with us (we were the first foreigners he'd ever met), we ended up having to take a taxi because there was no bus. As signs of life gradually trailed away, it became apparent why we were alone. We passed a graveyard, where we noticed a circle of fifty *chapka*-topped men, bowed in respect.

'No women?' we asked our driver.

'No – crying is not allowed at Kazakh funerals, so women can't come. The women stay at home and cry.'

No woman, no cry, then. Russians were also forbidden.

Most of the 20,000 women – among them eminent intellectuals, musicians and ballerinas – were imprisoned at ALZHIR simply because their husbands or relatives were the 'Enemy of the People'. Some 7,620 perished during their five-year sentences of hard labour.

'Astana is the city of the future,' said a survivor filmed for the accompanying documentary. 'Its people are so lucky not to know about the repression of the past.'

It was true – Astana was a rare capital for looking forward.

A cautious silence was observed on the way back until Mary's supervisor called (on Mary's day off), asking for something. Ever conscientious, Mary proceeded directly to her laptop at home, and we agreed to meet later. In a modern, expensive and deserted shopping centre, I managed to get online to confirm my last two nights in Kazakhstan. In Karaganda, a small city 185 kilometres south-east of Astana, I'd be staying with Oleg, an intriguing 21-year-old Russian male with long flaxen hair who seemed to be channeling *Hellboy II*, and who described himself as 'pretty geeky about IT security stuff and pagan metal'. I was keenly anticipating some novel experiences. Karaganda had an amusing reputation for being the middle of nowhere – I wanted to know: what happened in the middle of nowhere? Given that Kazakhstan's tourist treasures were pretty thin on the ground, a stop in Karaganda seemed a fitting finale.

✪

Another invitation for dinner: this time from a Turkish guy whose couch I'd also requested, but who'd had too much work on to host. The evening wasn't a success because a) he didn't seem that friendly, b) we didn't really see eye to eye and c) he never referred to his glamorous – and objectified – girlfriend, present as nothing other than his cute little baby. I couldn't wait for it to be over; Mary too, it seemed.

They drove us home in his BMW 5 Series through fantasy-thick snow, with great frozen golf balls thudding onto his windscreen. Such was the night, this was easily the highlight. And Mary was the night's saviour – together, we could write it off as one of those nights. Without her, it was all my fault.

29TH NOVEMBER

Sergey and Yelena had given us the name of a home stay in Korgalzhyn, a village 130 kilometres south-west of Astana, near the Korgalzhyn State Nature Reserve, a UNESCO World

Heritage Site. I did wonder whether really Mary would prefer to go to a Verdi opera she'd expressed interest in, but she 'could go to that any time'. Manners had a funny way of cloaking the truth. I was hoping that over the weekend they'd melt away.

The bus dropped us off at a sleepy, ice-speckled crossroad; beyond that was a perfectly one-dimensional horizon. A few white and blue-painted cottages were scattered in the near distance, so we approached the only building that wasn't – the Reserve's small museum. In a deserted corridor we bumped into an old Russian, who, without any verbal exchange, took us directly to our home stay. Without knocking, he pushed open one of the unlocked cottage doors and called up to someone.

Tonya, a sanguine, blue-eyed Russian in her fifties, greeted us vigorously in Russian, as if we'd met before. A CB radio was crunching words in the background, a young girl in giant slippers was sweeping the cork floor, and, in the kitchen, a budgerigar was babbling away. Tonya sat us down at her old but spotless kitchen table for tea and thick wedges of airy white bread. The homemade jam was made from the apples on the tree outside, she said, pointing out of the window. But instead my eyes fell upon the decaying carcass of an oven. I went to wash my hands at the kitchen sink, but the tap was dry.

The act of returning to the capitalist system (and paying for accommodation) exposed what a narrow furrow couchsurfing ploughed – one of Westernised youth, with money, computers, English and ambition. This was quite easily the most charming and homely place I'd seen all trip – a real home, with children's artwork and painted pistachio shells decorating the staircase. At the heart of it was a veteran homemaker who used a CB radio for a mobile, had conversations instead of computers, and who, in place of money, applied her imagination.

Since the world's most northerly colony of pink flamingos (and the Reserve's main attraction) had better sense than to stick around for winter, we asked instead about the possibility of horse-riding. Or rather, Mary did – there was a lot of: 'Mary, would you mind asking …'.

Tonya popped out, returning five minutes later with Valerio, her jovial, ruddy-faced husband. Nothing was really explained, but we were ushered into the back of Valerio's old, smoke-coloured Soviet 'Buhanka' van (meaning 'loaf' in Russian, given that these vans looked like motorised loaves of bread). It was also the source of the CB radio – Valerio was a warden on the Reserve. We set off on the road to nowhere across the frost-covered, rust-coloured tundra. Happiness tingled in my stomach – we were off on an unknown adventure with somebody else's granddad.

'Anyone seen a horse round these parts?' This seemed to be the question asked as we stopped at the few signs of civilisation during our drive through – finally – nomadsland. We pulled up at a ramshackle bungalow.

'Do you think that's a wolf?' Mary asked, pointing to the leftovers of a kill in the shallow snow: one leg, a tail and some coat – there wasn't much to go on.

We drove several miles further to a small farm, whereupon Valerio got out and spoke to a woman in a shawl. We'd have to wait, but Valerio implied promise. I romanticised about a nomad's return.

Who'd have thought that epiphany lurked in nothingness? We waited for over an hour, without any word – no texts, no quick calls – or knowledge that our patience would bear fruit. With a peach-pink sun low in the sky, and winter's sting starting to penetrate, we suggested driving on.

'What do you mean?' replied Valerio. 'Where would we go? There is nowhere to go.'

There was nothing for it but to empty our minds and tune into the steppe's slow rhythm. Having nothing was liberating – it was meditatively calm. As Kissinger said: 'The absence of alternatives clears the mind marvellously.'

A stampede of horses passed in a cloud of dust – a gift that only came to those who stood still. And then, back to nothing again.

Suddenly, Valerio grabbed the binoculars: 'He is coming!'

Twenty minutes later, a young, powerful Kazakh came into focus on a horse sweating in submission. I couldn't break my gaze from this Turkic Disney prince – raven hair, wide almond eyes, caramel skin offsetting perfect ivory teeth. We were invited into the two-room farmhouse to sit on the kitchen floor and eat with the family (his twenty-year-old wife, their baby and her parents). Were we German? they asked – Stalin had deported much of the population of Russian-dwelling Volga Germans to Kazakhstan during World War II.

Neither of us were remotely hungry, but we were benevolently forced into eating three plates of fried, sliced potatoes and great hunks of white bread: 'It's cold outside – you need to prepare yourselves.'

We were in for *some* ride, I thought to myself, with a rush of exhilaration.

This was the family's winter house, we established. They weren't exactly nomads, more like pastoralists, moving their herds seasonally. After drinking three bowls of tea made with creamy, fresh cow's milk, I asked for the toilet: the wife led me outside and into a large, open outhouse with a dirt floor, and pointed at one of its four corners.

And now, what we had been waiting for – a thunder across the infinite Kazakh plains on a wilful stallion. Our Disney prince walked me to my steed, a sleepy-looking pony not more than thirteen hands. I mounted, and he led me away, still attached to his leading rope – maybe, I thought, he was taking me to the start point. But no, after thirty seconds we looped round and returned to the farmhouse. Then it was Mary's turn. A Blackpool donkey would have been wilder – perhaps they thought we'd never seen horses before.

We might not have got the wind through our hair, but Mary and I laughed to our very bones. With a smiling shake of the head, they refused to accept our money.

'Please – let us pay for our potatoes,' we insisted. 'Or a gift for your baby – please.'

Eventually, £2.50 was happily parted with.

Our life lesson in simplicity continued into the evening back at Tonya and Valerio's. We sought more pleasure from more food, eating a simple pumpkin soup and fried meat-cakes (like fishcakes, but made with a meagre ration of unspecified meat). Their eight-year-old granddaughter, Valeria, whose divorced mother was currently 'sorting things out' in Kaliningrad, gave us a scratchy *dombra* recital. Kazakhstan's favourite instrument might only have two strings but it was very hard to play, we'd been assured. We watched Russki *Stars on Ice* (surely an absolute, not relative, thrill), and there was even a brief power cut to keep us grateful. It was probably the most normal – mundane, even – night in, but I was right in the moment, struck by the extraordinariness of ordinariness, soothed by simple comforts, and liberated by the total lack of psychological complication. That, no doubt, was in part achieved through paying our way.

It dawned late on us that the living room was also where the entire family slept, and that we were sitting on a little girl-sized sofa-bed and eating into their sleep. We, of course, were given a lovely, proper, small bedroom upstairs, with red gingham bedding and pink, synthetic curtains, which we scurried up to. There was no bathroom in the house, just a wooden banya (a tiled box-room with wooden benches and a slatted floor) and a downstairs toilet and basin. I went to bed feeling uncommonly centred. The happier I was, the quieter the callings of my heart, I realised.

30TH NOVEMBER

Food was the panacea, it seemed. We stockpiled our stomachs for the journey back on a late breakfast of blinis, apple jam, biscuits and bread, only to find that at noon, it was lunchtime. We somehow found room for Tonya's virtually vegetarian *plov* (so frugal was the meat), followed by sweet curd-filled pancakes. But all this communal eating did earn us plenty of airtime with Tonya.

We steadily built up to the delicate matter of the Soviet past. Tonya had been born in Belarus, and came to Kazakhstan with her family when she was six for Khrushchev's Virgin Lands Campaign. A mammoth agricultural plan launched in 1954 to produce grain on 330,000 square kilometres of steppe using some 300,000 farmers, by the 1960s it had failed, causing widespread soil erosion and crop rot.

'Yes, they were good times!' she said, clapping her hands. She called out to Valeria to fetch the photographs. They had been well paid, well housed and had good power supplies, she said. From Valeria's stack of photos, Tonya carefully pulled from a plastic folder a proudly preserved page of a book.

'That's me!' she said, pointing to a young girl in a family portrait.

The book from which the page was torn was called *Happiness in Virgin Lands*, and it was sent back to Russian and Belarusian families to show the success of Kazakh migration.

'We were happy! We all had the same opportunities. We used not to have to worry. There were free sports, concerts and games for us Young Pioneers. Now there is nothing for the children unless you pay for it. All they have is TV. Being clever and ambitious won't necessarily get you anywhere.'

But what about freedom in Soviet times?

'This isn't freedom!' said Tonya, slamming her hand on the table. 'We can't do anything.'

So with communism, the people weren't free; now, with rampant capitalism, nothing was free.

Tonya wanted to show us the museum, where she ran children's craft classes funded by a German environmental NGO.

'Wow!' Mary and I chorused, spinning our heads around her classroom. Hope and positivity winked and sparkled at us from hundreds of colourful collages made from fish bones, orange peel, nutshells and painted dough, framed in old chocolate boxes with ring pulls for hooks. Valeria seemed to have made the majority, so we bought a couple (half the money went to the child). No, they weren't pretty, but they were a touching picture of resourcefulness in the face of great boredom and scant assets.

✪

Back at Mary's, the time was right to ask to put on a wash – finally the conditions had been met. Firstly she had a functioning washing machine. Secondly I could deal with my underwear out on show. Thirdly – crucially – I felt welcome. My first wash was a private celebration. Then I introduced her to couchsurfing.com.

'You don't have to say yes to every couchsurfer – it's completely on your terms,' I advised.

I showed her my inbox to illustrate the mechanics, but, as if electrocuted, she physically recoiled at the potential breach of my confidentiality. Maybe Mary was too private for couchsurfing.

For our farewell dinner I bought chicken, which turned out to be pork, salted fish which was practically fished salt it was so salty, and a box of chocolates, which turned out only to be fit for picture framing. Back in the controlled environment of her kitchen, I compared our first night to our last. I was still suspicious that she was saying what I wanted to hear, but I knew this game – that had been me in Urumqi. This was a hazard of couchsurfing – the preservation of guest-host relations at the expense of a meaty debate. Seeing Mary's decorum reminded me of what I was trying to leave.

CHAPTER 14

KARAGANDA: A DAY IN THE LIFE OF A PAGAN METAL-LOVING IT GEEK

It would be an optimistic enterprise that tried to profit from tourism in Karaganda. Kazakhstan's fourth-largest city, with a population of 500,000, was known for coal mines and labour camps. That is, Stalin established a vast network of labour camps for the purpose of extracting coal without having to pay wages. The industrial city of Karaganda was no destination. My coach comrades consoled themselves with en-route fags and vodka, while I became hypnotised by the flash-frozen panorama outside my window, which, over four hours' drive, developed like photographic film from miserable patchy earth into a morose Russian blue.

Some might have been intimidated by the sight of two black leather, steel-toed Grinder boots with two-inch rubber soles stomping towards them; the fine blond curtains of Norse God hair swinging sinisterly; the bitterly cruel case of cystic acne looming into view. But for some reason – maybe the relaxing effects of having just spent five days with one host, maybe the eventual de-sensitisation to the weirdness of couchsurfing, or maybe simply Oleg's instant aura of ease – I seemed to slip right into his fold. Mellow and genuine, yet bright and out-there, Oleg seemed resilient to Karagandan gloom. However, given that his Grinders just couldn't keep him upright on Karaganda's glacé pavements, perhaps it was that I couldn't quite take him seriously. Sexual tension certainly wasn't going to be a problem.

Passing a noticeably Russian population, we walked – he skidded – to the bus stop, and boarded an overflowing bus to his home. As the bus chomped and rocked through the traffic like a hungry hippo, Oleg and I alternately chatted and shared the silence contentedly. I found it easy to respect the honesty of a prime nerd: he studied computer engineering and IT security; he liked 'Veeking' metal and pagan mythology.

So was Viking metal popular in Kazakhstan?

'No, it's not – it is very popular in my apartment. Actually, my mum don't like it.' Oleg spoke as if via Stephen Hawking's voice simulator. Monotony was unusual for a Russian. Perhaps, I wondered, he wasn't so temperamental, but more rational and scientific.

We disembarked on to what resembled the edge of a void: in the distance, across a hoary no-man's-land, stood a bank of surly Soviet blocks. Beyond those, the highway headed into distant cloud. Isolated in steppeland, no wonder Karaganda had Timbuktu status. I followed Oleg across the wasteland into an estate in ugly beige brick. At five tenge (three pence), the lift was beyond both of our current means, so we walked up to the eighth floor.

An immaculate, brown, motel-ish hallway, decorated with a Königsberg calendar and an ethnic mask, would have been put to use as an ample bedroom in most Soviet flats, but Oleg and co. had no cause. An only child, it was just him and his mother. He opened two narrow stained-glass doors on to a set straight out of *Abigail's Party*. A huge, velour tiger-print sofa complemented the blended brown furnishings, wooden cabinets and net curtains. This was the living room and it was all mine – his divorced mother was away in Belgium 'seeing a friend' for two months.

'She has gone to relax. There is no work to find here,' Oleg explained.

'Is he her boyfriend?'

'I don't know – it's not my business but she goes a lot.'

'Wow – most children would want to know, wouldn't they?'

'Ah – I am not a child,' he smiled wryly.

Now nearly 4 o'clock, it was *obviously* time to head to the neat, pink-wallpapered kitchen for homemade borscht with pork, followed by homemade meat patties with mash and onions. Both were deliciously comforting once liberally sprinkled with salt – Oleg didn't do additives. Putting an entire slice of lemon into his mouth, pith and all, he said, 'I don't like things that I didn't made myself. I'm trying to healthy life.'

He didn't drink vodka, or even beer, obviously – though he didn't say so – to save his skin. He was too much the gentleman to point out that my *Merci* chocolates would be useless here. I suddenly felt rudely empty-handed.

Oleg's mother worked in the pharmaceutical industry: I wondered if that was why his fridge was full of intriguing-looking phials. His father was a miner, which threw me – Oleg was unquestionably middle-class.

'The coal is very high quality here,' he explained, holding his hair away from his face to eat. 'But,' he added, 'a lot of people dying every year.'

What made it so dangerous?

'The human factor – they don't care about anything. They drink a lot and do a lot of amusements like make fire. Then they are caught in explosions. It's a really big problem.'

Oleg was not Karaganda's number one fan: 'I don't have anything here that connects me with the city, except my parents and grandparents.' Had there been no Soviet Union, he said, he'd have been born in the Ukraine. One set of grandparents had come to Kazakhstan with the Virgin Lands Campaign. His other grandmother was from Königsberg, the capital of the ex-German Russian exclave of Kaliningrad: 'So I am a mix of Ukrainian, Russian, German and Belarusian. Now I think I'll leave this country. Kazakhstan is a village,' he said dismissively.

Couchsurfing, it seemed, was all part of his master plan. To pursue his dream to study in the 'Veeking' land of Scandinavia, he had to pass an English exam. Perhaps just by chatting to him, I was buying my borscht. What did a 'pass' cost, I asked, with a knowing look.

'I don't know – I never paid,' he shrugged. Maybe £10 per exam, he reckoned: 'The educational level in Kazakhstan is very low.'

I was flooded with admiration for Oleg for changing his fate, but I was distracted by a more pressing concern – whatever did one do on the edge of the middle of nowhere?

Oleg was evidently something of a self-starter – before I'd even looked up, all the plates were cleared and cleaned. Since eighteen, he'd had a 'nomadic' nerd's job, working late evenings or early mornings from home for a Russian company that made anti-virus software. I *had* to ask him if he could hack. As if telling his mother, he explained that he did know – it was essential for understanding security – but he wasn't interested. He had much more diverting things ahead, like programmers' conventions with his remote colleagues: fourteen guys and one girl would agree on a place to meet. Previously they'd been to the Ukraine, Moscow and Egypt – the provenance of his ethnic mask.

Here was the thing: I wasn't friends with people who went on programmers' conventions and who used chatrooms to discuss assembly language and black metal. Oleg's considerable appeal was precisely his anti-appeal.

'I think you will be pretty bored if you hang out with me,' he smiled at me with raised eyebrows.

But all boring things were novelties first time around. Weren't they?

What were Oleg's plans for the rest of the day?

'Well, it is getting dark so we don't have to go out,' he said, sounding relieved. It was 5.30pm.

'Oh … Ah …' I hesitated. 'Maybe we could go out for air later?'

Or maybe that wasn't the done thing at -12°C? The suggestion went unanswered. It seemed to be time for his internet hit so he took to Mission Control in his single bedroom where three live monitors sat in a row with a Notebook computer bringing up the rear. He set me up with his Wi-Fi name, *tuska* (meaning 'pain' in Finnish) and 31-digit password, and we both sat in our respective rooms connecting with the world.

I re-established communications with China. I was *very* excited about my next stop, Chengdu, capital of Sichuan province, and home to an important panda-breeding centre and my first native Chinese host, a bright, beautiful and with-it law student. Chengdu was fifty miles from the epicentre of the May 2008 earthquake that hit 8.0 on the Richter scale – the fallout was ongoing and reported to be catastrophic.

And look, there was Mary! She'd signed up to couchsurfing. That was at least a sign that, even if I had bullied her, she'd enjoyed it. But then she herself suggested she had masochistic leanings.

'Okay, we go out now.'

This couchsurfer had to act fast; but I was ready since there were few vanities I could perform. Without the mercy of the sun, Karaganda by night and by winter was not for the weak. The wind blew a ghostly, snowy powder up the highway and the atmosphere tried hard to prise us of all our heat. We took a bus to the main drag, Bukhar Zhirau Avenue, named after an 18th-century poet and advisor to Ablai Khan, Genghis Khan's great-grandson. Here lay all Karaganda's totems to whatever triumphs and champions that a city which only had coal to be proud of could muster.

'Karaganda is a typical Soviet city,' said Oleg, as a ten-strong coal-truck motorcade rumbled past. Our tour had begun. 'Soviet shops, Soviet buildings, Soviet minds – people don't think for themselves.'

Its high priest was, as for all ex-Soviet cities, Lenin. Oleg and I stood beneath the domineering, constructivist idol while his mighty gaze faced Moscow. Oleg's words poured scorn: 'Lenin was wrong. Communism suits the lazy, the people who can't be bothered to get a job – the government just gives it to them.' Capitalism gave people an incentive to work hard, he argued: 'It is better if you go and get it.'

Oleg was doing just that.

Behind Lenin's back was the local headquarters of the world's fourth-richest man, Lakshmi Mittal, whose coal operation ran from here. His coal fed the vast Karaganda Steel Mill in nearby Temirtau (where a young, humble Nazarbaev once worked) and which Mittal also now owned.

'He is very unpopular,' said Oleg, a look of disgust descending on his leonine face. 'He pay very low salary and don't give anything back to the city.'

Accusations of slave labour were rife, and dangerous working conditions causing grisly industrial accidents, including one in 2004 where an explosion caused twenty-three fatalities, were common. Kazakhstan's thorny transition to capitalism saw exploitation and gross inequality. Was this progress?

Now standing outside the towering, neoclassical Miners' Culture Palace, I couldn't grasp the incongruity. But apparently there were also dedicated miners' playhouses in Soviet cities such as Kiev and Kirovsk, where they'd put on plays and exhibitions about mining for anyone interested – they surely couldn't afford to be exclusive. Across the main drag was another classic Soviet sculpture: a grandly oversized and geometrically abstracted ... lump of coal, held high above the heads of two proud workers. What about when Karaganda's coal ran out?

'It is not a concern,' Oleg said robotically. 'Kazakhstan have to sell these resources to develop, otherwise we are poor like Kyrgyzstan and Tajikistan. Now we have the living standards of Ukraine.'

Who was I to judge?

Oleg eyed the unlit beyond with suspicion. 'We go no further. This is Old Town – it's dangerous after dark. There are gangs. They steal.'

Our industrial tour was over so we took the bus back. Oleg didn't like Chinese buses – they were too small for his beanpole frame. A Kazakh boy automatically offered his seat to me – and

I realised the bus was too small even for a 5'6-high girl. I scratched the ice off the window. 'The window will be solid white by winter – you can't even scratch it,' Oleg said.

I thought *this* was winter. Much, much worse was yet to come.

✪

And so I got to spend the evening in a programmer's bedroom. Here I discovered the key to killing time in the middle of nowhere: the computer. A picture of a pallid gothic model dressed in mourning clothes, with multiple nose and lip piercings and long, black witchy hair looked out from his monitor. I had to ask: was Oleg a blond Goth?

'There are not any Goths in Kazakhstan. I think you have in London?'

'Yes,' I said. It was like telling a small child about a fairy kingdom. 'A *whole* town of them!'

'I like very much.'

I knew I wasn't his type. I was safe.

That night, I saw another side of Oleg, as a wholesome grandson in sunny photos at his grandparents' dacha where they grew strawberries, apples, tomatoes, potatoes, onions and garlic. And I got to see Kazakhstan in summer – verdant, light, smiley (though some of it was still weird-core – like his grandfather eating garlic like apples). Gardening was part of the Soviet make-up, Oleg explained. During the USSR, they were each given six *sotki* of land (600 square metres). Some villagers here were so poor, they grew their own vegetables so that they didn't need any money.

Did people got depressed here?

'No, we have fun,' he said defiantly. 'I have friends who went to Moscow who were crying. It doesn't get hot here actually but it is light.'

It was admirably optimistic.

But Oleg knew his options for escape. 'The Russian government has a programme that allows us from Ukraine, Belarus and Kazakhstan to move to Russia. There are regions that need people, and they help you find job and accommodations.'

Like Kaliningrad, which looked 'truly European', which is why Oleg liked it. And it had forests: 'We no have in Kazakhstan'.

Plus, I said triumphantly, there was couchsurfing.

But no, Oleg couldn't couchsurf in Europe. He was legally required to have every night accounted for in a hotel. Europe suddenly sounded like Uzbekistan. I felt ashamed of western mistrust.

Having exhausted his entire photo supply, there was nothing for it but to go to bed. I lay between the contradictions of kitsch tiger-print and a heavy camel-wool quilt: 'It doesn't look so good but it's really warm,' Oleg explained.

I thought about Oleg, a fish out of water, desperate to derail his destiny, yet still honouring his hometown. His couchsurfing hosting status was 'Definitely!', but I was only his fourth in a year. But I knew Oleg was going to make it. He was too independent of mind, too mature to linger in a rut. I looked forward to the next day with amusement – what on earth were we going to do? I was happy to put the challenge into Oleg's hands. I was relaxed here. Perhaps my Britishness was starting to lift. I had almost forgotten about trying to do the right thing.

2ND DECEMBER

'Morning! I'm going to make some porridge!' Oleg announced. And Turkish coffee – he had a sophisticated taste for coffee and had stocked up in Egypt. Of course, I wasn't sophisticated enough to let the mud settle to the bottom, but still, it warmed me, as did Oleg's uncomplicated generosity.

'Okay, we go out now.' Oleg was impatient to get to the market to buy fruit and vegetables. 'You can buy everything in the supermarket but these are much more healthy,' he said, swinging on a new-looking, charcoal sheepskin coat. 'The super-market, they make everything look alike.'

He'd be right at home in new Camden.

It was -15°C outside, and the air was finely speckled with trace ice-dust, illuminated by a crisp, cold sun: 'I bet you don't get air like this,' Oleg said, looking pleased.

I was *really* pleased, I said, that it was -15°C.

Oleg looked at me disdainfully. It was tourist folly, of course: a local would never be so flippant (not least when the mercury hit -40). But it was an exotic thrill that made me feel like I'd crossed a frontier. My legs felt like I'd forgotten to put my jeans on, my fingers stung after just a couple of seconds of exposure, and the sharp, arid air tickled my throat when I inhaled. When I pressed my nostrils together, I could feel the frozen moisture crunch. It gave me a warm glow of satisfaction. I recalled the tale about Kazakhstanis monitoring strangers' nose-tips for frostbite – till now, I'd presumed this was myth.

'Actually frostbite is really a problem with alcoholics, because they don't feel it happening,' explained Oleg.

So while vodka was evidently not the anti-freeze it was presumed to be, it was still very much considered an aid to self-help, like in Russia. There weren't nearly so many alcoholics in warmer South Kazakhstan.

And what about the homeless? They went into the city's underpasses apparently. And drank.

And so to the outdoor market, where fresh produce had been preserved in nature's refrigerator.

But Oleg, you're about to buy frozen persimmon.

'Yes, but they taste sweeter this way.'

As I started photographing the piles of fish, frozen into rigor mortis, and the cauldrons of market food obscured by their own steam, people started jumping into frame.

'They're very excited,' Oleg explained, as one, two, three … four stallholders stepped into the line-up. 'It's a big shock to see a western girl here.'

I couldn't understand why I was so conspicuous in this multi-ethnic nation. Oleg was blond and blue-eyed after all.

'You just don't look like you're from here,' he said. 'Russian girls dye their hair yellow. They dress differently.'

Maybe those girls were on to something, digging their trashy heels in like spikes. But for some reason, I didn't feel out of place. That, I guess, was the Oleg effect.

Laden with apples, clementines and persimmons, we crossed Karaganda's urban sprawl to return home. As he unlocked his vault-like front door, I asked why everyone in the former Soviet Union had such heavy steel doors. Crime obviously:

'In the time of crisis in the early 1990s, there were a lot of criminal people who stole a lot. There were no jobs and no food then.'

So trust in strangers was by no means a given here – couch-surfing was *really* radical.

There was a danger in having unlimited internet access, I realised, as Oleg and I instinctively drifted to our portals. But it was his call, I thought, and I was happy to hang around – being on line was so comforting. So the rest of the day was a complete unknown: this no longer unsettled me; it was like being in a game. Who knew, maybe this – me and my laptop – *was* the rest of the day.

The Emperor was grumbling that London was so cold he was wearing two pairs of socks. *Two pairs of socks!* London didn't know cold. Only putting myself out here made me realise how soft I was, how easy London had it. London's middle classes were like spoilt children – always wanting more, not respecting enough, forgetting to count our blessings. I was grateful for this recalibration. Oh – and The Emperor had decided to go on holiday to Cuba over Christmas and New Year. That glorious reunion at Heathrow airport – the impatient meeting straight off the plane, being swung this way and that – was going to have to be erased. I suddenly felt a bit silly for over-romanticising our détente; he hadn't been think-ing along those lines at all. Why should he? Officially we were no longer. Or were we? We'd suspended that unbearable decision. This news was another moment of essential recalibration.

'Let's go to the museum,' Oleg said, going through the Grinders-and-coat routine. 'It is okay,' he added, 'if my friend comes?'

Yes! I was intrigued – another computer scientist.

We took a bus to town and a stroll through Karaganda's Central Park, where a faded Soviet fairground – a children's Ferris wheel, a carousel and a giant *matrioshka* – was unsuccess-fully inviting attention.

'I think every city should have this,' Oleg said.

This was my invitation to delve more into the human side of Soviet history. Everyone I'd spoken to had glorified those times, but wasn't his family scared – wasn't everybody – when an ill-advised joke landed them in the Gulag for a 'tenner', a ten-year sentence?

But no, Oleg had 'read books' saying they were happy times. Though he knew his mother's mother had been forced into the Virgin Lands Campaign, he hadn't known her very well.

'It's difficult for West to understand Soviet times,' he said, after I'd pushed for more.

I wondered if Russia's failure to acknowledge and apologise for Soviet terror was so that it allowed for more of the same, with disappearances and deaths of dissenters.

'They just don't want have enemies in the government,' Oleg said, in justification. 'These people are used to the old style and they still work like this.'

The combination of Slavic pride and propaganda was impenetrable.

Looking like he wasn't accustomed to daylight, a Russian adolescent in a black hoodie was waiting for us in the street. This was Nick, who, according to Oleg, knew more about computer security than anyone (not least since Oleg had missed his lectures for me – I felt a little guilty about that). It was time for Karaganda's Museum, where our newspapery tickets were printed with the price '10 kopecks'.

Oh, there were plenty of Soviet artefacts still in existence, Nick and Oleg laughed. Then, standing in front of some Nazarbaev memorabilia, they laughed again, about the president's lifelong right to be in power.

'But us Russians would be in trouble if someone from South Kazakhstan got into government,' Oleg said soberly. 'Lifelong is good for us.'

We saw a pickled, Cyclops-headed baby, a victim of the radioactive fallout from Semey's Test Site. We saw space-food tubes from the Baikonur Cosmodrome in West Kazakhstan, now under Russian command. We saw medals that were 'Awards for

Mothers With Many Children' (with a population of fifteen million, there was room for growth). And yes, they said, as we passed a display to local lead, copper, zinc and Mittal's steel, it was pretty much true that every element of the Periodic Table lay in Kazakhstan's soils. As if the museum had run out of positive things to celebrate, one glass cabinet was filled with pretend ice cream made by a local company.

'Russians like to eat ice cream in very cold weather,' Oleg said, relishing my surprise.

Nick wanted junk food, Oleg didn't, but Nick won out.

'Some people think that Kazakh fast food is made with cats and dogs,' said Oleg, provocatively. 'The west are so stupid: they believe in vegetarianism like it is a religion.'

I tried to explain about cruelty to animals, but it wasn't in their mindset, he said. I judiciously ordered fish, and then we all headed home.

It was 7.15pm when the police knocked on Oleg's door. The president was coming to town, so they were looking for men with guns – apparently a hunter had previously lived in Oleg's apartment.

No payoff?

'The police here are too lazy to ask for bribes,' Oleg said, sounding indifferent to news of the president's imminent arrival.

Oleg knew that we still had one ace to play. *My* slideshow. He loaded my photos on to his computer, and we looked through all seven weeks' worth. In what turned out to be an unanticipated bonus, I got a local perspective on my experiences:

- The waiting room of Novosibirsk Hospital: 'If you get a disease in Kazakhstan, it will be your last – if you ill, you go to Russia, or Europe.'

- The *dombra* recital in Almaty's Folk Musical Instrument Museum: 'We have this on all our channels. Fifty per cent of air time has to be in Kazakh language. The radio programmes are clever – they do this at night.'
- Kazakh hospitality on board a train: 'I am sneaky: I never take food on trains.'
- Mary's *Merci* chocolates: 'Oh, so everybody get this?'

As predicted, the danger in being relaxed was being presumptuous – too late, I realised I'd never replaced Oleg's redundant chocolates. I was leaving at the crack of dawn to return to China, and Oleg would be left without a gift. Social anxiety at least would have made me think of this – it had its uses. I prepared for farewells, but Oleg said he'd wake for my 6.40am departure (these Slavic hosts!). I went to bed at ease – I'd be leaving on an undramatic high. That was more remarkable that it sounded.

3RD DECEMBER

After offering me to make me breakfast (I spared him), we said goodbye like teenagers, hands in pockets. I'd made indiscernible movements towards a hug, but quickly quit – I didn't want to break our pact of easiness. Oleg didn't have relationship issues. He wasn't 'ill'. He didn't harbour a confidence crisis. There were so many personality parameters that could clash in couchsurfing, but we seemed to have escaped them all.

'See you in Europe,' I said, encouragingly – and I hoped I would. Oleg had made nowhere somewhere.

CHAPTER 15

CHENGDU: ALL A-BORE TO THE K-HOLE

4TH DECEMBER

Set in a luscious, fertile basin, Chengdu was supposed to be China's fourth most liveable city, famed for its teahouses and informal gatherings around its spicy hotpots. But it also had a population of eleven million. As my full bus drove through Chengdu's pretty, willow-lined avenues, my immediate neighbour hucked and snorted, three women shout-talked into their mobiles and a salesman at the front of the bus talked loud, fast and interminably at us through a microphone. I felt crowded and sick. I was looking forward to my host's inner sanctum.

Except that I was having a little trouble locating it. My texts and phone calls went unanswered (I had the wrong number, it turned out), so I asked a young mother. Touchingly intent on helping me, we wandered down a homely-looking lane together under a sunless sky. With among the least hours of sunshine in China, Chengdu was reputedly *even* less sunny than London. Eventually an elegant girl with layered hair and a waisted mustard parka called out. 'Are you the couchsurfer?' It was Lin, my 25-year-old host. I wondered why she didn't use my name, but the thought took low priority: I was connected again.

Through an ornamental gate, under two red, onion-shaped paper lanterns, Lin led me into a verdant courtyard. Try as it might, the foliage couldn't conceal the Sino-Soviet block's iron caging and utilitarian greyness.

'I've got some other couchsurfers staying,' Lin said brightly as we scaled seven flights of stairs. 'A Spanish girl and a guy, but I don't know where he's from.'

It seemed strangely uninvolved not to know, but so what? I had support.

Like scattered pearls, a dozen white balloons in various states of deflation clung around the edges of Lin's large, wood-panelled living room, huge for one girl, especially given that most stayed with their parents until marriage. But the party was over, evidently, and there was no sign of any surfers. Lin extricated herself from her fourteen-hole white leather Dr Martens (fake, she said) and I followed her in sitting cross-legged on her folksy Tibetan mats at a drape-covered coffee-table holding all the tools for making tea, including a kettle – it was the nest of a sensualist.

'You're in the right place,' Lin smiled, ceremoniously pouring me a ping-pong ball-sized cup of Fujian green tea. It tasted of delicate flowers. 'Chengdu is really relaxing,' she continued, in a strong Chinese staccato. 'There's a very huge foreign community – about 20,000. Our slogan is "Chengdu is a city that you'll come to and never want to leave." Chengdu doesn't exclude anyone. We have Muslims, Tibetans, Chang, Ye …' She gracefully lit a cigarette, holding it between fingers topped with chipped, black-cherry painted nails.

'I'm going to put on some crazy Ukrainian music.' She sauntered off to her bedroom, from where the sound of loud pagan chanting and drumming started up. 'The genre is ethnic chaos.'

I nodded like I knew.

Her phone rang. 'Okay, well have a great trip. You're always welcome.'

It was the Spanish girl and unknown man – for some unspecified reason, they'd decided to leave early. I felt a twinge of loss: the pressure was back on the solo performing seal again. Lin poured more tea. I drained my cup instantly for a shot of warmth – sitting in my jacket, hat and gloves, I was still shivering. Two days prior, eleven ten-year-old schoolgirls in the neighbouring province of Shaanxi had died of carbon monoxide poisoning after lighting a charcoal fire in their dorm to stay warm. Now I understood.

I tried not to flinch as Lin announced – out of the blue – that she and her Irish boyfriend were into ketamine; all the kids were in China.

'Cool,' I replied obligingly.

Her boyfriend, she said in a tone suggesting infamy and cachet, was the one with the bloodied nose on couchsurfing. But I hadn't noticed him – I wasn't looking for ex-pat males. And, she said, there'd probably be ketamine at her party that weekend.

Suddenly K-holes – Ketamine-induced out-of-body experiences – and bloodied noses and acting cool flashed before my eyes. I smiled with resignation. I had to be prepared for anything.

So why was she having a party? It was a leaving party. She'd been offered a month-long internship in another province's regional office of Xinhua, the government's official press agency – an outfit that Reporters without Borders called 'the world's biggest propaganda agency'.

Lighting another cigarette, she said, 'I always wanted to be a journalist. These journalists are very popular. Everyone is afraid of them, that they will tell the government bad things.'

A ketamine party for a Xinhua send-off? Not a good news day for propaganda.

Lin had clearly given indoctrination the slip. 'You cannot say any bad thing about Chairman Mao,' she explained. 'Most of my parents' generation hate him. In school we are taught "Great Leader – without him we wouldn't have freedom."' But her parents had been 'victims' of the Cultural Revolution, and were sent for years to a rubber-tree farm in the rainforest near the Burmese border, where they had to 'carry burdens of over 100kg' and were fed only rice and bananas. Her parents were considered 'young intellectuals', but they were just fourteen-year-old students.

'Both lost the chance to get education,' she said, hugging her knees. 'Both broke their health.'

As a result of chronic malnutrition, she said, her father had had two-thirds of his stomach removed.

'Isn't this boring you?' she asked, wrinkling her nose.

No! No way, I assured her. Maybe I looked bored, but actually, I'd slipped into a trance, captivated by my beautiful, hip new host, shocked by her honesty. But then, being cool always involved some amount of rebellion.

It was almost a duty to address the Sichuan earthquake, one of the world's worst environmental disasters. Lin had been to the epicentre, working as a translator for a German journalist, 'just discussing the problems of housing and food.' She'd felt the earthquake right here in her home, but she just thought she was stoned.

There were still massive problems, she said, chewing her lip, with 20,000 still missing on top of an official casualty count of 70,000, and millions homeless – they were now resorting to underground trains for beds. Some of Lin's friends had lost entire families. I quickly dismissed the creeping cold in the face of the reality around me as I was, yet again on this trip, reminded to count my blessings.

Lin sprang up from her mat: 'I'm going to see if my neighbour is in.' He was European; they shared a roof garden and parties. It was a bonus living right next door.

Regardless of wealth, the squat toilet was evidently the preferred Chinese way. What's more, Lin's washing machine drainpipe lay *in* the toilet. And in an open bin were sitting some unabashed used tampons – reality came with the couchsurfing territory.

The neighbour wasn't around. Lin returned as I was leaving the bathroom: 'Don't open the bathroom window,' she advised. 'Or rats get in.' There were rats in the kitchen too, apparently. It didn't seem very far away from rats running free over the entire apartment. I tried to think of earthquake victims.

✪

I suspect the original plan *wasn't* to invite me to her send-off dinner with her parents, 'a very well-known, now retired businesswoman' and an owner of a construction company. But with the other couchsurfers' mysterious, premature departure went my babysitters. I wasn't to mention couchsurfing – her parents would be paranoid if they knew where I really came from. Instead, I was a much less dangerous 'friend from the internet'. Her American-born Chinese friend was playing a gig later, where I'd meet both the Boyfriend and her Brighton friends who'd told her about naked bike rides and Maori poi juggling.

Past golden gingko trees and leafed bamboo fences, rickshaws laden with fecund flowerpots and women balancing baskets of clementines from each shoulder, we strolled the couple of blocks to her parents' house. Lin wanted to know about my worst experiences (always juicier than the good ones). I told her about losing Ollie.

Lin's expenses were much cooler – two surfers had hit on her; one, an American, even calling her a stupid bitch when she refused. But they'd had a big argument beforehand about how she'd ignored him and had only spoken Chinese with her friends when he was around. I couldn't speak for unwelcome advances, but I'd been an ethnic minority of one on many occasions this trip. Isolating, yes, but it was one of the prices to pay. There was always a price, inside or outside the monetary system.

Old Duck Soup was just the kind of restaurant you'd go to with conservative, middle-class parents. As I surveyed Lin's parents' middle-aged friends, I realised that instead of providing a sanctuary from unsavoury slurping and deep, throaty sniffing, couchsurfing brought me right to it. But if these people were at it, it was obviously acceptable conduct. Even Lin chewed noisily with her mouth open. It made me think more gently about the people in the street. Couchsurfing had done its job.

I wasn't making much noise, however – there was little I could say in Chinese. I sat inert and observed the endless toasts. With whatever was going – glasses of *baijiu,* soda cans, even teacups – they'd hold their drink in both hands and clink. Despite two weeks' acclimatisation in China, I still felt so alien to all of this. Maybe that lasted years.

Relief at being able to hold a conversation again at Le Café Paname – a French bar with pretty cocktails, velvet settles and cerise painted walls – was surprisingly short-lived. While the Chinese-American, with hair two-foot-long on one side and shaved on the other, experimented with beatbox over a lute-shaped Chinese guitar, I was introduced to the gang. The Brighton girls were there, as was a mulleted Boyfriend and a dreadlocked Australian guy. They were all couchsurfing hosts, and all (save the Boyfriend) studying Chinese at university. The couchsurfing had been short-lived, because they were all agreed – most couchsurfing guests were boring.

'I have a blanket ban on Polish couples,' said one Brighton girl, with two plaits spilling from a beanie the colour of red onions. 'Invariably boring.'

The Boyfriend was feeling caustic. The violent nosebleed in his profile picture was a deterrent, he said, because those who didn't get it bored him till his 'gonads dropped off'.

The Brighton girl was going to post a naked picture of herself on her profile, but then spared us: 'I thought it would attract the wrong type.'

Lin, fortunately, wasn't available for comment, as she was entrenched in another conversation. I suddenly became aware that I might say something disgustingly boring.

If couchsurfing had an elite, this bunch wanted it.

'Just by being on couchsurfing,' said the Australian, 'you cut out a lot of the population already. But then only a few are really that interesting.' As a host, he heard the same old story, and the same old route, time and again: Xi'an, Chengdu, Kunming.

I froze – no prizes for guessing where I was going next. I was a couchsurfing cliché! But you had to go to Xi'an, for the Terracotta Army, to Chengdu for the pandas, and Kunming? Well, 650 kilometres south-west, it was the capital of a province that bordered Tibet, Burma, Laos and Vietnam and was home to all of China's fifty-six recognised ethnic groups. I hadn't even realised I was being unoriginal. I dropped my head, catching sight of my sensible merino-wool thermal layers. There wasn't room for my cosmopolitan currency in my rucksack.

So what else did they notice about guests, I pushed, inviting trouble.

'Well,' said the plaited Brighton girl, a look of exasperation elongating her face. '*Lots* of them end up showing off.'

But, I thought to myself, wasn't that how people responded under pressure?

'In the last year,' the Australian added, 'loads have joined couchsurfing, but they're all the wrong type – boring and unadventurous. They used to be much more independently minded.'

The Boyfriend, after having just dropped – yes, dropped – his trousers to show off – yes, show off – his red stripy long-johns, offered his assessment: 'Couchsurfing is like the Beatles – very good at the start, then it sold out.'

If this lot were right, couchsurfing had reached a critical mass and was now filled with amateurs like me.

I hobbled off to talk to Andrea, an Italian couchsurfer working in Shanghai who'd got in touch with Lin for local information. He was a fellow guest of sorts (with a hotel room) and was sitting alone. We shared a blissfully boring, unpressured conversation together – he was here on business, selling professional Italian hairdryers to the Chinese. With Andrea, I was judged as a person again, not on my couch count or the craziness of my route. Liberals could be incredibly narrow-minded.

✪

'Have you done crystal meth?' Lin and I were back at hers.

An implosive pause gripped the room.

'Nah,' I replied: 'It sounds really, umm, boring.'

Crystal meth was vile – a hardcore drug that to me screamed try-hard. Lin then produced her DIY water-bottle bong – like, she really was *that* cool.

'Oh my,' I said. 'Is that the time?' After all, I had my *own* bedroom to indulge – okay, a bare room with a bed so austere it resembled a line drawing. The rats were on my mind, and the temperature had plummeted (even further) – it was the perfect excuse to sleep in my clothes. And the plan for the next day? Nothing. At last.

5TH DECEMBER

Throughout this trip, I'd usually only slept five or six hours a night, often less. There was always something to disrupt it: shared beds, punishingly hard floors, convulsing trains or just the cortisol-inducing shock of another new camp. Exhaustion was my constant companion. But in chilly Chengdu, I clocked up nine hours. I felt foggy with rest. Lin got in ten (she'd clearly resisted the bong). In red quilted Snoopy pyjamas and spectacles, she was cosy, not cool, that morning. And after disappearing into the kitchen behind a smoky blue haze, she re-emerged holding two plates with crisply fried eggs and plasticky sliced cheese on toast ('China can't do dairy,' she apologised). Sharing the apartment's one fork, we ate on the mats and spiritually re-grouped – over superficial things like train times and directions, but it was time together, just her and me.

Had I known how long it was going to be before I next saw Lin, I'd have been much more reluctant to go and explore. But Lin had work to do, and I'd be in the way. As well as her own studies, she taught political theories and administration law to sophomore students in a private college. She had to prepare an exam on constitutional law, 'the dream world of freedom of speech'. Also with her own fashion boutique, Lin fitted right into that over-achiever mould. We didn't make any plans and agreed to speak later. But 'K-day' was the next day, so I assumed that night we'd chill. I should have known better than to assume.

No space for introspection, the novelties of Chengdu's external world demanded all my attention: an elderly male security guard wearing frosted coral lipstick; two youths playing street badminton using the road as a net; small speakers disguised as rocks in the streets playing happy muzak; dentists displaying their skills – drilling even – in shop fronts. I fed my hungry soul with unidentified Chinese foods, eating anything that couldn't be translated by the eye – sweet rice-flour balls, sesame-seed floss cakes, snow plums … A rumbling stomach in China was a matter of great excitement.

My phone rang. It was Andrea the Italian. Did I have any suggestions for live music, maybe jazz? I wondered why he thought I'd know – then I realised: this question was originally for Lin. I didn't, of course, 'but if you find any, tell me.' Ciao, we said.

After I'd ticked off a poet's gardens, a Taoist temple and some Sichuan opera, Andrea called back with a lead. Meanwhile, and quite late in the day, Lin texted. She had to meet 'a few people', and she'd be 'staying at her parents'. She'd left out a key and would be teaching till 6.30pm the next day. What to make of it? The correct answer would be nothing, but I, of course, started adding it all up …

Waiting for Andrea in Bookworm, a hip, ex-pat café-cum-lending library, I bumped into the Chinese-American musician with the absurd hair, filing his pointy nails with a diamanté file. 'It's for my music,' he said grandly.

Suddenly, we were three, all connected via Lin, and at least two of us snubbed by her. The musician eventually shook us off for some other musicians, leaving Andrea and I to lean happily on each other. He explained why he didn't couchsurf in people's homes: 'I don't like this person who say, "You can take anything from my wardrobe." They are too trusting – they should pay more attention to who they deal with. I don't trust people, let alone strangers.'

It was true – couchsurfing required a denial of such instincts. Perhaps that was just too much for Italians. Andrea had couch-surfed in Europe: 'It's a completely different experience,' he pointed out.

I believed him. But then again, every couch had been completely different. It wasn't just about nationalities, but personalities – even surfing in your hometown would be intense.

Home alone, I went straight to bed. I didn't understand the abandonment (perhaps it was just cultural) but it made me lonely. Clutching my phone as if it were an animate object, waiting for it to speak of news and non-news from home, I mentally counted down the days. Again.

6TH DECEMBER

K-day. And a hideously early start to make it to the Giant Panda Breeding Research Base for feeding time, the only time these cuddly sloths were awake. They performed perfectly, childishly eating leafy bamboo like lollipops. I pretended to myself I was with a British group, talking to them with asides and observations, to ward off the loneliness. I wasn't picky.

Back in Chengdu, I tracked down the Tibetan quarter – noticeably poorer, rawer and friendlier. I was given a personal performance of some ah-so Jackie Chan moves by four grinning street urchins. I became embroiled with an affable Tibetan shopkeeper in a game of Hacky Sack in the street, resourcefully adapted from a shredded plastic bag. And I drank yak butter milk (it tasted … yuk) in a pretty Tibetan restaurant, where I bought the beguilingly named 'eight-treasure cakes' for Lin, hoping Tibetan warm-heartedness would carry in a cake. I was going to need Lin onside for the night ahead.

✪

After thirty-six hours' estrangement, Lin and I met again across the Tibetan mats. She was vague and remote. She put the cakes down without looking at them.

'So how was your night last night,' I asked, leadingly.

'I can't remember – oh, I was playing Fight the Landlord. It's a card game. I lost lots of money.'

She didn't seem interested in talking. Maybe she was down about leaving her boyfriend for a month (in which case I felt for her – it was hard for hosts always to put on the cheer). Or perhaps, as I suspected, I was like a Christmas present she'd grown bored with – like the American, and my couchsurfing forerunners. With my merino-wool layers and touristy ambitions, I don't think I passed her cool test. Chengdu was supposed to be inclusive, but inclusivity never sat very well with cool.

✪

The location was the suitably sceney Jah bar, a riverside rasta, ahem, joint, where some bongo players were taking themselves quite seriously. And was everyone melting into ketamine casualties? Well, I certainly wasn't offered any. I hawkishly surveyed all suspicious movements – the urgent phone calls, the mid-evening cycle runs, the wobbly behaviour – but it was pretty low-key.

I was in a good position to observe as I stood alone, bearing a coping smile, while Lin fluttered amongst the groups. Timing was both my friend and foe: I had an invitation to a party but I was – rightly – the least of her concerns. The closest we got that night was when she came over to confiscate the Boyfriend with whom I was in tense discussion.

I'd been trying to defend the Xi'an-Chengdu-Kunming trail, which the Boyfriend abhorred so much he'd explicitly banned it on his profile.

'You should be stopping at the villages,' he said fiercely. 'It's not natural to travel this fast.'

But these cities offered cultural importance, conversation and brain food, plus, with more couches, there was more chance of staying with a native. After all – here we all were in a city. It seemed hugely hypocritical.

He checkmated me: 'I'm not a hostel and I can take who I like.'

But he had a point – I'd clung safely to city life, dodging the pitfalls of getting lost or abandoned in a village. I had no idea what awaited me – getting to one became my new ambition.

I pondered the Boyfriend's dismissal of couchsurfing's new wave. Was this the beginning of the end? Or the end of the beginning? But couchsurfing was too radical to become mainstream. Perhaps it wasn't that couchsurfing had become less interesting, but that the Boyfriend, having hosted 'fifty or sixty' people, had by now heard all the travellers' tales. Hosting, surely, was subject to the law of diminishing returns. The Boyfriend was no doubt eligible for inclusion in that couchsurfing elite – those tired with the façade of universal appeal, who understood a photo of a naked bottom or a bleeding nose.

Getting on with everyone required the shelving of controversial opinions and anti-social habits until such time that it seemed appropriate to introduce them – it really was classic first-date territory. That need to adapt, and be inoffensive, stifled one's sense of self. I thought of Mary, Saviour of Astana – the polar opposite to this take-it-or-leave-it attitude. In her will to please, Mary and I might not have had heart-of-the-matter debates, but I felt entirely more cosy – that was the trade-off.

It was a relief to be liberated from social Siberia by Mark, Lin's Chinese-Australian friend. Mark was preppy and earnest – I was no longer engaged in a (losing) competition of cool. He'd just returned from couchsurfing in India and Iran. He was glad, he said, to have stopped 'bumping around'. How well I knew the feeling. Mark was a godsend of validation: all my bad experiences, which made me think I was just rubbish at couchsurfing, Mark – a well-adjusted, experienced couchsurfer – had had too. So he too had failed to click with much older hosts. He too had lost his patience with people who never shut up: 'Sure, there are cultural differences, but sometimes it makes you want to scream.' Mark, I learned, had lived with Sustainable John in Chengdu – my links in the network were growing. Emotionally deprived, I found myself fighting the urge not to rest my head on his shoulder – no, not like that: I was just at last comfortable and understood in Chengdu. Mark spoke human.

Lin wafted past, trailing her fingers across our backs, in a louche manner.

'How are things?' I asked.

'What do you reckon?' she shot back with a withering look. She continued straight on to the next table where she lunged in for a hug, knocking over all twenty-odd beer bottles on the table. With Lin and I now on completely different wavelengths (and not solely down to whatever was her stimulant of choice), Chengdu had come to be about Lin's friends, not her. I was lucky really, of course. I was living a local life, I had good company and I should be grateful. I had another eighteen hours before Kunming – I wondered how much of that Lin and I would share.

7TH DECEMBER

'Coffee?' The stern, shaved head of Lin's European neighbour had popped around my bedroom door – he'd let himself in. The original invitation, I'd heard, had been for Lin and the Boyfriend, but they were clearly in hiding that morning. It sounded like an order, so I obediently followed him next door for fresh, strong filter coffee.

Again, I found myself in the welcome surrogate care of Lin's friends. But it was still weird: the neighbour – Alex, a forty-something malcontent leftie – seemed intent on watching an ear-splitting version of the Mafioso film *Gomorra*. Was I expected to take up the film half-way through, or to compete with sparkling conversation? Eventually, after enough interruptions from both of us (it seemed the neighbour had already had quite a lot of coffee), the film was demoted. Alex explained ex-pat survival in China.

'The idea is to keep a low profile,' he said, his distant eyes fixed on the screen. 'It makes life easier. The system only applies to its own people. Communism is very Confucian – it's the only way to control so many people. Us Westerners don't have to follow their rules.'

Alex compared China to Franco's Spain in the 1970s: 'We were having wild beach parties and no one gave us any trouble.'

I peered at him – tattoos, a fresh scab on his forehead, hedonist's complexion: this man had lived.

A dozen red roses were slowly dying in a vase: Alex' Chinese ex-girlfriend ('well, maybe girlfriend') had come to stay.

'It's very strange,' he explained. 'Most girls don't have sex until the age of twenty-one, and at twenty-five, their mothers start suggesting husbands. Maybe eighty per cent of marriages are arranged. In China, they're much more with the idea that they'll never be happy.'

This girl's parents clearly didn't approve. Resting a bristly chin in his hand, he said, 'I didn't realise the complications. Her parents can't see the point if the guy doesn't have a car or an apartment. It's about status: cultural problems are solved with money.'

But I was still thinking about happiness. I was still struggling with the fact that I *should* always be happy out here, free, not at work. Perhaps the Chinese were on to something – it was like Wittgenstein said, 'I don't know why we are here, but I'm pretty sure that it is not in order to enjoy ourselves.' Maybe accepting this would quieten that constant state of dissatisfaction with The Emperor, with the trip, even with each couch. Placing less importance on happiness might clear the way for other experiences. I relaxed into the sofa.

In China, that 'other experience' was the glow of the greater good.

'Say a worker gets 700 yuan (£70) for working seven days a week at the Olympic Stadium,' Alex explained. 'This man has a very unhappy life: he never sees his family and he works extremely hard. But his basic feeling is national pride.'

It made me think: I didn't need fresh grass – I had it all already. I just needed to be a bit more Zen about my expectations.

Before the neighbour could launch into another coffee, I thanked him very much and returned next door, aware that I should spend my last day with Lin. I called out into the frosty silence. Lin appeared from her bedroom, 'about to go out,' she said casually. We went through the motions of farewell, exchanging an empty hug. I shouted out a goodbye to the Boyfriend. He didn't get up, but simply called out 'Safe trip' from beyond. Feeling unresolved and misunderstood, I thought forwards, to Kunming, where another chance awaited – a 27-year-old Norwegian male journalist called Jo (my native option had never responded).

As I climbed down from the top floor apartment, I tried out my new, stepped-down, no-need-for-happiness attitude. Couchsurfing hosts weren't ever going to be instant best friends – it was already a lot to ask that they'd act as conduits and innkeepers. I had to stop expecting them to replace Ollie. I had to stop expecting the couchsurfing hype.

CHAPTER 16

KUNMIN9:
THE TRAVELLERS' TEASE

8TH DECEMBER

Twenty-four hours on the hard sleeper to Kunming was more 'hard' than 'sleeper'. A hard sleeper was a bunk in an open carriage: no doors, no privacy, and where workers played cards loudly, drank *baijiu* and farted unashamedly. But after the ego-checking experience of Chengdu, I was content to stare at others' lives. Out of the window was picture-postcard China, a mythical mist swirling through clever little paddy fields meticulously tended by farmers in coolie hats. I knew I'd crossed into the province of Yunnan in south-west China because the sun had come out. Yunnan meant 'south of the clouds'. By the time I'd reached Kunming, people were using brollies for shades.

If Diet Coke were casting for a Norwegian fisherman, Jo would most certainly be on the shortlist. Tall and streamlined, with sandy stubble and long, dark blond hair, he wouldn't even need styling: his craggy oatmeal sweater looked like it had been knitted by a fisherman's wife.

'I wish it had,' he said, in a flawlessly Americanised accent.

But looks weren't the reason I was here – honestly. Despite

a taciturn profile, he had heaps of good references, a flatmate, and a spare double bedroom. And he'd been couchsurfing with his mum.

I found an instant distraction – as we stood in his large, sun-filled lounge, furnished with a fancy black-leather, three-piece suite, I had to concentrate hard to avert my eyes from an artless drawing of a naked woman with circular breasts, splayed over one of the clean, white walls. You couldn't seem attractive standing by this portrayal of woman.

'Do you know of any couchsurfers in Yunnan's villages?' I blurted out.

'It's very difficult – there's nothing around,' Jo replied, impassively.

It was a brief vindication. So it *was* difficult to find couches in villages near kunming.

'And, umm, have all your other couchsurfers come from Chengdu?'

'Not all of them – some come from Guilin.'

Guilin, 775 kilometres east and towards my final destination of Shanghai, was my next stop. Why were we all doing the same route? Maybe it was a good one.

We danced around in conversation, covering the essentials. His room-mate, Daniel, was Polish and used to work in trade – logistics or something. Daniel was also expecting a couchsurfer that day, from Australia. They'd lived there since August and were both studying Chinese. It looked like they'd been there for longer, I said, glaring at the circular breasts. They'd had some wild parties, he replied. I was getting the facts, but I was going to have to work a lot harder for some Norwegian feeling.

'Is it okay if I make some tea?'

'Everything is okay,' Jo said, like it was his catchphrase. Selecting the cleanest of all the dirty mugs, I eyed the washing-up – soon it would be mine. I liked washing-up out here. It was a fail-safe gesture.

Jo sat by the window and logged into his silver MacBook – he had work to do, 'real work'. He was waiting on news of his scoop for a Norwegian daily. He'd just exposed some Norwegian sponsorship of a Chinese coal business: 'They're supposed to be ethical,' he said importantly.

It felt grounding to be in the company of someone who seemed to be doing the right thing.

Perhaps I'd like a solar-powered shower, he offered. And he had Wi-Fi.

I felt happy. Out here, it wasn't difficult to make me feel that way, though increasingly, that happiness was becoming easier to disrupt.

A tabby moggy eyed me warily through the frosted-glass shower door as I took off my clothes. I agreed with the cat – there was something perverse about being intimate in someone else's private space. I usually dragged out bath-time, as it was also rare down-time, but since the solar option was just a hot hose, I didn't hang around.

✪

'Are you ready to go?'

I was always on standby and I was longing to get outside. Kunming was my trip's most southerly location – it was 15°C outside. Jo wanted to go to the Flower & Bird Market to collect a jacket, so he led me through the town, providing a factual commentary throughout. We rolled down his street, lined with silk cheongsamed girls trying to lure us into their smart restaurants. His rent here was expensive – 2,000 quai (£200) a month, the same as the average urban salary. The reason? The twee and popular Green Lake Park, so-called because the willow trees' reflection seemed to turn the water green. I felt quietly proud to be staying in one of the best parts of town, even if it was an ex-pat privilege.

Kunming's population was a very manageable 'five or six million', and it wasn't long before we found the Flower & Bird Market, an indoor arcade full of wooden trinkets and clothes stalls. No, they didn't sell birds and flowers here, Jo said, but they did sell dogs.

To keep or to eat?

To keep.

Had he eaten dog?

Yes – they had it from time to time. It was like lamb. He didn't see a moral difference between eating dog and sheep, he said coolly.

Had he eaten cat?

No, but he'd grown up with cats.

I didn't pursue the moral difference between eating cats and eating dogs, but it seemed to exemplify the confusion over animal rights in the west – really, people should be vegan or omnivores. But like playing golf with the boss, I preferred to let my host win.

We arrived at a stall where a woman was selling colourful ethnic jewellery. They chatted in Chinese and Jo recovered his North Face jacket that he'd leant her when she was cold. I really should have been smitten, but Jo was too aloof to love. Instead the event gave us stuff to talk about – she was from the Vietnamese Yi tribe, Jo explained; there were many in Yunnan.

Were there ghettos?

Not really: the Communists did a very good job of getting everybody to integrate.

Oppressively?

Only maybe with the Tibetans. Or they would make it worth their while financially to 'Hanify'. The Muslims were more oppressed because they were visibly different. All Yunnan's minorities were vulnerable. Bordering the Golden Triangle (that naughty, opium-producing crossroads between Vietnam, Burma and Laos), Yunnan was China's most HIV-affected province, with 80,000 people infected, mostly through sharing needles.

Jo was immersed, knowledgeable and seemed to care. Neither of us, I was sure, was bothered by the nuisance of attraction. The day ahead was still a total mystery, but gone was the tension and pressure.

'If you want to understand the world, you go to China,' said Jo.

He'd come to China for that reason two-and-a-half years ago, taking a Masters in Chinese politics in Shanghai. He argued he was taught the reality, not the dream, though it sounded like party line – no acknowledgement of the 1989 Tiananmen Square massacre, and Taiwan and Tibet were seen as belonging to China.

'Wasn't that China's version?' I wondered out loud.

'The west always compares China to the west,' replied Jo authoritatively. 'But if you compare China to China in history, things are so much better.'

I thought of Gareth and Beth in Xi'an – they'd all become Chinese sympathisers. I admired their immersion.

After a stroll through the food market, Jo stopped for his customary fruit smoothie, shouting me one too.

'Pineapple has been proved to make sperm taste nicer,' he announced, holding a full glass of crushed pineapple.

Well I wasn't expecting *that*. I blocked the suggestiveness and chattered on as normal. But Jo had to 'go and watch what was happening' with his exposé.

I was good with a little break.

✪

We reunited at Jo's local restaurant, the Red Bean, where we found – according to Jo – Kunming's best ex-pat band. This was Lush, comprising three raucous young jazz cats from Argentina, and Christina, a Chicagoan vamp. Suddenly we had company, including their two Chinese fans, for dinner.

'Do you wanna know what they're saying?' Christina whispered to me.

The boys had been hooting away in Spanish.

'They're asking the Chinese girl if chilli affects Chinese people as much as westerners when they, y'know, do a Number Two.'

And the answer? No, apparently.

'What's the Chinese euphemism for Ones and Twos?' Christina called out.

'Sing a song,' said the Number One Fan. 'When we want to go for a pee, we say we want to go singing.'

And Number Twos?

'Dancing!'

The band had been asked what they didn't like about Kunming in a recent interview. 'Well, you know how much the locals stare at westerners?' one started. 'Well, in the urinals, they *really* stare.'

The table exploded into laughter.

A chicken's claw landed on my plate.

'Welcome to Kunming!' Christina cackled.

'If you eat too many chicken claws,' explained Number One Fan, 'they say your writing becomes really messy.'

'If you get the claw,' Jo deadpanned, 'it means you get a prostitute that night.' He'd had the claw a few times, he said.

'Worth repeating?' I asked.

Jo picked it up with his hands, and in a bare-faced act of manliness, proceeded to suck on it.

'How is it?'

'Like chicken.'

Things could be so brilliantly uncomplicated with men.

But we had a few more factors to add to our equation – we were going to meet Daniel, and his Russian (no longer Australian) hitchhiker in Halfway House, a hip music bar. Meanwhile, Jo explained about unequal opportunities in China. He'd been paid to pose as an American businessman for a Chinese-American company's corporate propaganda. They didn't even care that he wasn't American – they just wanted western credibility. They wrote him a speech and took photos of him shaking hands, conducting good white-man business, and paid him about £300. It turned out to be an entire industry, and if you could live with yourself, you could make a living from it.

Roger, Jo's young Swiss environmental-engineer friend, came to join us. He had an appointment the next day with a Chinese TV camera crew who'd be filming him cooking some Swiss dish ('stew', he promised) for the Christmas special of a popular cookery programme – for £50. He'd previously starred in a fertiliser commercial, where he, the smart westerner, posed signing a contract. Some ex-pats, he said, got work just sitting in offices, enticing potential customers. Jo knew someone who'd worked in a perfumery as a 'chemist' (no experience required), mixing potions in test tubes behind a shop window. There were agencies and even a scouting hotspot.

Invisibility would have been useful when we met Daniel's gang of hardboiled travellers – one with improbably long dread-locks, one under-nourished and all in black, and Daniel, wearing a fake Adidas 'Addicto' zip-up top. And the Russian had arrived: Bulat, a 22-year-old Buryatian who stuck out in his reassuringly bourgeois Burberry spectacles.

I would have been happy just to listen to them. The spidery black-clad one explained about potlatch. Based on the native American feast, it was a regularly held free party – yes, often with free food – which his friends took turns to curate.

'It's the perfect metaphor for how artists raise the level against capitalism,' he said, grandly.

Daniel told us how he'd hitchhiked in Scarborough, and had stayed with a Christian family who'd hoped, as a Pole, he'd be a devout Christian.

Was hitchhiking really so rubbish in Britain, I asked.

No, he shrugged, France was even worse.

We relocated to Jo and Daniel's kitchen. Jo quickly retired from play, while the spider was feeling confrontational – an unspoken no-no in couchsurfing (or was that just my British rule?). But then, the spider would rather eat his own hair than couchsurf, despite the fact he'd be on Daniel's sofa that night. He didn't have to play by our rules.

'Couchsurfing,' he proclaimed, 'is a cult. I don't like staying with random people. Every time I've been couchsurfing, I've been raped.'

Which of course he hadn't: his point was that the price was too high.

'I'm prepared to pay the price of inconvenience or compromise,' I said, compelled to defend couchsurfing, 'for the fact that the people want to give their hospitality.'

'Hospitality?' he snorted. 'Hospitality is another word for hotel prostitution.'

It felt ironic to be arguing about couchsurfing with a hardcore anti-capitalist.

'Maybe,' I said, flushing. 'But couchsurfing is a solution for both sides; both host and guest can benefit.'

'Benefit?' Daniel joined in. '*Benefit*? There's no benefit for the host. I host because it's no trouble. I don't expect anything else.'

'All hosts have motives,' I said, quietly. 'Otherwise they wouldn't do it.'

Perhaps, I thought to myself, the tough traveller in Daniel couldn't admit to being lonely or wanting to meet other travellers. Bulat was no help at all, he just laughed when everyone else did. He maintained that protective state of detachment; he seemed to understand that no-need-for-happiness attitude. I still couldn't help but jump right in, hoping for friendships with my hosts – wasn't that ultimately more rewarding? Except that it was failing.

'Have you ever had sex with your guests?' the spider asked, arching an eyebrow.

'A few,' said Daniel, coyly.

So sex was a benefit. Irrelevant – the spider had already moved on to other topics for attack: like my bourgeois Moleskin notebook and duvet boots.

When the argument jumped to whether Mongolians founded or destroyed Beijing, I took my cue to duck out of the bear pit.

Avoid hardcore travellers, I muttered to myself, once in the confines of my own, now-freezing room. Tough, and such snobs. I admired them though; they rose above physical or emotional hardships. Chengdu had made me fully aware of my place in couchsurfing's amateur division. But us beginners weren't so bad. We were appreciative, we were still surprised by kindness, we didn't take things for granted – I bet the spider hadn't brought chocolates. Besides, didn't good guest behaviour come from the soul, rather than a certain number of experiences?

Word from The Emperor – he was sick and in bed and wishing I was with him. It was an overt reference to the state of being 'on' again. We were now texting at least daily. I didn't stop to rationalise it; I indulged it, I needed it. It was deeply, primally soothing.

9TH DECEMBER

Kunming's streets started buzzing at dawn, with the Hui Muslims' call to prayer, the seagulls' call for breakfast, and the street hawkers trying to call louder than their competitors. At 10am, I put my ear to the door and heard a merciful silence: Jo and Daniel had gone to their class; the spider had scuttled off somewhere. Bulat was washing his socks. Kunming didn't seem to do much planning, but Jo and I had arranged to meet for lunch, and then Daniel and Jo were meeting a local ex-pat magazine editor to discuss a photo-story they'd shot up some mountain – I could come if I was interested. Having missed out in

Chengdu, I was not taking time spent with hosts for granted. Meanwhile, I caught up with couchsurfing.

'I am very sorry to tell you that I am not available any more.'

It was my Guilin host, who I'd been really looking forward to staying with, given that he was native and lived in a tri-generational set-up with his mother and children.

'You told me you have an alternative,' he went on. 'so I answered another guy.'

I'd done no such thing. What I had done was over-complicate matters by saying, 'Please let me know if it's possible to stay, otherwise I'll find an alternative.' After that, I vowed to talk straight, and mounted a new search, heading straight for the top: Guilin's City Ambassador, a 28-year-old Serbian and 'full-time lazy person' called Goran. But he made no elitist noises – he'd even quoted couchsurfing's mission statement on his profile: 'It's not just about finding free accommodation ... We strive to make a better world by opening our homes, our hearts, and our lives.'

The temptation to find out-there hosts who'd take me out of my comfort zone and into a thrilling new world had been silenced for the moment.

★

At lunch with Jo and Daniel (who seemed to have forgotten Bulat), I was instinctively drawn to the stranger. Zahi, who made up the foursome, was a smiley Israeli also studying Chinese. As strangers, we could paddle in the neutral waters of getting-to-know-you; he wasn't going to give me a hard time. I explained couchsurfing to him.

'I suppose it's a crazy idea,' I concluded.

'We have a saying,' he said. 'If it's stupid and it works, it works.'

Lunch was a lesson in how difficult the Chinese language was to learn. Zahi explained there were thirty-two – yes, thirty-two – meanings for the word *shi shi*. I was taught some of them: 'timely' 'test meal', 'solar time' – whatever that meant. Jo would play squash later, or 'wall ball'. Badminton translated as 'feather ball'; ping-pong was onomatopoeic, so it was apparently the same in Chinese. 'Immediately' literally translated as 'on the horse', and 'fuck' in Chinese really meant 'bitch' – 'the thing you want to fuck'.

Foreign swear words came up time and again on this trip. It was the easy, impartial conversational fodder of the young.

✪

In an office that looked like the builders were due back any minute, a bearded young American was holding fort, clutching a pencilled crossword on a manila notepad. This was the editorial office of an ex-pat publication, and Jo and Daniel had come equipped with words and photos of their 5,394 metre climb up the mountain Haba Xueshan.

'Are you the editor?' I asked the American.

He looked behind him. 'I guess so.'

'So you do the crosswords?'

'Yeah, man,' he said, tipping back in his chair. 'I used to do them stoned but there'd be at least one mistake a month and everyone complained. I don't think anyone does them any more.'

Jo had another story he wanted to write: a day with Kunming's homeless.

'Yeah, man,' said the editor, 'I've heard there's Mafia behind them – y'know, they give them somewhere to stay, and the beggars bring in the money.'

Jo and I had seen a remarkable quantity of beggars on our stroll, though they didn't seem to be making any money.

'And child trafficking,' the editor continued. 'Woah, that is *massive* in south-east China. There's a story about a woman in the mountains who had twelve babies. She doesn't keep any of them. She takes them into Vietnam – maybe they can forge birth certificates easier there. Then they're brought back to China.'

'What about censorship?' I asked.

Oh sure, he said. They'd had to take out the word 'Mohammed'. They'd had to remove some stats about sexual proclivities. They could *never* write about the Dalai Lama.

Jo mentioned he wanted to do a piece for the 50th anniversary of the Tibetan leader's exile.

The editor shook his head. 'Man, if you do, you'd better leave town for a while.'

But Jo, a sympathiser, was thinking from the Chinese perspective. 'That side just isn't heard in the west.'

In the interests of damage limitation, I kept my western thoughts to myself. You couldn't take on these boys without a solid case.

But one question was burning into my consciousness. We left the editor's office, and Jo and I went to buy our train tickets (he was making his way to the Philippines for Christmas). I wanted to know Jo's motive for hosting – after all, the boys could make back some of their rent by letting out my room.

'We like having couchsurfers around,' Jo said, reticently. 'And we can afford it.'

'You'll have a hard sleeper, right?' Jo was going to ask for my ticket for me.

'Yup,' I said. I didn't want to expose myself as a wimp.

Jo couldn't recommend anything to go and see in the city – Kunming's attraction seemed to be its sizeable ex-pat scene, so while Jo went for 'wall ball', I wandered aimlessly. Beyond Green Lake Park, Kunming was brashly commercial with a claustrophobic crowding of concrete. I thought about the countryside – I'd seek it out from Guilin, in the sub-tropical province of Guangxi in south-east China. Except I still had nothing confirmed in Guilin. I started to wonder – how much nerve damage had couchsurfing caused me this trip?

When I could take no more argy-bargy in town, I retreated back to Jo's where Bulat wanted to talk, and I wanted to concentrate on finding my couch. I humoured him for a while until his arrogance began to infuriate me. Telling me how he'd studied economics and had taken a course in film art, I perked up.

'I'd like to do a course in film art,' I said.

'Why would you want to do that?' Bulat retorted, cracking his knuckles. 'You should follow your feelings, not what you are told to think.'

But Bulat, remarkably forbearing, had been alone all day. I pondered his approach. A hitchhiker and an indefinite traveller, he was just after free accommodation. It looked liberating, eliminating the need to like one's hosts. But then, Bulat didn't seem to have the emotional gaps – of Ollie's absence and heartache – that I was dragging around with me.

After a tip-off from Roger at Halfway House, I found a couch in a village called Xingping – I'd go there after Guilin; it was just 40 kilometres due south. My host liked climbing mountains! He played Chinese drinking games! He lived with his wife! Request couch! The find was a huge burden off my mind – I had to know the country couch before going home in … ten days!

Had I not invited Bulat to dinner with Jo and me, he'd have been abandoned for the evening, too. Never mind if Bulat was arrogant – and with his impervious pestering, annoying – couch-surfing depended on karma. Installed in the Red Bean again, we – or rather Jo and Bulat – discussed Chinese and Russian 'democracy', concluding that both countries needed strong leaders.

'China,' said Jo, 'takes its example from Russia as to why you shouldn't change to democracy overnight.'

But he fell silent as he checked his mobile.

'Everything okay?'

'I've got a weird situation,' Jo announced.

'Can we help?' I said, cheerfully. 'We could be your advisory panel.'

'Too late. I have a bedroom appointment.'

'A *bedroom* appointment? Not even a living room appointment first? Straight to the bedroom?'

'Yes,' he sighed. 'It's complicated ...'

'Is this appointment taking place in *your* bedroom?'

We shouldn't be around if that were the case.

'Yes, but don't worry – you don't have to make yourselves scarce.'

Yes, we did. Though not quite in time. Hiding in my room on Jo's suggestion ('I think she'd appreciate the discretion'), I smelt the scent of a woman, and froze as if I didn't exist.

'This is pretty stressful, this ... "thing",' spoke a woman's voice in a velvety native English. Maybe she had date fear, but she sounded audibly distressed. I waited until I heard Jo's door close then ran to grab Bulat to leave. A pair of black leather knee-highs were lying by the front door.

Bulat and I weren't going to be lasting friends, but he was at least someone to laugh with. It was a small karmic payback. So what to do? Check out the best ex-pat band in town, surely.

Lush had a residency at a nightclub called Soho, where we found locals partying for their lives, ingesting rows and rows of beers and spirits. An over-styled Chinese guy with cyberspikes was singing frenetically into a microphone, but Lush were nowhere to be seen.

I was rather embarrassed for Lush when we eventually found them upstairs in a godforsaken gig space. The truth behind being Kunming's best ex-pat band was that they were only really popular among ex-pats – and two Chinese girls. And the ex-pats weren't out that night.

'The only people here are waiting for a table downstairs,' Christina pouted.

Bulat and I exchanged pained glances: how long should one give for a 'bedroom appointment'?

10TH DECEMBER

I was stuck in the bathroom. The sliding door had fallen off its rails and jammed. Should I yelp for help? Smash the glass? Climb out the fifth-floor window? Finally, after half an hour, I managed to squeeze like a cat through the narrowest opening. Problem-solving and survival out here was all part of my 'personal development'. Was resolving all these little incidents shaping me? Only London would tell. Meanwhile, impending disaster in Guilin had been stalled – for the moment. Goran had agreed to host me. He had a British flatmate. And he was an Ambassador so he couldn't be too caught up in cool. Couchsurfing was starting to look as bipolar as my relationship with The Emperor. Maybe I was the link?

'Don't you feel slightly … abandoned?' I asked Bulat, who again hadn't been invited by Daniel to the lunch that a few of us were going to.

'No – it is okay. Daniel is traveller. He don't want spend time with guest.'

Getting my head around this arrangement was probably going to make my trip far easier, but I was a romantic. I believed in more. I took Bulat under my wing,

A students' banquet of deep-fried fish, lily roots, garlicky greens and some surprisingly moreish chewy tofu was shared between Jo, Daniel, Bulat and me, and some of their ex-pat student friends. Jo mentioned how 500 screaming Chinese tourists had broken his Zen sunrise on Yellow Mountain in Anhui Province, prompting a discussion about society under dictatorship. There was a connection: group behaviour. People conformed, and no more so than in China, hence all the screaming on the mountain. Plus there was the psychology of power. Power so quickly went to people's heads. The Stanford Prison Experiment saw students play out the roles of prison wardens and prisoners; it had to be aborted after six days because the students playing the wardens behaved so cruelly. And absolute power corrupted absolutely. There was a perverse logic to dictatorships – to the rules of Mao, Stalin and Hitler.

★

The blokey mess had been mounting up, I noticed, as Daniel, Bulat and I were having tea in the kitchen. I was leaving in a few hours for Guilin and was having a gratitude rush. But I felt shy – clearing-up felt so righteous. As I apologised for what I was about to do, I became caught up in one last battle.

'It is not about washing-up, it's about paying back by hosting,' Bulat sniffed.

I disagreed – why couldn't I pay back in the short-term.

'I know it's not about linear transactions and tit-for-tat,' I rebuffed. 'But it doesn't stop me feeling indebted. This is my way.'

'The linear transaction is staying in a hotel,' Bulat said, imperiously. I wondered what Bulat had given? But then what had he taken? Bulat and Daniel were both cool with the free accommodation arrangement. Their way was totally leftist. Perhaps those leftist principles were more alien to me than I realised; instead, by paying my way with gifts, I was living more by the spirit of market norms.

'Nice lovecuffs.'

I'd gone to say goodbye to Jo, who was sitting at his desk in his room. There they were, a pair of red fluffy handcuffs on a chest; impossible to avoid. I quickly launched into a small speech about what a nice time I'd had. And that I'd appreciated the battles, however personal.

'Yeah,' Jo nodded slowly. 'They're straight-talking guys.'

Politically correct, circumspect Britain didn't like to bite deep into issues like these guys did. Even Paxman was seen as shocking. We were indirect, avoidant. These personal attacks had been hard work, and therefore, good for me. Still, I was glad to go.

CHAPTER 17

GUILIN: TROUBLE IN PARADISE

11TH DECEMBER

Guilin looked like a pensioners' resort. That wasn't such a bad thing: in place of homogenous communist blocks were frilly buildings painted Miami hues of pink, peach and aqua, with jolly, striped balconies and jaunty palm trees waving agreeably. With a temperature of 20°C, Guilin wouldn't make for a bad retirement. But its real attraction was its karst formations – a gorgeous, otherworldly landscape of leafy limestone humps, hundreds of metres high. Plonked all around, Guilin's developers would just have to work around them. A tiny city by Chinese standards (its population just nudged 600,000), it was massive in Chinese tourism: most Chinese people visited once in their lifetime.

It was hard to distinguish between the effects of the cardiac exercise of five flights of stairs and that familiar sense of performance anxiety. Looking freshly scrubbed and shaved, Goran shook my hand and then retreated to his laptop in the small, bloke-ish living room piled high with electronics, cables, and DVDs. He introduced me to his middle-aged flatmate, Des, who was on the sofa – my bed for the night – drinking beer at 2pm. I parked in an armchair in front of a glass cabinet containing a young iguana called Jesus – or 'Hesus, as in the Latino bowler in *The Big Lebowski*,' Goran explained, in a bored, American accent with faintly Slavic gutturals.

I presented my chocolates with a generous grin.

'I don't like so much sweet things.' He lit a Chinese cigarette.

Was Goran in a bad mood, I wondered. Hungover, it soon emerged. He'd had so many flaming shots, he'd been sick. He looked pained – maybe normally his eyes weren't always so heavy, his face so forlorn. But it didn't matter. Des was fired up and on his soapbox.

'I'll warn you – I am o-pin-ion-ated,' he blustered from the sofa, with an estuary maw.

Des seemed to have two opinions: that Britain was very, very bad, and China was very, very good: 'I won't 'ave a bad word said against China.'

'What do you think about Tiananmen Square?' I prodded.

'People in glass houses, right … People from the British Empire can't criticise the Eastern Empire.'

'May I ask – why did you leave the UK?'

'Don't go there,' he warned, a deep groove appearing between his brows. 'You don't 'afta go there.' He pulled on his cigarette.

This was prime bait – I instantly wanted to go there.

'In the UK,' Des continued, 'you get up, 'ave breakfast, go to work for eight hours, come 'ome, lock the door and turn on the TV. That isn't life.'

Des sank his beer, and asked me: 'How would you say 7/7 was reported?'

'Well, I guess it was over-reported.'

'*Exactly!* See – the west is feeding the fire with bad news.

Chinese papers only have good news – why make Chinese people's lives unhappy by telling them the shit stuff? I won't contradict the government because they're doing their best for the country.'

Goran, silent till now, spoke briefly to support his friend's opinion. 'You can open up the Reuters website here, but not the pages on China.'

Des wholly agreed with China's apparent preference to publish bad western news and good Chinese news: 'They want the Chinese to look at the west and think, "You crazy bastards!"'

Des turned to Goran: 'What time you starting drinking, then?'

Goran grumbled something and left for the kitchen, where there must have been a hundred empty beer bottles. If they were an unlikely couple, beer was their bond. I was going to have to mobilise my drinking boots.

Des stormed on, comparing the States' reaction to Hurricane Katrina to the Chinese response to the Sichuan earthquake.

'Thousands of Chinese converged on this area for the love of their country,' he trumpeted. 'Now you wouldn't get that in the States, and never in the UK.'

Des was thumping my patriotic buttons.

'Well,' I said defensively, 'people talked about a return of Blitz spirit during the 2007 floods.'

'The last time we saw the Blitz spirit,' he said, shaking his beer bottle agressively, 'was in 1973 on the Queen's Birthday. Every street in the UK organised a party, and while we were out party-ing, houses were robbed. Thatcherism made everybody greedy.'

Not that Thatcher came into power until 1979, but Des evidently didn't need hard fact when there was so much hot air.

'And you don't see greed here?' I said.

'Yeah, but the Chinese don't shit on their own doorstep.'

Des was quite high on fight and beer now.

All introductions were surreal, given that total strangers from different worlds were suddenly obliged to get on, but this was runaway. And Des wasn't even my host. That no combat rule – in the face of such blinkered opinion and national attack – was feeling strained. I willed Goran, who I *did* want to talk to, to come back from the kitchen. I could hear hot fat spitting and crackling – someone's lunch was on its way.

'I had to get away from Britain,' Des ranted, 'because I couldn't watch the news anymore with all that bias.'

'So you came to China for openness and objectivity,' I rejoined.

'I don't care about it,' he said vaguely, puffing his chest. Rational debate, I realised through clenched teeth, was impossible, when he just said whatever was convenient to his argument.

Never was I so happy to see a mountain of hot, crispy French toast. As Goran distributed it, I tried to steer the attention his way.

Where was he from in Serbia?

'Novi Sad.'

But Des grabbed it: 'Do you think what happened in Yugoslavia could happen in the UK?'

It was as if Des wanted Goran to say yes – it would prove him right.

'No,' Goran tutted. 'What happened in Yugoslavia was the result of being suppressed for forty years, when we couldn't say anything or we'd be shot.'

Goran acted like Des's long-suffering spouse, but it was a relatively new arrangement. Goran had moved to Guilin in

March, when he joined couchsurfing and started teaching at the same school as Des. So he wasn't really a 'full-time lazy person'.

Des wrapped his hands around the back of his head and inhaled deeply, saying: 'I am all about quality of life and I've got it all right here.'

'But don't you feel you like you're cheating sometimes?' said Goran, his brow furrowed. 'Like this lifestyle has to stop at some point, and you have to go back and face the bills?'

'I left because I couldn't be what I wanted to be back home,' Des said, leadingly.

There was a serious reason why Des couldn't go back and I was determined to find it. Maybe alcohol would spill it.

But first, I wanted less Des, more Goran, who, it transpired, was a reluctant Ambassador. Guilin's previous Ambassador didn't want the honour anymore and had put Goran forward. But, like his forerunner, Goran now wanted a break from couchsurfing.

'I had 200 people marching through over three or four months – the stories repeated themselves with most guests.'

My eyes widened in mild horror to hear the law of diminishing returns in action.

Goran went on: 'Sometimes I felt like a whore. People would stay for a week, spend one hour with me and leave a reference saying how great I was.'

'Oh, there was that really self-centred Chinese girl,' said Des, back in play. 'One girl, right, came into my room when my door was shut and used my computer. She could see what porn I was downloading.'

I laughed.

'You can laugh, but I was 'n' all.'

'Shall we go to Rosemary's?' Goran sighed.

Anywhere – Des's constant noise was making me feel claustrophobic. Rosemary's was an ex-pat bar in town, which required a walk through Guilin's red light district. As we passed the *Bladerunner*-esque, dark and murky massage parlours, Des said in a low voice, 'It's the same with everything in China. If you need to know, you know. If you don't, you don't ask.'

Des seemed to know.

We were joined in Rosemary's by an American manufacturing entrepreneur, Chris, and his Chinese wife; Gloria, a fruity black Kenyan teacher with a love of brandy, a hearty laugh and a heavy heart; Kevin, the previous City Ambassador – a young Chinese student; and Diana, a groovy and mellow fifty-something teacher and couchsurfer from Australia.

Predictably, Des carried on where he'd left off, with a beer and his simplistic line that China was far superior to the UK. Restricted by couchsurfing etiquette, I sat back. Who was going to challenge him, I wondered.

'Look,' said Chris, tersely. 'You make the UK sound like hell on earth. Christ, wake up and smell the coffee.'

'Britain is more controlled than China,' Des argued, getting louder. 'It's just that we attach more importance to what we think is reality there.'

'If someone spouts bullshit in the west, you can say so.' Chris was getting worked up. 'Here it's all about saving face. It's about *guangxi* – it means 'relationships', and it's huge between businesses and government. If I have more power than you, then you talk 'happy talk' to me. Happy talk is bullshit, and that's how they do business. Eighty per cent of them don't believe in it but they do it to save face.'

As if in a murder-mystery party, we were all drawn in, whether we liked it or not. Other conversations were attempted, but all paths led back to Des and his blind love of China. Like a good fight, just watching it activated my adrenaline.

'Yeah well, most of my UK schoolmates got cancer because we were surrounded by steel and chemical works,' said Des, in a typical tangent.

'You don't think there's cancer here? Man, you're *describing* China,' said Chris, exasperated.

Goran was on his mobile – it sounded like it concerned my couch.

'I'm sorry – I already have a couchsurfer. I can see if anyone else could take you …. Okay, I'll meet you at mine in thirty minutes.'

Whoever it was had impressive tenacity.

Goran had to go, he announced: 'I have to meet a Russian hitchhiker.' It seemed I'd be sharing the living room with them.

Well, I knew it wasn't Bulat. Maybe Stasya?

'Yes – you know her?'

My old ally! This was further grist to the city mill – coincidences were surely much rarer in villages.

The party's crashing anti-hero left abruptly and drunkenly with Goran. The large hole was quickly filled by Chris.

'I'm astounded Des doesn't read a newspaper. If he knew the reality he couldn't say this shit. The point is,' he said firmly, 'Des is bitter because he couldn't be an alcoholic teacher in the UK.'

There – Des was out. It was so simple. I wondered how many of the others at the table 'cheated on life' out here, as Goran put it.

'No girl would look at Des in the west,' continued Chris, the veins on his forehead throbbing. 'I mean – no girl would look at me. I feel like a fucking king here.'

China – dirt cheap, abundant, with easy work for degree-less teachers and minimal interference from a state disinterested in ex-pat activity – was a new colony for escapists.

But the underside wasn't so rosy. Chris, with nine years in business here, and a Chinese wife, had seen it.

'China is moving at a camel's pace on a social level. My wife has no freedom. Des thinks this country is happy. Are you kidding? *Who* is fucking happy? They can't be gay, they can't be religious, they can't be themselves. They study so hard at school, but there aren't enough places at university. They pay, they cheat and they still can't get a job. Des says he feels safe here – well, the Chinese don't feel safe. Six years ago the Family Planning Committee broke down the door of my friend, eight and a half months pregnant with her second child. They cut her open and put a needle in her unborn child's head.'

The table drew a collective gasp. Then Gloria piped up. 'But your friend is breaking the law – if you live by the rules, you're fine. Abortion is free. Okay – it's very wrong to kill babies but why not take pills?'

'They're too shy here to talk about sexual stuff. They don't have sex education because it's frowned upon. They can't complain here. Kevin is not an idiot. He knows his place. He knows it's better to pretend that China is this great utopia. But China is not the Olympics.'

Kevin wasn't hanging around, he said: he'd travel for a few years and then get to Poland. A relative's friend lived there. Or Mexico, where he had a Canadian friend. I felt for his optimistic shot in the dark.

It was like watching a live documentary – I had fallen quite passive, gripped by the revelations. Chris had more to get off his chest. He'd seen child labour used in manufacturing one of his products, and the audits were a travesty – he'd discovered that the fire stations in his factory were simply props, and that it would cost 500,000 yen to install real ones. He'd had to print eighteen months' worth of fake timecards because his workers refused to work shorter hours.

'No factory can pass an audit,' he revealed. 'But you can if you pay 20,000 yen. It's what Wal-Mart and Toys 'R' Us do – that's why they pay a third party so they can keep their hands clean. In Shenzhen, there's even a factory that's just for show – the inspectors know too, but so long as they do their job, everyone is fine with it.'

'*Stas*ya!'

It was like an old friend from home had come to visit. But then, couchsurfing had redefined the concept of friendship. In the field, with our shared experience, Stasya *was* my old friend. We might not have been close, but it was easy. I jumped up and hugged her. She seemed … drained. But she had new pink hair – DIY, she said. Like turning from one drug to another, I lapped up her arrival as a pleasing diversion. I wanted to hear all about hitchhiking in China.

I could have just shut my eyes and listened to the lullaby of Stasya's tuneful Russian voice.

'Mmmm, if Chinese man stops by the road, it's because their car is in trouble,' she explained, sipping a thrifty glass of boiled water. 'If foreign girl stands by the road, they think you're in very, very trouble. It's very big difference to Russian hospitality – my drivers buy me so much food so I don't die and then fifteen minutes later, they buy me dinner. They can't believe I'm not hungry. And nobody speak English so it's really …' she threw out her arms with grand melodrama, 'theatre!'

But no one had invited her into their home: 'Actually, that would be very strange for them.'

I wanted to squeeze her in congratulations. Leaving one's comfort zone was directly correlated to the reward of adventure.

Across the table, I caught Goran's eye. With all these other protagonists, we had still barely talked. But Kevin wanted to take Stasya and me to see the 'world's largest artificial waterfall' at the Waterfall Hotel, which was switched on for ten minutes each evening. Then someone wanted a donkey burger (sadly not a euphemism) from the street – this would do as dinner. It turned out to be sweet and tender, not unlike my nibble of horse. Next, Gloria wanted to buy some miniature brandies for the (short) walk to the next bar, so I tagged along with her.

How was it to be black here?

'At fust it was difficult,' she said, in a rich Kenyan accent. 'They said, "Oh you smell". After a while, I said, "Oh you smell too."' She screeched with laughter.

Gloria taught out in a village, which was boring, she said: 'Just a school and some rice fields.'

Eccentric, honest and warm, Gloria was immensely, immediately, likeable.

The Chris Show was still running when we regrouped in the next bar, but I resisted joining in, otherwise I'd never get to Goran. But I was curious about Diana, a 52-year-old divorcee with a salt-and-pepper pixie crop and two adult sons.

'Couchsurfing has brought the world together again,' she reflected, as we stood at the bar table together.

It was words like these that made couchsurfing sound like a cult, but she was right.

'Society is segregating,' she said. 'We only live within our groups. It's nice meeting people from different countries – you realise we all have something in common.'

'Isn't couchsurfing all a bit uncomfortable?' Chris chipped in.

'Yes!' I wanted to cry.

'Well, we work around each other,' said Diana, nimbly. She paused, adding: 'I put it like this: when they walk in, you shake their hands and when they leave, you hug.'

That was a nice way of putting it.

Without Des, I liked this little gang – informed, immersed free thinkers, without the affectations of trendies or travellers. But I knew Goran the least – I was avoiding him, I realised, because he was a single Serbian male a year younger than The Emperor, and it all felt too ... dangerous. Not that Goran came close. Kind, genuine and not unhandsome, he still couldn't touch The Emperor.

'What about one night stands?' Chris asked again.

'There is always a question of that,' said Goran.

I rocked with the double-take.

'I don't want to put this pressure on my guests,' Goran continued. 'So I wait for them to suggest it.'

I didn't like the news – I didn't want to have to think of Goran like that, nor him me.

After a few more sharpeners, Gloria, Goran and I found ourselves at Guilin's 'fresh, new' nightclub, Ragazza. Finally, Goran and I were pushed together. Stasya had gone home – clubbing often didn't appeal after weeks on the road.

Goran, I realised, *was* the Lebowski Dude. We finally talked, tête-à-tête, at one of the numerous bar tables, as we supped on beer and cocktails. Something of a drifter, he'd taken full advantage of white-man privileges since arriving in China in 2004.

He'd been quickly scouted by an American, asking him to 'name his price'. $1,000 a week, said the savvy Goran. Done. His job was to 'take photos' at an American carnival in China. They wanted eastern Europeans, Goran explained, 'because we are cheaper than westerners.' He'd also worked in clubs as the western 'manager', then taught himself how to be a TEFL teacher.

'You can learn on line in a matter of hours,' he said, dropping his shoulders in shame. 'And my English isn't even perfect. I make a lot of mistakes.'

That downcast countenance never really left Goran. Perhaps it stemmed from a disappointment in himself? Perhaps the pain of his war-torn homeland? Or perhaps it was caused by the very lonely pursuit of drifting.

Stasya was still on Goran's computer when we got home. We had to choose between the sofa or a mattress on the floor. Now 3am, it didn't matter. I wasn't going to be able to sleep. The longer the day, the harder it was.

12TH DECEMBER

Was it deliberate, I wondered, that at 8am Des clopped about in his fancy shoes, cooking bacon and whistling into our sleep? I had my suspicions. He was off on a party weekend, so I buried myself under my sleeping bag until he'd departed: that, alas, was the last we saw of him.

One of us was responsible for a toilet blocked with what looked like muddy river water. Such things happened in homes, so such things happened when couchsurfing. It was at least an incentive to leave Goran's sanctuary. Goran had provided breakfast: filter coffee, a glass of full-fat milk each, and mini pastries;

we had Wi-Fi and no will to leave. I even put on a wash – a sign of a good atmosphere.

What should we do in Guilin, we asked Goran, lazily leaning on his knowledge. Would Goran like to come with us? (I didn't want to be another couchsurfer that treated him like a 'whore'.)

'I don't do sightseeing,' he said, with Slavic directness.

I liked that – now.

Goran's if-you-only-do-one-thing recommendation was Seven Star Park, Guilin's serene, if over-produced, 137-hectare city park filled with karst towers, limestone caves and manacled, photo-op peacocks. It was a perfect, cloudless day, and a benign sun warmed our wintered faces. But there was an entry fee to pay. Stasya didn't do entry fees. From her bag, she produced an official-looking stamped document in Cyrillic, which apparently stated she was part of a charitable foundation working to save the world (or something like that). It was pure Krotov, the Russian hitchhiking guru who also recommended cadging a lift by offering a torn-up bank note, which would then be refused. After the Chinese ticket office proved nonplussed, Stasya beckoned me through a gap in the broken wall.

'Hello?' A builder was shouting at us as we illicitly entered the park.

Stasya waved her arms in the air at him: 'Hello!'

Genius – why not deflect the unwanted attention by throwing unwanted attention right back. We pushed on, wandering without direction, untangling the stifling effects of couchsurfing. Stasya was tired: she was over couchsurfing's constant social demands.

'I hate always having to entertain your host with interesting stories,' she said. 'Sometimes I don't want to talk; I just want to sleep.'

She wouldn't couchsurf in her next stop, Yangshuo (we would be close! Both still in Guangxi province, Xingping village was only ten kilometres away). Besides, she said, she wanted to think about her future. It was true – there little space for personal contemplation when couchsurfing.

I devoured Stasya's every word – we'd only have a few hours together before she left that afternoon. I was leaving for Xingping the next morning. I knew nothing about it other than the guidebook's one-line description: 'a picturesque village on the Li River'.

Stasya understood implicitly the psychological drama of couchsurfing. It was as if my soul was being aired in a warm, light breeze. And she showed me The Life Vicarious.

'There's one guy in our hitchhiking community who only spends $300 in half a year – but he is eating only rice,' Stasya said.

But of course, it wasn't just about economy: plenty of hitchhikers could afford to buy a train ticket but wanted the experience. She laughed as she described the hiker type kitted out in new, expensive equipment, trying to persuade drivers they needed a lift. Stasya didn't have that problem: her black plimsolls, with one green lace and one orange, were falling apart.

'They come from China,' she chuckled. 'I think they choose to stay in China.'

Stasya's Chinese was far superior to mine by now – as a hitchhiker, she was really on the ground. I admired her fortitude: she was exposing me! But the hitchhiking community was a large, widespread and 'very close' support system, she said. She'd be spending Christmas with them in Cambodia or Thailand.

The Seven Star Cave – an underground limestone world full of stalagmites and 'tites – became our approximate target, and, eventually, another cost. Stasya and I were on different budgets, so I just bought her ticket without consultation, only to discover she was in the process of inveigling some locals into buying our tickets at the local rate. We played in the pitch black, exploring and imposing dramatic silences. Alone, I'd have been purposeless; with Stasya, I stopped questioning – her presence made me present.

We ambled back at an almost reverse pace, willing the day to extend.

★

Goran's toilet was still muddy and Goran now had an upset stomach, so, after a curious, protracted intimacy when Goran took down his underwear from the line so I could hang mine up, I was starting to feel like I knew too much. Goran and I would meet later for his couchsurfing dinner so I stepped back out with Stasya to see her on to her bus – she was even taking a break from hitchhiking.

Alone again, I loafed along the wide, smooth Li River, pecking at some fragrant and powdery Osmanthus flower cake. Guilin meant 'forest of Sweet Osmanthus', so-named for its ample coverage of the nubby little flowery trees. I fed off the meditative rhythm of half a dozen fishermen who fished its waters together yet neatly spaced apart, like semibreves on a musical score, each settled in their own quiet zones. I envied them – since Ollie's departure, I had either been very together with, or very apart from people. On my way to meet Goran, I overheard three young American guys wondering where to go for dinner. I couldn't help feel smug without such needs.

Guilin's couchsurfing group that night comprised Diana,

Gloria, and JC, a sensible 31-year-old Frenchman. Goran was disappointed – low attendance figures seemed an ongoing problem. Goran took us to Guilinese, a restaurant set out like a giant food mall, where whatever we wanted was on the menu. Overwhelmed, I submitted to the others' choice – pork dumplings, sticky aubergine, fried rice and slippery, garlicky greens. And to their conversation: plans for Christmas in Guilin. I detected a lingering sense of melancholy and emptiness – perhaps Christmas reminded them of what they'd left behind. I didn't want to tell them how much I was looking forward to going home for the festivities – Christmas couldn't have more meaning for me.

Then we were three: Gloria, Goran and me. For my last night before my river ride to Xingping the next day, we settled in Rosemary's, where Goran shotted tequila and chased with beer and Gloria cupped her habitual brandy. I was glad for the low attendance – I wanted to hang out with Goran. I wanted to find out what had happened to his Slavic fire.

Perhaps it had been extinguished during his twenties. Goran's home town, Novi Sad, was Serbia's second city and a major target of NATO bombing during the 1999 Kosovo crisis. His apartment had been 300 metres from NATO's very first hit in Serbia: Petrovaradin Bridge over the Danube. And that was just the beginning; the city was left without power, water and communications.

'So what did us young people do?' Goran asked calmly. 'We had really big parties. Life was so cheap – we didn't want to stay in our basements. The government fixed it to keep us happy – alcohol was easy, buying food was less so. It was bread and circuses.'

Having ridden BMXs professionally, Goran quickly spent all his cash, 'trying everything', he admitted.

And Gloria – she hailed from the Kisii tribe of the town of Bosongo in south-west Kenya.

'Bosongo means "belonging to the white man",' said Gloria, indignantly. 'I have issues with British men for the pain they caused my country.'

I avoided her gaze. But Gloria had moved on: 'Life in China is better than Kenya.'

Goran, Des, Gloria – maybe others – all united by alcohol and all colonialists of a kind, were living a life in hedonistic exile that they couldn't lead at home. Perhaps it was why they defended China – it was a very Chinese state of mind: let me do my thing, and I'll let you do yours.

CHAPTER 18

XINGPING: SO VILLAGE

13TH DECEMBER

China's great human migration – 130 million villagers heading to the production lines over the course of three decades – started to reverse in 2008 in line with export demand. I joined the contraflow back to the countryside.

It was all right for me, of course. I was the tourist, so I found it stirring to observe orange pith drying in the sun outside crumbly, yellow-brick houses with holey ceilings so that it could be sold on (for a pithance?). I whooped when I saw water buffalo being herded by a shepherd in just his underpants. And when I saw a crowd gathering to witness the event of the year, a lorry unloading an oil drum, I practically cried out loud: 'So village!'

But just half an hour from Xingping, my fun was rudely interrupted by a text from my next host, Leo: 'We are now taking the train to Yunnan.'

Yunnan? Yunnan was the neighbouring province. I shook my phone crossly.

'Go to the youth hostel,' his message said. 'And you will find Axiang. She will host you.'

I imagined dinner for one and an empty youth hostel dorm. Now I was heading out to nowhere for nobody. So this is what happened when you went couchsurfing in villages.

Xingping had been put on the map when it was put on the twenty yuan note: a fact not lost on Chinese tourists who, according to Goran, would rush off the boat with their cameras to scramble to the position that matched the note's karst-tower scenery. On arrival, I realised that among all these surreal obelisks, there wasn't room for anything larger than a village in any case. Some of Xingping's buildings were said to date from the Qing and Ming dynasties, but as I wandered down a quiet, grey brick lane lined with simple, low, white-painted buildings, it was hard to distinguish which had just been built very badly and which had been built a long time ago. I rubbernecked in through open doors, to see abacuses on scrubbed wooden tables, scalped basketballs serving as buckets, and Mao posters in pride of place by the TV (the real rural god).

At the hostel reception, I found a cereal bowl containing a little water and three sad goldfish, and Axiang, a tall, young girl in a white sporty zip-up top and relief-effect wrinkled jeans (as all young Chinese people were wearing). Her long, neat hair was carefully tied into a schoolgirl's ponytail, while her high eyebrows and structured face suggested an ethnicity other than Han. Eventually, after speaking very slowly indeed and finally remembering Leo's Chinese name, Liu, I managed to make my introduction. Axiang was – I think – the 21-year-old niece of my absent host's wife. She smiled amiably and said, 'Home now?'

Past various shops, including 'Monopolying shop of tree root carving and jade article', Axiang led me through Xingping's main road, a gritty dirt track. Shopkeepers and passers-by called out affectionately to her but we were busy trying to communicate. I only fully grasped the extent of our language barrier when, expecting to arrive at her parents' farm where she and her brother also lived, we turned off the street into a grain store, and upstairs into an empty apartment.

Any lingering cynicism about being obliged to be involved with the youth hostel – which would surely involve some kind of profiteering – melted right into my boots when, with the ungrudging flourish of a 1950s housewife, Axiang made up my bed. I had a clean, empty twin room to myself – new-ish and charmless, but with a view on to the karst hills.

'Shower?' she said.

I followed her through a kitchen with no sink, fridge or any cooking facilities save a pressure cooker, and into an empty room with a hole in the floor for a toilet. Outside stood a three-foot high gas canister. Axiang demonstrated how to get hot water by opening the gas.

'Bad smell,' she said, frowning and waving her hand.

Goran had told me there was a big problem with people being poisoned to death by leaking gas canisters – this was the reality of under-developed village life.

So where did her parents sleep?

'Yunnan!'

And her brother?

'Yunnan!'

Without Leo, would this be the extent of conversation in Xingping?

'Do you hungry?'

Yes, I could do hungry. It was dark when Axiang walked me to the youth hostel's café, situated on Xingping's other main road, the narrow lane. When I saw the exposed brickwork, bamboo furniture and clean table linen, I didn't mind the possible profiteering. Besides, maybe it was the only choice. It was empty save one twenty-something Chinese tourist flicking through her digital camera. Apparently keen to connect with man again, she translated for me when it was obvious that Axiang and I were struggling to understand each other. The kitchen closed at 7.30pm (*7.30!*), and Axiang would be working at the hostel till midnight.

'Why don't you order something sensible like a sandwich,' said the Chinese tourist, overhearing me order 'taro'.

Because I wanted to know what taro was. It turned out to be a local tuber that tasted in between a chestnut and sweet potato – deliciously crumbly, sweet and nutty. She introduced herself to me – Evelyn, a Taiwanese girl who'd quit her job in Shenzhen to go travelling.

'So what is there to do here?' I asked.

'Oh, everywhere shuts at 7.30. There's no nightlife.'

I didn't want nightlife, I just wanted somewhere to go.

'People go home and watch TV.'

That would do. I soon realised that chancing upon Evelyn was a small miracle. She knew the only place to hang out – the youth hostel – and was the only person I could hang out with. Being alone when I wasn't meant to be alone was so disappointing.

'This is amazing to see historical architecture,' said Evelyn, pointing up at the disintegrating houses as we drifted back. 'In Taiwan, we don't see so much old buildings.'

Old meant poor.

'We look very wealthy here,' she warned. 'Watch yourself.'

Through the unlit lanes, Evelyn located the empty youth

hostel, where Axiang was back on duty at reception: an optimistic shift given that the last bus in was at 6pm.

So this, for today, was countryside couchsurfing: Evelyn and I sat 'together apart' in a comfortable silence for several hours on a wooden bench in the youth hostel's common area. We were alone but for two Chinese girls near us, quietly zoomed-in on their laptops. The peace was almost shocking. Finally, there was space to think. Or, even, not to think.

A message from Stasya! She was thinking of coming to Xingping the next day. She would share this peace well. Perhaps she, too, was looking for some kind of constancy, someone to whom she didn't have to explain herself from scratch. I responded with encouraging noises. This funny little place was somehow looking after me.

In three days' time I'd be in Shanghai, my trip's finale. Its couchsurfing scene looked typical of China: mostly over-experienced ex-pats and a few novice natives. How about, I thought, a safety shot and a wild card? There was the 28-year-old Italian Nomadic Ambassador, Manfred, with 150 references who, going by his Chinese name of 'Bei XiaoFei', suggested some amount of cultural participation. And the thirty-year-old David, a married Chinese Protestant in the missionary position – 'full of love' because he'd finally found God. The car-crash voyeurism, I must admit, amused me. Was I going to get bible-bashed?

My mental ceasefire was briefly disrupted.

'Want tour tomorrow?' It was Axiang.

'No thanks, but perhaps a game of ping-pong?' This was the perfect diversion, surely – no English or Chinese necessary.

She gave me a searching look.

'Ping-pong!' I acted it out, I drew it for her.

'Aaah! Ping-pang Ch'iu!'

It was agreed, and after an abortive attempt to ask for her address (there wasn't one), and saying farewell to Evelyn who was leaving the next day, I went home.

✪

At first, I thought the enormous spider on my bedroom wall, that spanned at least ten centimetres, was a plastic joke. Then it twitched. I ran.

I leapt into action, hunting down a jam-jar trap large enough to contain it. Obviously, by the time I'd returned, it had disappeared – into my rucksack? Into my bed? Into my nightmares. I looked in the living room – perhaps I could sleep on the sofa. No sofa. As I froze in my bedroom, desperate to sleep, I understood that this was the kind of challenge travelling was supposed to throw at you. Now I was supposed to solve it.

Goran – maybe Goran would know if it was dangerous. I started composing a text ... I couldn't send Goran a text. I sent it to Leo. He never responded. I sent a simplified version to Axiang, who was staying at the youth hostel that night.

'NO!' she wrote. 'Dont can then hurt.' And then, a few minutes later, 'I come to home.'

'Is it a friend,' I asked.

Axiang didn't seem in the slightest bit worried by it when she got home, which, while reassuring, left me with the small matter of a large spider at large in my room. Eventually, I gave up trying to control the situation. It was a realisation of far-reaching implications. What happens when you stop worrying? Maybe nothing.

Perhaps I should try it.

14TH DECEMBER

I survived the night and the suicide shower to be able to squeeze a few more facts out of Axiang. She was from the Dai tribe (closely related to Thai people). She showed me a Myanmar bank note for 1,000 kyat ($1), which the Dai tribe spent in Yunnan. She showed me mythical-looking photos of her in colourful, long dresses in lush grasses and on bamboo rafts. When you couldn't take conversation for granted, making these small steps was hugely warming.

We both 'did hungry', so she took me to 'nooduh' – a noodle kitchen up the gritty track. With its makeshift roof and a bloke watching telly in the corner, it felt more like someone's house. Communicating and eating was too much for breakfast so we ate our spicy peanut noodles in complicit silence. Details of the day ahead were firmly trapped behind the language barrier. I wondered what on earth I'd be doing. Axiang led me to the youth hostel café. My dumping ground? No – she returned after a brief disappearance with two ping-pong bats and some balls. I clasped my hands together in the universal sign for joy – her English might not have been up to much, but she was fluent in hospitality.

A lone thirteen-year-old was shooting baskets in the empty assembly ground of Xingping's school. With three cement-clad blocks for ping-pong tables and old greying planks for nets, Axiang and I arranged ourselves at either end of the least ramshackle one.

Pop, pop, pop!

'Sorry!'

Pop, pop, pop!

'Sorry!'

Axiang and I batted away contentedly under a clement, over-cast sky, bound together in Olympic universality. I mimicked her Chinese-style grip, but it didn't prepare me for when the thirteen-year-old strode over, took Axiang's bat and took me on.

'Sorry, sorry, sorry!'

His serves continuously flew through my elbows. He gave up on me eventually, and Axiang and I pop-pop-popped until her phone rang.

'Your friend café.'

Tracking me down in Xingping was well within Stasya's considerable travelling talents. We found her tending a mug of hot water at the youth hostel's cafe, threatening to play on a *hulusi*, a Dai bamboo flute with a gourd wind chest. It was pure Stasya. Axiang had to work, so I distracted Stasya with a walk through Xingping.

I found myself a weather vane to Stasya's blithe breeze. Coloured by her sense of adventure, we meandered through Xingping, truffling for treasure. We would take the smallest alley and see where it led, push open doors into houses, workshops, mahjong circles – nobody seemed to mind or care.

Across the Li River, where bamboo rafts waited patiently for summer tourists, we found juicy farmland crammed in amongst the limestone humps. In a colour-saturated oasis full of orange trees, banana trees, chilli bushes, strawberries, and plenty more mysterious flora, I had an urge to harvest.

'I want to pick an orange,' I whispered, high on the oxygen. 'But there's that local watching us in the distance.'

'I was thinking the same,' Stasya giggled.

The life we witnessed here was about as far away from my

London life as I'd seen all journey. I was sad not to have made it into a Russian village, I said.

'Mmmm, it is so sad,' Stasya lamented, as we passed a string of lumpy, handmade sausages drying in the wind. 'Sad you don't go, but also sad in the villages. All young people leave, so now it is only old people. They all drink alcohol and the farmers can't get nobody to work with them. It's tough – there is often no running water.'

We headed back to Xingping, as Stasya had to catch her bus back to Yangshuo. Her mood seemed grey – the only work she had found in Thailand would keep her in food but not money, so she was contemplating returning to St Petersburg. She was stressed by the not knowing. Here was the contradiction of free-dom: we could be whatever and wherever we liked out here, but without routine and givens, we were subjected to the very drain-ing effects of constant flight. Routines didn't have a good image, but not having to think about, say, where to sleep that night, freed the mind to travel to other places. I found it so unsettling to be so far away from the roots that I had grown for so long. And Stasya, as a hitchhiker, travelling indefinitely, had even fewer knowns.

As we stepped out from the undergrowth, Stasya, smirking, yanked up her jumper to reveal a pale, ample ... orange. This was her swan song – I knew I wouldn't see her again. It was a bitter-sweet goodbye: I felt sorry yet blessed.

Now what? Without Evelyn, what prospect for another night in the youth hostel? Perhaps I should make a run for Yangshuo, the nearest town. On couchsurfing, I'd seen a private English college there that traded bedrooms and two meals a day for up to ten couchsurfers prepared to spend two hours at their daily

English Speaking Club. And I loved those opportunities – they presented an engaging mix of learning new perspectives and national validation. But I couldn't meet their conditions as my train for Shanghai left before it started.

I took a path – any path – and headed uphill. I wanted to touch those eerie karst hills that surrounded Xingping like an invasion of monstrous green ghosts. I walked and walked, passing the circular, stonewall burial grounds and into the wilderness where butterflies perched on tiny purple Alpine flowers and where birds, veiled by fir trees, filled the air with song. For three hours, I didn't see or hear man, or even the mark of man. In China, this was a total luxury. The clearing in space and in my mind was like the refuge of meditation. This was worth the harangue in Chengdu.

The beauty of a village is that it doesn't take long to conquer. After twenty-four hours, I had done all I could do, and all without the need for motorised transport. I was thinking about that English college. And the prospect of another night with the colossal arachnid. I called the college and spoke to a Chinese man called Gary – yes, it was fine to come that afternoon. I hurriedly bought Axiang a gift box of local cakes and explained I was leaving. She opened and closed her mouth like a fish coming up for air. But it wasn't that Xingping was worth leaving, more that the college was worth visiting. Villages were for peace, cities were for people.

CHAPTER 19

YANGSHUO: THE SCHOOL OF LIFE

Leaving quaint Xingping for the backpackers' paradise of Yangshuo felt instantly regrettable. I cringed at the majority rule of young westerners sporting their new tattoos, dressed in ethnic threads, queuing for pizza. This wasn't real China, but a safe white enclave. Fortunately I had a different Yangshuo to go to.

At the end of a calm, evergreen-filled avenue running parallel to a still canal on the edge of town just before the soaring karst peaks took over entirely, a sunshine-yellow banner was stretched across a tall white house. 'Zhuo Yue English College'.

It was Sunday, and deserted. A couple of dogs played in the courtyard by another giant banner: 'English only!'

I weaved through some plastic curtains into the Teaching Department.

'Hello?'

A young east-Asian woman appeared. I spoke carefully and slowly: 'I'm looking for Gary. I'm a couchsurfer.'

'Oh, sure,' she said briskly, in an American accent.

She left me in the office looking at Level 4's topics – work-related stress, conspiracy theories, corporate hospitality.

'Gary, someone's here for you.' She returned and introduced herself: Mia from the Philippines – she was a teacher here.

Wearing a navy tracksuit and askew but modern black spectacles, the 21-year-old Gary seemed to be jogging on the spot, or was he just running over with energy? I shook his warm hand.

'Hi!' He flashed a melon-slice grin.

Gary had the temperament of a spaniel just freed from his kennel: bouncy, cheery and seemingly happy to see *anyone*. It was infectious. He took one of my bags and led me out of the school.

As we walked through the Yangshuo dusk, I apologised about my early Shanghai train. Maybe I could help in the office? In the school kitchen? Maybe I could play badminton or ping-pong with the students?

'No problem!' said Gary, bobbing away. 'You can speak with my high-school friend Serena – she wants to practise her English.'

In a dark side-street, too narrow for cars, Gary opened a house door on to a living room and introduced me to Serena, who was watching a TV game show. Gary disappeared while Serena and I were left to chat.

'Nice To Meet You!' she enunciated, like a recorded message. Tripping up on small talk, it quickly emerged that there wasn't much English to practise. Gary returned and I handed over my gift box of local cakes. I had to find a way to get out of speaking nursery rhymes with Serena – I wasn't going to learn anything about China this way.

The school's modern accommodation block where its residential students stayed was just opposite. Inside, each step we climbed was emblazoned with an English expression. As we stepped over 'Let's hope for the best', 'Let me put it this way', and 'Take it or leave it,' and up to the second floor, I asked Gary if any other couchsurfers were staying at the moment.

Oh yes – they always had couchsurfers. Three had just left that day, and two remained. I'd be sharing a room with Stephanie from Quebec.

'Stephanie?' Gary knocked on a door off a central, enclosed courtyard. No answer. Stephanie from Quebec was going to have to remain a mystery, although her possessions – clothes, bags, snacks – had laid claim to both single beds. It wasn't a large room, and whatever space there was had been filled with new, three-star frills: a large TV, a DVD player, drawers and wardrobe, and, my favourite, a hot-and-cold water dispenser, for tea on tap. And this was my first couch with an ensuite bathroom (it even had a western toilet). This was a great deal for couchsurfers. But then it was a business transaction – couchsurfing gave the college those esteemed westerners.

Despite the luxuries, it was the room of an itinerant: cold (metaphorically and physically), damp and with no natural light. There wasn't much to stay for, so I left with Gary who got me a good price for Yangshuo's river-borne folk musical that night and a curious hot corn juice (essentially pureed sweetcorn chowder – sweet, creamy and gloopy).

'So will I see you tomorrow?' I asked, reluctant to lose my jolly guardian.

But Gary would be working so he gave me Serena's number. I was going to have to think fast.

✪

It was midnight but the sun still shone in room fourteen. Stephanie, a pretty, 21-year-old Chinese-Quebecoise, had scaled back her land grab and was now on the far bed, ready for some co-guest therapy. As she fed me wild-harvested kumquats and told me about Zhuo Yue English College, I basked in this girl's radiant, even-tempered energy. But first, she had lost some money in the room. I felt implicated. Theft and mysterious disappearances happened between strangers with no ideological connection. The possibility hadn't been an issue this trip.

Stephanie was a week into a month-long stay, she said in a mellifluous, French-Canadian accent – a month was pretty normal at Zhuo Yue. She seemed fully conversant with alternative travel options, before here having worked on an organic farm in the Cantonese province of Guangdong (just east of Guangxi), through the volunteer programme WWOOF (World Wide Opportunities on Organic Farms).

Organic farms in China?

In embryonic form, yes – forty Chinese hosts had signed up on the website. In return for working five or six hours a day, she had had free accommodation and food. Couchsurfing at Zhuo Yue sounded like an infinitely easier deal.

Avoiding the more bumpy option of staying in strangers' houses, Stephanie had mostly used couchsurfing in China to find travelling companions, and, through this, had had an excellent week with a Chinese-Australian girl. She was sick of shallow, fleeting encounters, she said, and wanted something more profound. It resonated: with most hosts capping guests' stays to three days, I was longing to root down.

Stephanie was having a little less success with 'companions' in Yangshuo. There was a guy she liked here: 'So I said to him, "Y'know, if you want to get closer …". But the concept is so strange to them. I was really surprised – I thought everybody would be getting together here.'

I was also surprised (and secretly entertained). Was that a typi-cal Canadian come-on? Stephanie was beautiful, with luxuriant, glossy hair, chic side-swept fringe, a smooth, peachy complexion and captivating tear-drop eyes.

'But nobody here thinks of anything more than friendship,' she continued, popping a kumquat in her mouth. 'They are very traditional, very simple-minded. This guy just sees me as a younger sister.'

I learnt a few more things from Stephanie: that there was only a six-hour window for hot water here, and that I'd missed it; that Zhuo Yue was – apparently – the best English School in Yangshuo (there were at least five in town); and yes, there *was* something I could do to make myself useful.

'You can call up the old students and ask them how they're getting on, what they're using their English for.'

Stephanie had done some office work for the college, including that very task. I was encouraged that after just one week, Stephanie was a fully paid-up member of Team Zhuo Yue. I thought back to Gary – there were no tensions here, no judgments or criticisms. The college looked like an extremely fun place to be. And I was glad not to feel such a freeloader. I could be useful at last.

15TH DECEMBER

'What do you normally have for breakfast?' Stephanie asked.

Stephanie was walking me to school (she didn't need to go to school, she was just helping me – she was on her way to the clothes market to buy 'pants').

I usually ate whatever was going – chaos had consumed any routine. But I liked things from bakeries.

'Oh – they have these delicious buns,' she said, smiling her perfect white teeth at me. 'I'll help you buy one if you like.'

I liked. Her considerable Mandarin (she spoke Cantonese as well) procured me a thick, doughy steamed bun stuffed with caramelised sugar and peanuts – it was dense, deep and plump, with a sweet, nutty crunch. That, I decided, was what I should normally have for breakfast.

Just where were these little godsends coming from, I wondered. As we passed through a part of Yangshuo completely free of backpackers, Stephanie primed me about Zhuo Yue. Its residential students were young professionals, she said, aged between eighteen and forty, mostly from the cities of Guangzhou and Shenzhen in Guangdong province, who'd worked for a few years but who wanted to earn more: 'They really dream of opening their own business. They're so motivated.'

The vision was rosy.

'Good morning, Charles!' Stephanie said lushly.

We were in the school's administrative office, a modest room with three desks and a small, round meeting table. Charles, a bespectacled Chinese man dressed in a charcoal suit and charcoal turtleneck, beamed from behind his desk. As if by teleportation, in the next second he was right by her side, hip to hip: an act that she received with – literally – open arms. I was transfixed as they flirted.

'You must stay longer,' Charles urged, still in her hold.

'I would have to have a proposal from you, Charles.' Stephanie pressed her face next to his. 'I would have to have you down on one knee for that.'

Was this, I wondered, the 'older brother'? It couldn't be – it was too overt.

'Romance' was short-lived: there was business to do. Stephanie introduced us – Charles was Zhuo Yue's 27-year-old manager. We shook hands, and Charles warmly welcomed me in. As a one-dayer, I was not much use to them, but Charles – just as Gary had – greeted me with plenty of warmth. Perhaps they were saving face. China's goodwill act of face-saving – concealing one's true feelings to protect others and avoid conflict – was really rather British. At this level, I liked it.

Stephanie set me up with my task, sitting me down at the meeting table with a spreadsheet of names and numbers and a printed script:

'Hello, this is [Your Name] from Zhuo Yue [jo-yoo-eh] English School ...

Is this a convenient time?

How has your english [sic] been since you graduated?

Are you still learning English now?' etc etc.

The ultimate goal was to encourage previous students to return for another course – I was going to be telemarketing. Charles had some tips: 'Try and get into a conversation with them. Ask them how about the weather, ask them how about their job. Talk a good level for their English.'

I nodded devotedly. I was looking forward to this. It would be like a one-on-one English Club. Given that I was the only native English speaker around, I was excited to be using my best asset and spreading some real, proper English. But it was too early to call, Charles decided – I should start at 10am.

Was there anything I wanted to see in Yangshuo, Stephanie asked. This girl was unstoppably nice. Yes – the farmers' market sounded interesting.

'Oh yes,' she nodded. 'It's the most explicit market I've seen in China for meat. They have dogs. Cooking dogs.'

My guidebook simply said it was 'dark and atmospheric'.

Chinese farmers didn't do much face-saving – it was much

more honest than a western farmers' market. I saw those dogs: cooked, ready to cook and ready to be killed. A slaughtered dog had been slung up outside the very cramped cage of five resigned hounds. At another stall was the even more shocking sight of two bald, stiff, and roasted dogs that looked like they'd been flash-cooked mid-snarl. I positioned my camera for a photo: 'Two yuan!' growled the farmer. So China.

✪

'Hello, this is Fleur from Jo-yoo-eh English College! I was just wondering how your English was coming along since you left the college.'

'Uh? Uh?'

[Repeat lines one and two.]

'Ha ha – I sorry. Very difficult. No understand.'

'Ah – okay! Hello. This. Is. Fleur. From. Jo-yoo-eh. English. College! How. Are. You?'

'I working.'

'Oh. Sorry. If. You. Are. Busy. There. Is. A. Forum. On. Jo-yoo-eh's. Website. Where. You. Can. Practise. Your. English. Shall. I. Spell. It?'

'J-O-H-N'

'Ah, lovely, thank you very much, John. Welcome back to Jo-Yoo-eh when you have free time!'

My best asset wasn't much use. This had been the eleventh nuisance call I'd made, except most of the numbers didn't work. When Hawkin (call number six) actually answered, I was so shocked, I forgot who I was calling and fluffed my lines.

My brush with marketing left me feeling rebellious. I went outside, where I spotted a British teacher.

✪

'Hello,' I said, as minorities spotting fellow minorities did. We chatted.

'Oh, you've been doing that ring-round,' he said. 'It's a complete waste of time – com*plete* waste of time.'

Few of the numbers worked apparently because Chinese people changed their mobile numbers frequently. I returned to the office with a new sense of uselessness,

Fortunately, a call came through on my phone for Charles, so I was – literally – off the hook. I leafed through their brochure– western men with travellers' beards pictured in classrooms and discussions. The college was using their investment well.

By now it was 11.30, and that meant lunchtime. I was pointed in the direction of outside, where I came across Stephanie chatting to Gary. She'd had lunch with the real big brother. I was surprised to hear she'd chosen dog. It was soft and juicy, she said nonchalantly. She was deftly cracking sunflower seeds in her mouth, spitting the husks on to the floor – Stephanie had so quickly gone local.

I gingerly stepped into a single-storey outhouse to find a liberal spread: green beans and minced pork, bamboo and black beans, raw tomatoes with shredded omelette, and a vat of rice. Alone, I felt a bit of an impostor, so I quickly latched on to some-one for conversation. 'Missy' was nearest to me, a thirty-some-thing Philippino teacher with an Australian boyfriend who ran his own bar in Yangshuo.

'Bar 98 – do you know it?' she asked.

'Umm, no, but then I'm probably Yangshuo's briefest visitor.'

'Ha ha – most people end up staying,' Missy said kindly. One of her friends had come for two days, 'and that was five years ago.'

'It sounds like Goa,' I said, pecking at my rice with chopsticks.

'Yes, I suppose it is,' she said. 'It's certainly not like China here.'

Missy scooped the remains of the rice into a bin-liner.

'It's for my Cocker Spaniel,' she explained.

I'd seen him playing in the yard earlier, shortly after my visit to the farmers' market, I said.

'Oh yuh,' she said, 'one of my students wrote a poem about my dog.'

'How sweet.'

'Well, no – it wasn't like that. It went, "Delicious dog/So sweet and tender …".' It was a dubious honour.

With one hour before my train to Shanghai, I returned to the office.

'How are you doing with that list, Fleur?' asked Charles.

Rumbled. Actually, one former student had said he *should* come back, but I'm sure he was just saving face. I told Charles just the first part and blushed when Charles instructed Stephanie to come back after English Club and finish the job.

Despite not paying my dues, the loss was all mine. Most references on the college's couchsurfing profile were breathlessly euphoric, mentioning 'profound experiences', calling Zhuo Yue their 'second home', and overstaying their visas. Beyond the opportunity for cross-cultural exchange and free accommodation, there was something so welcoming about this place. I wondered if it was all down to saving face – which, in this instance at least, elevated relationships into a mutually nice, happy union. That begat a kind of loyalty; no wonder couchsurfers were so happy to hang around. In Britain, we only saved face until resentment, anger or suspicion kicked in. For my pathetic efforts, Gary gave me a big, easy cuddle, and Charles shook my hand cordially, sending me on my way with a Zhuo Yue English College shopper. I was almost – but no, not quite enough – sorry to be on my way to Shanghai.

CHAPTER 20

SHANGHAI: CHRISTIAN CRIMES

16TH DECEMBER

I'd been saving the most cosmopolitan place – Shanghai, pearl of the Orient and the reputed 'showpiece' of the world's fastest-growing economy – till last. As I disembarked Shanghai's gleaming metro, a marshal whistled loudly in my ear. Nothing personal, that was just how China's most populous city (the second most populous in the world) herded its twenty million inhabitants. I crossed the road and walked right into a commotion with a taxi – I jabbed a finger at the flashing little green man; he sounded his horn at me. Motor evidently triumphed over man in Shanghai; I stepped aside. And, just near my new couch, I passed a modest fast food joint. Outside, a cheaply suited man was shouting into a microphone to lure passing trade. Shanghai's biggest environmental problem was said to be noise pollution. Ironically, I wanted to scream.

Changning District, just west of down-town Shanghai, was industrial, but not cool-industrial. Ugly, grey twenty-storey buildings had recently been dropped in any old how around an angry, six-lane street. Still, exteriors didn't usually bear any relation to the heart inside.

Manfred was much smaller and more approachable than his profile suggested. I was expecting a lofty skinhead with a cat's ear in his mouth, as I'd seen on his profile, but I was learning not to take those filters too seriously. Manfred's black hair had grown to a much more sociable, scruffy Caesar cut, framing a pleasant bearded face, while Rupert the cat – named after the one-year-old Stewie's stuffed-toy confidant in *Family Guy* – still had both ears.

'Would you like some Pu'er tea?' he said, in a thick Italian accent, flanked by a pretty Chinese girl, ShuShu.

No one said, 'Yup, that *is* a wig ShuShu is wearing,' so I pretended to go along with her kinky porn hair – very long and very fake, shiny and black, with a strong fringe and loose, bouncing curls. I presumed she was Manfred's girlfriend, but couldn't help but wonder if they'd met at a Special KTV.

The tea was from Yunnan, ShuShu explained, like herself. The colour of stewed maple leaf, it tasted mellow, earthy, and welcoming. Manfred instantly supplied me with details on the best place to buy it. Wig apart, I quickly felt 'in'. There was no tension, no hovering question marks, and Manfred had already given me a spare key. As they playfully ribbed each other like kittens, I slowly adapted. The wig, I realised, was a joke. I was relieved to be wrong. Even in my last city, I couldn't get rid of my snap judgments, these instincts for ordering the chaos.

Catching sight of my Zhuo Yue bag, Manfred revealed he'd spent two-and-a-half weeks at the English College. And before coming to Shanghai in August, he'd also done drunken karaoke with Gareth and Beth, and knew the Chengdu gang. Couchsurfing might have been 'creating a better world', but also a much smaller one.

So was Manfred a teacher?

'No,' he said, mildly put out. He was a translator, and was learning Chinese.

It wasn't the first time I had forgotten a host's profile, but then my plans were often made weeks in advance. I recalled he had a young male Chinese-American flatmate, yet to show, but details about Manfred? Gone. The amnesia was mutual, however. Along with the Ollie leg yarn, I'd often lean on the story of my mother cavorting around the skies in a single-seater aeroplane. No one recognised it from my profile; none of us read them properly.

'But then she happened,' Manfred continued, pointing to ShuShu.

ShuShu was twenty, and off to study German in Germany (there were 'so strict rules' at Chinese universities, she explained: 'It is not very enjoyable'). They'd met couchsurfing, her as his guest in September.

'Because it's against the rules,' Manfred said, talking to me but gazing at her, 'I didn't touch her, but sent an e-mail.' A suggestive email, he admitted.

She returned in any case, without having read the e-mail.

Manfred wanted to go to the market to buy ingredients for dinner for his local couchsurfing friends: Sam, a British guy, and Mark, a German. Except, with a cat to play with, and all those new conversations, the market was deferred, until, two hours later, Manfred's shy flatmate Eric, a 26-year-old from New York, showed up. He was laconic but present: 'Maybe Fleur would like to see the market too.'

Yes, I would.

'And maybe ShuShu would like to take her wig off,' suggested Manfred.

Finally, the joke was out. She wouldn't.

All four of us ventured out to the market: no dogs this time, just live frogs the size of a man's hand.

'We should not be shocked by what other people want to eat,' said Manfred, wisely.

✪

'Shouldn't I move my rucksack out of the way?' I asked. I'd just dumped it in the kitchen.

Manfred insisted it wasn't in his way, and I believed him; he seemed bigger than such trifles. But I had a subtext – I needed to meet my couch, to remove that dull ache of homelessness. And there it was, upstairs on the landing: a small, cream pleather sofa, wedged in between the two bedrooms and bathroom. It was touching that hosts multi-tasked their homes like this so altruistically.

'I'm undressing the onions,' said ShuShu, as dinner got under way.

'I won't look,' Manfred replied, busy at the sink.

'If you look, you will cry.'

Sitting around the repro dining table was a bunch of pure couchsurfing stereotypes – all middle-class idealists, for whom life was comfortable enough to be idealistic. Sam, a honey-coloured 27-year-old teacher with a public-school accent, volunteered for Hands On Shanghai, a charity that comforted hospitalised children. Eric worked in environmental finance, determining whether ventures were worth investment. Mark – well, he was a 21-year-old programmer and took great exception to Zhuo Yue English College cashing in on couchsurfers. Manfred himself was a 'communist', he said from the hob,

✪

while conducting a four-pan symphony. 'I hate money – I believe in sharing.'

Which right now seemed to be more a case of straight giving. A platter of blue and white tofu arrived at the table, which turned out to be tofu and 1,000-year egg (that was the blue bit). It wasn't really 1,000 years old, but 100 days, preserved in a clay cocoon to produce silky, jelly bruises that tasted explosively eggy – the blank tofu diluted it. A multiplicitous glass-noodle salad arrived, with sprouts, peppers and sesame oil, and a subtle pork mince and mushroom dish. Everyone dived in. The Italian had made an authentic Chinese spread, and no one was prepared to wait.

'I'll eat when I've finished cooking,' Manfred said from his galley, with hostly largesse. Manfred just seemed to be one of those natural, happy hosts – my safe bet was paying dividends.

Meanwhile, Sam and Mark had gone decidedly cool on couchsurfing – these friendships had transcended that. More and more people had joined, they said, but 'not the right people'. There were too many empty profiles, people just after free accommodation. Some requests they received were even addressed to other people. London – another big city, attractive to tourists and with steep accommodation costs – would also surely be beset by this problem. Mine and Ollie's cheerleading grins were going to have to go – I needed a filter too.

I confessed my dread. If I didn't like hosting, how to pay back my twenty-odd couches?

'Don't give money,' Manfred entreated, finally at the table. 'That money goes straight to Casey Fenton.'

Fenton was couchsurfing's young, nomadic founder. Manfred wasn't the first naysayer: there were enough even on couchsurfing's own forums, calling couchsurfing 'Casey Inc.'

and raising the 'serious issue' of fund mismanagement. What would couchsurfing – Casey even – have to say about this? I resolved to find out back in London. Maybe Casey and co. could tell me the best way to pay back – certainly no one here could.

As an Ambassador, I asked, what dramas did Manfred have to deal with?

Mostly girls claiming they'd been harassed, he said. It was often a misunderstanding between shy girls and Asian guys. There had been cases of rape: a western girl by an Indian man, and in Thailand a Pakistani had tried to rape a French guy. There were stories of guests squatting in hosts' houses. After my string of safe experiences, I'd rather forgotten about danger.

But why weren't there more native hosts?

'Chinese people's first thought,' said Sam, who'd been here for three years, 'is that couchsurfing is too dangerous. Their second is how much money they can make.'

As China became the lead topic, the evening turned into something of a teacher-and-class affair. Sam – who'd been in China the longest – took the floor. Manfred was more intent on playing. If he wasn't prodding ShuShu, he was swinging Rupert around by his armpits. Very Stewie. And I was happy to be passive. Looking forward to home, my mind had prematurely begun to disengage. Besides, Sam was a well-tuned, compassionate narrator – we were all engrossed.

Because Shanghai was only 200 years old – having established itself in the 19th century as a shipping port – the Shanghainese, Sam said, were obsessed with class. To hit a Shanghainese where it hurt, you'd say, 'You have no class.'

English was learnt as a status symbol. Just as well really – China's English teachers could barely speak English themselves, having grown up without any foreigners in their country. No surprise, then, that China's new colonialists – many with no teaching experience – got work so easily.

And what was Sam's source of knowledge? Cab drivers and workers, mostly. The less well-off were more honest about China than the wealthy. And he liked them older: 'In China you have to be thirty to have any life experience.' He'd talk to the homeless: 'The government doesn't like to help the homeless – that would be to acknowledge the problem.'

Perhaps that was the dark side of saving face.

'But China's main obstacle is the volume of people,' Sam explained. 'If the UK was so populous, it wouldn't be so polite.'

China had made even *him* aggressive, he said (gently).

After ShuShu had fallen asleep on plum wine, time was called. Once alone, I thought again about my return to London. Decision time on The Emperor was almost up. I thought back to our three-day experiment. I couldn't live forever in some kind of romantic purgatory, as we had for eighteen months. Maybe there was a better, easier fit for us. Perhaps our loss had already started to heal – we'd surely broken the spell. With perspective, it made sense. By now, The Emperor had arrived in Cuba – I had to let him know he was free. I tearfully composed the text.

17TH DECEMBER

I peeled my cheek off the pleather and took a shower, by now immune to the scum that would collect under my feet in hosts' bathrooms. I really should give it a deep clean, I thought, but I was eager to explore. Fully dosed up on company, I was good with going solo.

'How was the sofa?' Manfred asked, outside the bathroom. He'd be sleeping there imminently as he had a couple staying soon. Amazingly, he wasn't the only one to downgrade for guests – Diana, Goran and Sam did too. I *definitely* wasn't made of the same stuff. The washing-up, however, was within my means. I secretly cleared the supper detritus, and scrubbed the worktop so vigorously that a shimmer eventually peeked out through the grime. Sleeping on one's own sofa, like Manfred would be, must bring the biggest feel-good factor.

✪

'Miss! MISS! You come my shop! Just looking!' I'd fallen into the slipstream of Nanjing Road, Shanghai's Oxford Street (on a Chinese scale, of course), and had four or five hawkers on my tail waving laminated brochures of 'good plice' fake fashion. On the Bund's riverside promenade, the street-sellers were practically abusive. Culture had been obscured by capitalism. And the romance and beauty of the French Concession district, colonised in the late 19th and early 20th centuries by the Europeans, was fictitious. The reality wasn't beautiful, just Western. I was cross, and cross that I was cross. I was tired of travel's emotional vicissitudes.

✪

8.30pm at Manfred's: silence. I clomped about. Silence. They were in, and we'd agreed to meet for dinner, but I couldn't bring myself to knock (I mean, supposing …?) so I read in the kitchen, coughing at frequent intervals. Inevitably, couple-hosts were less available. At 9pm, Manfred emerged, still in pyjamas.

'Are you hungry?' he asked.

We'd go out for 'solids', he said, and return for his home-made onion soup – perfect! They'd been watching *The Empire Strikes Back*.

'I am educating ShuShu,' Manfred smiled. 'I hope to watch them all in the next two days.'

The sum total of Manfred's Shanghai sightseeing covered what I'd done that afternoon. Not that I blamed him. Home was the enemy of adventure – so often, I'd had to force myself out of my hosts' havens. Gareth and Beth told me they'd had guests that never left the house, just gorging on their DVD collection. If you weren't careful, couchsurfing took the travelling out of travelling.

'Solids' were tiny meat-cuts, mushrooms and greens stuffed on to wooden skewers, cooked at a local Chinese street barbeque.

'Try this chicken gristle,' Manfred encouraged. 'You can chew on the cartilage.'

I played safe with intensely salty and spicy barbequed lamb morsels and soothing duck broth. ShuShu and I used our skewers for a lightsabre fight – there was always child's play with these two. I was low on social energy – I felt lazy. And lucky.

Italian onion soup was a million tiny pieces of onion, topped with Parmeggiano-laden croutons – it was sweet, golden, deep. Where on earth did Manfred find Parmeggiano in China? His dad had sent it, he explained, along with sixty per cent cocoa chocolate and Lavazza coffee. In many ways, Manfred wasn't *tipico* – not least in his ready adoption of Chinese culture – but with his love of food, he was hard-wired Italian.

Some areas of Chinese culture were rather harder to infiltrate than food. Manfred and ShuShu, I realised, were half-way through their own *Romeo and Juliet* drama. ShuShu's father had summoned her home to Yunnan, unhappy about this cross-continental liaison. Would Manfred follow ShuShu to Germany? Her parents strongly disapproved, because – of course – she was going there to study. No wonder they'd shelved Shanghai tourism, their time was precious.

'Let us show you the way.' It was a text from David – the next day, I'd be swapping white pleather for the House of God, and I confess, I rather dined out on it.

'Don't let him give you the holy water,' Manfred mocked. 'It's like vampire's blood. Once you taste it, it's as good as being bitten.'

I laughed along with them. But then that was before my conversion ...

18TH DECEMBER

Waking to a silent house, I performed my ritualistic washing-up and deep scrub, and after fishing out the last, drowning toilet roll from the loo (was it me? Rupert?), I left for Shanghai Museum.

Having overdosed on Chinese calligraphy, seals, vases, and ancient currency, I sought refuge in People's Square, Shanghai's central park. Three separate groups asked me to take their photo, go to their hometown, go to the theatre with them, just have a drink there and then. Now that I wasn't on show, I was numb, despondent, saturated. After all that 'bumping around' with little respite, my cravings for home, now in sight, were screaming.

It didn't feel like farewell with Manfred. There was talk of KTV, and a lunch with Manfred's 'mentor' and fellow Shanghai

Ambassador, Philippe. I presented him with a bonus gift to my habitual chocolates: twenty toilet rolls, for having left him with none. I was also putting back into couchsurfing's bigger bank – these were the things I'd taken for granted throughout my trip.

'Oh, I'm sure that was Rupert,' Manfred said generously.

As Manfred, ShuShu and Eric sat around the dining table, I lingered quietly, reluctant to take on the unknown once more.

✪

I'd told David I'd be late, but still he arrived half an hour early to pick me up from his nearest metro. I sensed he just wanted to be there to catch my fall. Wearing a multi-pocketed gilet and spectacles, David spoke softly and calmly – his impressive command of English was clipped with short Chinese tonality, and he would pause thoughtfully before answering as we paced through the prelims. I was being a little aloof, waiting guardedly for the proselytising.

A loud Chinese cartoon was blasting from a giant and modern TV while David's mother-in-law was squawking excitably at his two-year-old daughter – there was no escape from Shanghai's noise. I was surprised and gratified to see another couchsurfer, seated on the large, modern L-shaped sofa in David's clean and spacious living room. Irving was a flushed and smiley 22-year-old International Relations graduate from Connecticut, looking for a job in green energy.

While David's wife (whom I knew only as 'my wife'), mother-in-law and daughter played amongst themselves, the men and I sat down to dinner. At a tiny table dominated by a large, electric casserole pot steaming with dumplings, seaweed, mushrooms, chicken wings and Chinese leaf, we filled our small bowls. While David looked on benevolently, Irving and I involuntarily launched into a one-to-one. I just couldn't help myself. There was something so healing about a burst of real English and western empathy. Plus, of course, it took less effort to be understood. Besides, Irving and I – by the magic of couchsurfing – were already connected. Irving had couchsurfed with Manfred, no less, in Florence.

Irving had also couchsurfed with his parents for six weeks across America as his graduation present (a present?).

Wasn't that hard?

He guessed so – but his mum usually got a bed, and his parents were really active couchsurfers, often hosting parties.

'It was hard having to be on the ball for six weeks,' he admitted. 'But the thing about couchsurfing,' he said, straightening his Lance Armstrong wristband, 'is that you just get amazingly lucky.'

Now *that* I knew about.

Irving's parents had stayed with Casey Fenton's father – so someone we knew had actually got close to the fabled Fenton.

'I know his dad is pretty disappointed that he's just drifting,' said Irving, through his 'Shanghai cough' (as the world's busiest cargo port, Shanghai's pollution was dire).

Perhaps Fenton's dad, of a different generation, couldn't grasp the concept of the nomadic entrepreneur needing just an idea and a laptop. But was Casey cashing in? The intrigue grew.

Ta-da – I presented my box of chocolates. David looked like he'd swallowed a lemon; perhaps he was cross I couldn't just accept his hospitality. He tucked them on the sideboard where they remained for the rest of my stay. Then, after clearing the table, my attempt to wash up was briskly refused.

Now all ensconced on the sofa, attention was duly turned to David. He was indeed 'full of love': couchsurfing, he said, was his favourite thing, despite Irving being David's first ever guest. His private English tutor – a Canadian couchsurfer – had introduced him to it.

'I guess you can measure the openness of China by counting the native couches,' David said, pushing up his spectacles.

Energised by my new native couch, my earlier mope had been quite forgotten.

David was keen to point out he wasn't so typical. He read a lot online; he thought about 'democracy and individualism'. He told us how he'd taken his daughter for her medical exam.

'She is under-height, so the doctor suggested we stretch her legs. He thought her personality was introverted, so he suggested we changed her personality. China wants everyone to be the same. Even if she is gay we don't mind. The most important thing in the Bible is that people are equal.'

There – David's first Godly reference. Except it wasn't really about God, but acceptance. David really was a very gracious, and deeply kind, man. My aloofness had been based on *what* he was, not who. That 'creating a better world' business? That was about understanding the person behind the colour or creed, which made it much harder to mock or hate. It was this that was my conversion.

'Are you tired, Irving?' David asked dotingly. Yes he was. It was ten-ish – the time had come to be introduced to my sleeping arrangements. Irving was sleeping in David's study in a bunk bed, but maybe I'd prefer the tent in the living room?

Tent, as in camping tent?

'Yes,' David replied. 'For a bit more privacy.'

Comfort trumped privacy. 'Irving,' I asked, as I lay above him, 'are you Christian?'

It had been bugging me all night – was that why he was here?

'I'm not very religious,' he said, diplomatically. 'Good night, sleep well'.

19TH DECEMBER

A text from the other side of the world. I'd expected The Emperor to have agreed with being granted his new freedom from me, but now I was left with the sense that I'd wrecked his holiday. He couldn't discuss it – or even think about it – out there, he wrote. But he'd started drinking tea, which reminded him of me. And sometimes, despite everything, a small smile would come to him, as he remembered our very great love. I felt bad, and *deeply* confused.

Breakfast had been neatly laid out on the dining table: chopped tomatoes and lettuce, ham, sliced white bread, a glass of full milk and chopsticks. Was it for me? David was out at his English lesson, his wife had gone for a walk, the maid was in the kitchen. It felt presumptuous to eat it, but Irving assured me they'd be insulted if I didn't.

I'd arranged to meet Philippe the Ambassador for lunch. Since couchsurfing was about sharing, I invited everyone: Manfred, ShuShu, Irving and David. David drove Irving and me into town. Arriving early, as was David's way, the three of us sat on a wall at the meeting point. Summarily chased off it by a security guard, we began to discuss corruption and injustice.

'China is a very complicated society,' said David, plaintively. 'Grocery stores have to pay protection both to police and black societies.' ('Black societies' was David's polite term for the Mafia.) 'The police need to collaborate with black societies. If there is not black society, who needs policemen?'

Schools, too, were prone to corruption: parents would ensure their children did well by paying the top students to sit their lesser children's exams for them; they'd bribe teachers with phone- and shopping-cards.

'Schools have all kinds of methods to absorb money from you,' said David.

He was considering home schooling for his daughter but he thought it was illegal.

'Are you ever scared?' I asked.

'I'm not scared – I'm annoyed. It's inconvenient to want to know the truth. The media is not easy to get to.'

I felt scared for him.

✪

It was an odd little lunch, on account of there being too many strangers around too big a table. Eventually, the strongest personality – Philippe, a thirty-year-old, Belgian-Chinese-French guy working in the garment industry – dominated while the rest of us asked appropriate questions. Except ShuShu and Manfred, who, like bored children, pinged each other's jacket cuffs.

Philippe was couchsurfing Establishment. Despite handing over the ambassadorial ropes to Manfred (because his new Chinese wife 'wasn't up for it'), it was still his show. But Philippe genuinely cared, and was trying to establish a proper community in Shanghai, and a permanent couchsurfing 'zone' – a kind of Cheers bar for couchsurfers to drop in anytime. He fed us some Casey gossip.

'I don't think he wants to be a leader. He's just a guy who had a really great idea.'

We lapped it up as he told us that Casey had been to the Burning Man (the most radical, ideological festival out there, where participants had to bring all provisions, even water, plus a showpiece, to the Nevada Desert). Casey had been 'like six times'. No wonder: the Burning Man was right on-message for couchsurfing. What's more, Casey had clearly reached celebrity status.

Philippe was getting there himself – he'd been the subject of an article in the State-run English newspaper *China Daily*, about his involvement in the charity project One Couch One Euro.

'It was a very simple way,' Philippe said, commandingly, 'of bringing some meaning to all this couchsurfing partying.'

Guests had to pay one euro, which he and other participating hosts would match. After a few months, they'd raised enough money (5,000 yuan) to buy a water buffalo. But the idea stopped there.

'I think there are a lot of individuals who could be doing more,' said Philippe.

Like us.

The restaurant cleared up around us. Manfred and ShuShu wanted to go to the clothes market to buy hot pants and Ugg boots for her sister. So, in good couchsurfing spirit, we all traipsed along. And like a long-suffering father, David dropped us off: 'Don't thank me, thank God.'

✪

Unnervingly, the security guard on David's block was expecting me, excitedly gesticulating like a children's TV presenter. What else did she know, I wondered. She let me in, and I hurried up to dinner (hot pork dumplings with sweet chilli sauce), which was, of course, waiting on the table for us.

Eventually, the conditions were right for our Christianity discussion. I'd deliberately waited for David to raise it again, and was pleasantly surprised how long it took. When he announced that he was going to church the next day, I probed a little further. He'd converted just one month ago, having met a Christian at his English teacher's party. But it wasn't so sudden, he said: 'I needed a religion to support my spiritual belief.'

But what about Christianity and the communists? Official churches were under strict regulations and had to report to the government and register their attendees. David, however, went to an underground church – or a 'family church', as he called it. Organised get-togethers were illegal, and prone to attack but, said David innocently, 'we are not organised – we are just a group of people who love each other.' There were apparently three times as many family churchgoers as official churchgoers.

Could I come? (Not since my childhood Christingle days, when churchgoing had been rewarded with satsumas, had I wanted to go to church.)

David rang his leader. No – it was too sensitive. They were 'afraid to bring danger upon me'. But I could meet them for lunch afterwards.

Manfred's KTV invitation came in by text just as David told us both his grandparents had died of starvation during the Great Leap Forward – he never knew them. We sat on the invitation, and listened.

'That's one reason why I hate the Chinese Communist Party,' he said quietly. 'Why I can't forgive. The whole country suffered under the one-party policy. We should have had much more happier childhood. Most the population hate the Party.'

David wanted to emigrate to Canada because, he said, he wanted to become a global citizen. He was worried there might be another 'major accident' like 1989. (Many Chinese didn't even know about Tiananmen Square.)

'In China I have no right to vote but if I just walk away, I can vote with my feet.'

As David attended to his daughter (letting rip three times without blinking), Irving and I conspired about getting to KTV.

'David, come to KTV with us!' we tried.

But he wanted to stay with his family, and, insisting on booking us a taxi, saw us off like his own children going out for the first time.

Irving and I quickly got to discussing important matters. Like how we were ever going to repay David. The chocolates had bombed and the maid did the washing-up. It was worse for Irving, to whom David had granted an extended stay. Well, Irving should be David's friend – it seemed David wanted that. I was going to have to deliver something much more meaningful than chocolate.

✪

Manfred and ShuShu were still at Mark's flat with Jenny, Mark's girlfriend, and Sam and his girlfriend. Manfred had been cooking dinner again. Irving and I explained about David. Sam nodded – he'd noticed there were lots of 'wide-eyed' Christians in Shanghai.

'It's seen as a foreign disease,' added Jenny. She pinned the blame squarely on the missionaries, who'd tell peasants they'd go to hell for not believing.

Mark looked David up on couchsurfing, and soon they were all falling about laughing. Irving and I fell silent in unmentionable, protective disapproval.

'I love that man,' Irving said, smiling uncomfortably. 'So don't be unkind now.'

They, too, had judged from afar.

Jenny had met one of couchsurfing's three other cofounders, Leonardo Silveira, in Buenos Aires.

'He had particular thoughts on communication,' said Jenny, 'that we should be socialising. And he'd ask really provocative questions, like "Do you really believe you have to love just one man?" At one Burning Man, he'd had a threesome relationship.'

In fame, there was a fine line between being aggrandised and demonised.

KTV was off, it was announced. It was too late, and Manfred and ShuShu had some *Star Wars* to watch before ShuShu flew home the next day. No one seemed particularly into Shanghai's nightlife, which apparently comprised superficial crowds following the latest trends into expensive, uninspiring bars. Manfred's dinners seemed like one of the nicest options going.

20TH DECEMBER

Goodbye Shanghai. After my breakfast of soupy, plain rice and fierce chilli relish, I went to meet David for our holy lunch. Right at the back of the restaurant were ten young Chinese around a large circular table. They all looked normal – hip, even. Like group therapy, each introduced themselves, in English: 'My name's … and I'm a Christian.'

All converted, as opposed to ethnic, Christians, they explained how the family church worked. There was no priest, and no church – the 'brothers and sisters' would meet at one of their houses and take turns to lead the Bible's teachings and hymns. Everybody was extremely enthusiastic, until I asked one of them her profession: she refused to say. Were they seeing more and more new members? 'We are not members,' she snapped.

Retreating from personal enquiry, I asked about China's spiritual vacuum.

'China needs God,' that week's leader boomed.

David explained, thoughtfully: 'After the Cultural Revolution, we were left with nothing. But the younger generation really needs something to believe in. To my understanding, the most important commandment is to love others as we love ourselves. It's simple. It's all about love.'

Everyone looked very pleased with that.

Spiritual sustenance finally over, the girl who'd snarled so un-Christianly sought me out to apologise.

'It's hard for us,' she said. 'We have to be very careful.'

I apologised for being insensitive. Really, I was glad for her assault: it gave me an insight into how it was to be Christian in China. David walked me to the metro.

What did his parents think?

They didn't know, he said. He had to find the right time to tell them – about Christianity *and* about couchsurfing.

Heading for the dark heart of consumerism for some Christmas shopping, I thought about David and his sudden new loves, Christianity and couchsurfing. What voids were they filling? Perhaps, as Sam had said, he was coming of age. I felt for him. However, thinking for myself eventually became impossible as I became indoctrinated into spending by piercing renditions of *O Come All Ye Faithful*, present-laden Christmas trees and even a young Chinese Santa waving the peace salute. No one seemed to realise they were partaking in a Christian festival. I bought my present for David, and hurried back.

✪

Irving was out, and over a Last Supper with David of yesterday's dumplings, crispily fried, I asked about the very great disconnect between Christianity and Christmas in China. Not that the same wasn't true of the UK, but at least Christ wasn't just a dirty word there.

'Christmas in China is a very modern fashion,' David explained. 'Chinese people are in a dilemma – they admire western culture and want to join the world, but they want practical things – money and health. It's not so easy to understand Chinese society.'

Or, indeed, for China to understand the west.

While I was packing in my room, David called my name.

'I have something for you,' he said, and with both hands presented a small packet: an ornamental bottle opener inspired by the Beijing Opera. I, in turn, presented my gift. His face immediately reset into one of irritation.

'You mustn't give us presents,' he chided.

Wrapped, I suppose it did look like a wedge of bank notes, but I insisted he opened it – a big wall map of Canada. Calling out excitedly to show his wife, I think he found forgiveness for me.

David drove that extra mile, taking me to my bus station – time for one last chat. Had he travelled? He'd been to Japan, he said, and liked it very much. This was radical for China, who viewed Japan as its archenemy due to Japan's imperialist invasions of the last two centuries. He thought the Japanese well educated, hardworking, hospitable and that they had contributed much to the world.

'But,' he explained, 'the government make people hate them.'

I loved that couchsurfing demanded an extended dialogue with people, like David, that I wouldn't otherwise encounter. In a country so moulded into group mentality, couchsurfing allowed individualism to triumph.

I was leaving a very different country to the one I'd arrived in. The only people who had something to fear were, sadly, the Chinese themselves. I could now attach personalities and critical thought to the automaton workforce I'd originally expected; I now had an outline of understanding. China was so different, complex and difficult for us western sojourners to comprehend, but that so many ex-pats leapt to its defence was telling.

CHAPTER 21

LONDON: THE DEBT COLLECTOR

After ten weeks, I had slept on:

- 5 floors
- 4 sofas
- 3 sofa beds (shared twice)
- 1 air bed
- 1 canvas camp bed
- 1 bunk bed
- 6 single beds
- 4 double beds (shared once)
- 12 rail bunks

in:

- 4 countries
- 12 trains
- 2 gers
- 1 kitchen
- 1 couple's bedroom
- 4 one-room apartments
- 1 hotel
- 1 hostel

From a total of twenty-three different couches, I'd had my own room ten times, two decent nights' sleep and zero sex scenes. I'd lost one caffeine habit, and gained one morbid fear of ever having a biscuit dinner again.

The cost:

- 15 boxes of chocolates
- 3 books
- 1 bottle of perfume
- 1 pair of traditional Mongolian slippers
- 1 bunch of flowers
- 1 bumper pack of toilet rolls
- 2 boxes of cakes
- 1 wall map
- 3 home-cooked meals
- 4 bought meals
- Plus new homes for the Hyatt Prosecco and statuette, and Polly's Turkish spices.

Pretty cheap, all things considered.

'How was it?' everyone asked.

'Strange!'

It was so very odd, landing in yet another stranger's living room, as if via H.G. Wells's Time Machine, and just getting along with whomever I found there. I'd just experienced twenty-five random acts of kindness, where the emphasis really was on random.

'Intense!' I said.

Try to imagine staying with your neighbour for three days, and then the next neighbour and then the next. Then imagine all that in Russia, China, Kazakhstan and Mongolia. I thought I could, but it hadn't prepared me at all. And the kindness! Like a secret society only visible to the enlightened, couchsurfing had punctuated the world with its welcoming. And, having had such access to other people's lives and other countries' cultures, I'd collected a whole catalogue of meaningful experiences. But was I glad to be back in my own bed – no more forced grins, no more unlikely-couple alchemy, no more claustrophobia.

Had I made real friends, they asked.

Some, sure – Lindsay, Irving, Donagh, Stasya. And for some of my hosts, I was having reciprocal hosting urges. But really, what they all wanted to know about was 'special friends'. No, there was neither the possibility nor the inclination. Had I broken my addiction to The Emperor? If that meant not obsessing about him and us, then no.

But there *must* have been disasters?

As Daniel in Kunming had pointed out, 'How you define a shitty couchsurfing experience depends on what kind of traveller you are.' Never endangered, my worst-case scenario had been not connecting with my host – the luxury disaster of a softie. Couchsurfing was like a reality game show, an extreme social experiment where success was measured in how we got on. As a perfection-seeker, I guess I took that quite seriously.

★

'The whole object of travel is not to set foot on foreign land; it is at last to set foot on one's own country as foreign land,' said the 20th-century English writer G.K. Chesterton so sagely.

How different London seemed: so clean, handsome, orderly. I'd returned to a glorified film set. And for some reason, the

Britons I came across – randoms in the supermarket, the RAC man, the woman who let me go in front of her – weren't the cold, driven and selfish types I'd recalled while away. But really, it was me who was different. As I happily chatted with people on the street, it suddenly struck me: where was my British reserve? Britain could be friendly if you invited it to be. I felt like I belonged to the world, and it to me.

How was Ollie? There was good news and bad. The good news was that he'd had the all-clear, the bad being that his consultant thought his leg was never infected in the first place. So the 'emergency' hadn't been an emergency – Ollie could have stayed with me. But alone, I'd conquered a bigger Everest. I'd solved my own problems, fought my own battles, and chosen my own way.

I'd returned somewhat re-wired. Accepting hosts as they were had made me more tolerant, and respectful for what I already had. I felt more confident, more robust. I seemed to stop caring quite so much about what people thought of me – couch-surfing was like aversion therapy, like chucking an arachnophobe into a pit of spiders. I'd finally climbed down from my mental attic. Perhaps I was even starting to become 'easy-going'.

'Couch available: own room with double sofa bed. Four days is too many. Maximum number of surfers: 3.'

I changed my photo to something much more mysterious, and asked prospective guests to put the word 'la-di-da' in the subject box – a trick to encourage surfers to read the profile and choose a host on compatibility, rather than just opening fire on all. Part of me was excited by the prospect of interesting, well-travelled, well-chosen characters, but most of me wasn't. I was still a private person, selfish about her personal space – my London life was crowded.

Of the fifteen requests I received between Christmas and New Year, only two attended to my password, one of whom – a Chinese girl – called me Tanja. I did consider the three Hungarians because I was curious about the country, but two weren't on couchsurfing and they wanted to stay for four days. Similarly, I said *nein* to three young German guys who 'just needed a roof over their heads' for New Year's Eve. *Non* to a French family of three who didn't know what dates they were coming. No to a 'Hi there!!!' message from a Mexican girl with an empty profile and a very full, low-cut vest. The vast majority of applicants were about twenty years old.

Where were the barnstormers and adventurers? It was coming up to New Year's Eve: hostels and hotels were full and expensive, and the weak pound made London attractive. My requests weren't about couchsurfing but free accommodation. Perhaps there was some elite tier where the cool people stayed with pro hosts. Or maybe the adventurers just weren't coming to London.

So I lowered my expectations, saying yes to an intriguing thirty-year-old Austrian mathematician with a taste for Immanuel Kant. He too failed to use my password, had never couchsurfed before, and wanted to stay six days (though would accept less). But he professed to go out of his way to help people: 'You could call it one of my kinks.' And, he promised, he was 'rather uncommon – weird, strange, even excentric [sic]'.

I liked unconventional people – surely he wouldn't be boring. Besides, there were other safety checks in place: 'Jorg' been vouched for twice by special surfers with vouching rights (actually his local friends).

I agreed to host him for three nights from New Year's Eve. His third night was coincidentally the day The Emperor would return from Cuba. But they wouldn't clash, because I'd vowed not to see The Emperor. *Just* in case, though – given my confusion – I informed Jorg I wouldn't be around that day. It was one of a number of pledges I'd made for my guests:

1. I would be unambiguous about how much time I could spend with them.
2. They'd be shown their sleeping place immediately (so unsettling not to know).
3. The fridge would be stocked, and they'd be invited to help themselves.
4. I would make a meal on arrival and try to provide a meal a day.
5. I would greet them properly. I thought of Diana: a handshake on arrival, a hug (if it went according to plan) on departure.

And how was I going to amuse Jorg? Was he expecting to tag along with me on New Year's Eve? Then he messaged to say he'd found a couchsurfing house party – I could come! A promising sign of independence. And an impressive advance payback. I was intrigued by London's couchsurfing scene, and now I had a couchsurfer to take me. But what about the rest of his stay? I lived alone – wouldn't we be bored? I engineered a dinner with my twin sister, who had a dog, two cats, a husband and a three-year-old daughter. Already, weirdly, I wanted to provide. What was that – host pride? The instinct to entertain was on both sides.

31ST DECEMBER

A towering, ursine figure stood outside my door in a sensible brown anorak holding a wheelie suitcase. Jorg had the look of a voluntary worker: square but smiley and engaged. And with an ostrich-egg head, a bristly DIY haircut and small eyes lost to a very long, very pink, hooked nose – all evidently airbrushed out of his profile photo – we were instantly spared the concern of desire.

I trotted through pledges five, two and four, and led him up to the top floor (usually my study) where he'd be sleeping. He dumped his bags, presented me with two tiny boxes of chocolate (he was keen to point out that the heart-shaped one had just been lying around at home). We settled in my living room for fresh minestrone soup, hunks of granary bread and some Camembert and Brie. He was awfully enthusiastic, sometimes emitting a high-pitched laugh like a kid on Christmas morning, but I felt comfortable. Jorg himself pointed out that he didn't feel like a stranger, but then he was way too strong to be shy. I, meanwhile, was fresh from training – this all seemed very easy and adult. Except he didn't seem to be eating enough.

'Eat more!' I urged. 'More cheese! More bread!'

I had some questions: firstly, why had Jorg come to London? Not for an arbitrary couchsurfing party?

In his clipped, precise accent, Jorg said he was here to see a friend from China, who'd also come to London on holiday.

Was there a romantic involvement, I asked cheekily. But no, she was engaged.

What else? Jorg was a maths teacher, and was helping to build his brother's house in an Austrian village. (Building one's own house was definitely a pattern.) He was a Dungeons & Dragons addict – he'd once played for fifty hours non-stop.

'With drugs?' I asked, amused.

'No!' he said, outraged. With excitement. Sometimes, he admitted, as they acted out their parts they'd let out a battle cry.

I let out a little laugh, but I was endeared. I loved how couchsurfing enabled those unlikely encounters.

I wanted to know about Austria – that was payback.

'My country is known for not being Germany,' Jorg said, with all the assurance of a live broadcaster. 'The German humour is very anal, very low-grade. Austrians have this 'we'll be all right' mentality – not that we'll do anything about it, but it all somehow works out.'

Pledge Number One came with the issue of the evening's plans. After dinner with my sister, I had a bit of a party hop – that couchsurfing party, hosted by a twenty-something Italian, one of London's veteran hosts, only started at 1am.

'A party hop would be good,' Jorg said eagerly.

But before I had to tell him that it would actually be quite tricky for him to come along, I was pleased to learn he'd be meeting his Chinese friend. I decided, silently, that he'd passed his interview and I gave him a set of keys. We could be independent.

After a couple of hours, I grew weary of the scenery; I wanted to be alone again. Still two hours from dinner, I set him up with some books on London, a giant map and TV options. He helped me clear up, and I introduced him to the fridge.

'Why are you refrigerating your chocolate?' he asked, in mock indignation. 'I should spank you for that, ha ha ha'

Incarcerating me in his giant, Brobdingnagian arm, he laughed alone. Aghast (and surprised to smell his unwashedness), I discreetly edged out.

As we retired to our separate quarters, I felt an obligation to keep my bedroom door open – I couldn't bear for him to feel excluded. After a lull, Jorg suddenly swung his head round my door, brandishing a camera, and started snapping away at me. Hosts should expect to have their photo taken – but papped? That was the end of the open-door policy. Shouldn't intimacy be on my terms?

✪

It was always a reality check introducing a third party to a couch-surfing arrangement. As soon as my brother-in-law James opened the door to us – Jorg now in his 'party' top, a blue Mega Man T-shirt over a thermal polo neck – I felt a twinge of embarrassment for pushing them into this absurd pact. It was safe to say James and my sister Chloe would not be couchsurfing's next sign-ups. Within the polite boundaries of dinner party conversation, they expressed their concerns: how did we know we could trust each other? How foolproof was the reference system? The one on eBay, after all, was self-serving and prone to unscrupulousness. Couchsurfing wasn't exactly rigorous.

For example, Jorg pointed out that if he was vouched for one more time, then he himself could vouch for people – despite having never couchsurfed before. But he was persuasive.

'Every person should have a friend in every country, then they won't want to fight them,' he said. 'If Americans all had friends in Iraq then they wouldn't have wanted war there.'

And with that, his peculiar presence suddenly made sense.

We had to get the party started. What plans had Jorg made to meet the Chinese girl? He'd meet her by a tube station. Which one? When? They hadn't organised that far. After some nudging from me, he called her. She was at London Bridge station already; we were in Putney. Feeling responsible for my charge, I drove him through sticky New Year's Eve traffic. I was completely under the spell of hospitality, until I realised I was running an hour late myself. Dumping him at the nearest tube station, we agreed to meet much, much later. Jorg planted two, too-close kisses on each cheek.

✪

My friends didn't want to go to the couchsurfing party – too many unknowns, they said, too much risk. At 3am, I finally submitted. Despite the struggle to get past the congested door, there was no problem falling into instant conversation As I chatted with two Turkish guys, Jorg slithered over for a python-like hug. I wriggled out.

'Are you Russian?' asked a very drunk young German, standing in my face. 'You look Russian.'

It was soon established that I was just one of three British people at the party; this really was like a support group for expats. There was something a little tragic about it, all these outsiders clinging together. I guess I'd been there, in Beijing, say, or Moscow, but in London, I didn't need to be. At 5am, I'd had enough. I found Jorg working very hard on a cute east-Asian girl in a tiny top. He'd stay, he said. Mega Man had hours left in him.

1ST JANUARY

'Thank you for an exquisitively [sic] lovely & exceptionally awesome first day. Thank you so very much. Jorg.'

Sadly, the note left out on my dining table did not have the desired effect. What with the hysteria, the flash photography, the

✪

spank comment and that tentacular grip, I was starting to feel cringed out. Already, I had hosting fatigue. I gave myself strict instructions not to let it show, and crept around the house so as not to wake him and terminate my peace. At about 4.30pm, I heard the floorboards creak, followed swiftly by an appearance of Jorg at my bedroom door in a top and just his underpants – and a very tight and short pair of pants at that. My crumbly old Georgian terrace wasn't exactly tropical, so what was he thinking? That I wanted to see him like that? Through gritted teeth, we, ahem, debriefed the night.

Jorg's next outfit seemed even stranger for New Year's Day: crisp beige chinos and a pressed beige, long-collared shirt, buttoned up to the neck.

Was he hungry, I asked – if I made him lunch, I thought, then my hosting duties were done. I knocked up some tagliatelle with a homemade bacon and tomato sauce, and obliged him a hairdresser-grade chat. His next trip?

Ja, he was going to travel around Europe with another friend from China. He winked mischievously: 'And, before you ask, yes there is a romantic involvement. I have a thing for Chinese girls. Or all oriental girls. They're just so cute. But then all girls are cute. Ha ha.'

I was keen to leave the girl subject.

'What about helping people?' I asked. 'You said it was your …' I hesitated, wincing, 'kink.'

'Oh, have you heard of the Free Hug Campaign?' Jorg had been giving out free hugs in Vienna. 'I guess you'll have noticed I'm quite a huggy person.'

I smiled unconvincingly. So they'd make a sign, hold it up and then wait for people to come to them.

'Lots of old people really need the kindness,' he said. 'The old women really want to talk. Others you can feel instantly relax when you hug them.'

The campaign was so couchsurfing, but *so* slimy.

'Now, tomorrow,' I reminded him, 'I'm not going to be able to spend with you.'

Dual thoughts were running in my head, Post-its were slapped across my bedroom saying 'NO!' yet my mind was solely occupied with thoughts of The Emperor's return. I was in thrall to my id. But it would be Jorg's last night and I didn't want to leave him in a Xi'an position. I suggested some activities, like a 'brilliant' place where he could stay till 3am. However, I was starting to realise that the dynamic between Jorg and me was dom/dom – whatever I told him, he had his own ideas.

After five hours of Jorg, I decided to go for a 'lie-down'. I lent him my laptop while I retreated to sacred solitude. As I thought about my hosts, I realised I'd done the same with many of them, placing all my entertainment needs in their hands. No wonder experience was a premium – knowing what it was to host, and to be a guest, gave the other half of the equation an easier ride.

2ND JANUARY

After waking up once more wondering which country and whose house I was in, I found Jorg – in his beige job-interview outfit again – dominating my kitchen. The washing-up had been done, he'd un-limescaled my sink, he pointed out, and was drinking tea. He'd paid back, but Mega Man was still blocking my kitchen. Three days was already feeling like too many.

'So!' I said, cheerily. 'What are your plans?'

He was off to spend the day in Greenwich with his Chinese friend, he said, though was vague about the evening.

'Don't forget that I won't be around tonight, I'm afraid,' I said, baldly.

✪

The Emperor called. After two-and-a-half hours on the phone, there was still so much to say.

'He can't come round,' a little voice upstairs repeatedly said. 'Stay strong.'

But I'd been waiting three months for this moment.

'Soooo, what are you doing this evening?' he asked, in an irresistibly charming voice.

'Umm. Nothing. Busy.'

No one had a bigger spell on me than The Emperor. But if Jorg was around, it would be a major host violation – and excruciating for us.

Irrelevant: I was powerless to resist. Waiting or refusing would be like standing out in the cold for the night.

It was always going to be a beautiful reconciliation – this was the easy bit. My heart soared in the bliss. But The Emperor had barely been round half an hour when we heard the tread of the Austrian. It was 9.30pm. After a knock on my closed bedroom door, I reluctantly opened it. Jorg breezed right in with rhinoceros-skinned entitlement (we were fully clothed, natch). I glared at him with the unmistakable non-verbal message of: 'Don't you get it?' He didn't.

'I have bought you some wine,' Jorg said, looking pleased with himself.

'Oh, thank you. That's kind.'

'Ja, shall I open it?'

'Umm, I'm not really in the mood for drinking.'

'Oh come on! You were drinking on New Year's Eve.'

'That was New Year's Eve.'

'Well!' he said, nudging The Emperor, 'we'll just have to drink it ourselves. Ha ha ha ha.'

The Emperor, caught in the middle, grimaced. I was going to have to step in.

'Look, Jorg – I'm very sorry, but we haven't seen each other for three months. We're not really around tonight.'

'Ah. Well. Okay,' he said, proudly. He turned and went upstairs.

The Emperor and I looked at each other and wheezed wickedly. But his presence lingered – if Jorg didn't understand doors, when would he be back? After that, we spoke in whispers. I was a prisoner in my own home.

3RD JANUARY

Knock, knock. Jorg was in my bedroom again. Were there no boundaries in Austrian bedrooms or something? The Emperor was naked and asleep in my bed. Having never explained this new arrival to Jorg, it didn't look good. I blocked Jorg's path and guided him out and downstairs. The air was stiff. I apologised and defended myself in the same breath: 'But I did say yesterday that I couldn't be around.' Jorg seemed combative, contradicting me over silly little things like London phone numbers and public transport, like he knew better. He was leaving today and would be back to collect his bags after visiting the British Museum. See you in a bit then, I said.

'Well,' he snorted, 'it's going to be quite a long bit.'

He shook my hand briskly. I was quite relieved not to be part of his Free Hugs Campaign. For the time being.

I reclaimed my laptop and study – now haunted with the invisible but very present ghost of his unwashedness. Obviously it was *utterly* indefensible to snoop through my guest's internet history, but when I saw that he'd spent the previous night in a Gothic bondage chatroom, morals were overruled by sensation. I immediately rewound the film – the 'spank' comment, the vice-like grip that came too close, too often, and Mega Man's hunger for Chinese girls, rather like a snake's partiality to rabbits. I shuddered.

At 6.30pm, I heard a heavy footstep thud up the stairs. Who was it – The Emperor? Jorg? I didn't like not knowing. It was Jorg, seeming much brighter. But I was struggling to concentrate on his tales because the threat of our impending farewell hug was like waiting for an injection. Once ready to go, Jorg stepped in till he was very, very close and then, putting both trunk-like arms around me, overpowered me as if about to lift me off the ground. Then he wiped his paddle-like hands over my back in a nauseating back rub, administering his 'therapy'. Now holding me firmly by both my shoulders, we were so close that all I could focus on was his hungry mouth. I prickled with disgust. He wished me well, thanked me very much and said he'd had a brilliant time.

I quickly changed my availability status on my couchsurfing profile – first to 'No' (out of revulsion), then to 'Travelling' (out of shame), then to 'Coffee or a drink' (out of duty). But Jorg wasn't all bad – he was gregarious, he presented an amusing life of hobgoblins and orcs that wasn't mine, and he was well-mannered. Over-familiar was probably better than impenetrable. The real issue was that as a host, there was a different dynamic than I'd experienced abroad. I had less incentive to love my guest, because I didn't owe them anything. All guests would be subject to scrutiny, because they'd have to deliver, in exchange for stepping into my space. This is what Stasya had complained of; now it sounded thoroughly reasonable.

I was disappointed to be able to confirm I wasn't as leftist as I'd hoped. Leftists were nice, sharing types. I was selfish, private, guarded – a product of the West and an island. Now I understood why couchsurfing was dominated by Generation Y. They still tolerated flatmates.

But, let's be honest, most hosts weren't paying it forward or backward; they were satisfying other motives. I wasn't remotely lonely, I didn't need to live vicariously through travellers, I didn't care to practise my languages, I didn't have children whose lives I wanted to enrich, I wasn't looking for sex. I wasn't against good conversation, other points of view and cultural exchange, but just not in my inner sanctum. Were I posted to Timbuktu – or Karaganda – I'd no doubt be glad to host; in London, it was just too much.

Struck down by my old nemesis, couchsurfing guilt, I still had debts to settle. Despite everything – sleeping in a kitchen, in a rat house, enduring a lovers' tiff, the dog turds, the skid marks, the monster spider, the crystal meth, the AWOL hosts, and (I almost forgot) *all* that social anxiety – I'd loved couchsurfing. Without all these Narnias, my trip would have been much more superficial. That much I'd hoped for, but I had no idea its toughness would be my therapy. The new, couchsurfed me was, I'm sure, why I could now negotiate The Emperor. Past the easy stage, relations were still rosy. Better than ever, even: there was gratitude, balance, and fun – because our differences stopped being such dramas. Epiphanies never usually lasted, but I had just really, really tested myself. The effects – being desensitised, forbearing, more outward-looking – had to be pretty enduring. I'd grown up. Yet I felt so young.

So – that debt. I tried to get hold of couchsurfing, and Casey. While I waited for the response, Manfred directed me to couchsurfing's finances page: 'What they say on that page is just what they want you to know,' he wrote.

2008 saw a tidy profit: the total income ($783,910.17) easily topped the total expenses ($645,655.88). $100,000 of that profit, they declared, was put in an 'emergency fund'. But what Manfred was really suspicious about was the Travel & Meeting Expenses ($89,820.27).

'When it says travel,' wrote Manfred, 'it means the travelling of Casey Fenton, who travels for free, paying for his tickets with donations.'

For that reason, Manfred was 'absolutely against donation and verification'. Verification – a $20 cost to prove you were who you said you were – generated almost ninety per cent of couchsurfing's income.

Casey Fenton, the media office told me, didn't do interviews. This was obviously a massive anti-climax, not least since the idolisation process had already taken hold. I got in touch with Philippe, to pursue a comment he'd made about Casey 'trying' to keep couchsurfing non-profit. Did he know any more?

'Non-profit is a complex notion anyway,' Philippe wrote back immediately. 'Where do you draw the line between the money going to some people's pocket and for the good functioning of the community? I heard Casey is doing both.'

But Philippe was more intent on updating me on Shanghai's couchsurfing scene, which now had weekly gatherings in the 'zone'. Over 120 people had come to the last party. 'Everything else really doesn't matter.'

He was right: the real point was strangers making friends.

I finally secured an interview with one of the three other co-founders, Harvard graduate Daniel Hoffman, a management consultant and 'the businessman' of couchsurfing. He gave me some perspective.

'Some people,' I said, 'Ambassadors among them, say Casey is pocketing the profits.'

'Casey receives a salary of $30,000. No one is getting rich here.'

'Yes, but they say it's the travel expenses that are murky, that Casey funds his personal travel from them.'

'Those travelling expenses are shared across the entire staff. Do you know about the couchsurfing Collective?'

'Umm, kinda.'

'It's a mobile office that moves around the world every six months. Right now it's in Costa Rica, before that, Alaska. It's an incentive for volunteers to work full-time without a full-time salary. So we get them to Costa Rica, feed them, house them, and instead of paying them $60,000, they get $15,000. Have you seen our finances page? Given what the organisation is doing, there's not exactly a lot of money here. We're much more transparent than most other companies.'

'So if you can explain all your costs, why do you think people are upset?'

'It's just conspiracy theories – I think it's pretty naive personally. Besides, the only cost to couchsurfers [verification] is optional and one-off. If members feel 'free' is too expensive, they can go to another site.'

I suddenly felt horribly churlish. Was this all I could say in response to this genius idea, the labour behind it, and the enablement of my twenty-three couches? I quickly thanked him, for everything.

Finally, I had to ask, what did Daniel think of the suggestion that the 'wrong types' were joining? Was couchsurfing being washed down the river?

'The best times are yet to come,' he said.

'Meaning ...?'

'Couchsurfing is about facilitating positive relations and inter-cultural understanding. The larger we get, the more effective we become at achieving our goal.'

It sent me into a reverie about millions and millions of couchsurfers doing just what I had done – as numbers grew, so too would cultural tolerance.

'But what about the new wave of members who just use it for free accommodation?'

'Because they're new members, they don't understand the value system, but the more they get involved, the more they'll get it.'

Still, without being privy to the back end of the business, it left me rather wondering which camp to back. Did I care? Considering it had a million members, these figures were microscopic – even if the naysayers were right, there wasn't exactly enough for Learjets and Lamborghinis. I was rather inclined to think that the founders deserved their expensed cocktails. The most important thing was that couchsurfing could afford to continue – it had to stay afloat. Not least because I wanted to couchsurf again. Just maybe not for ten weeks at a time. Or a honeymoon.